IMAGES
of America

CAVE CREEK AND CAREFREE

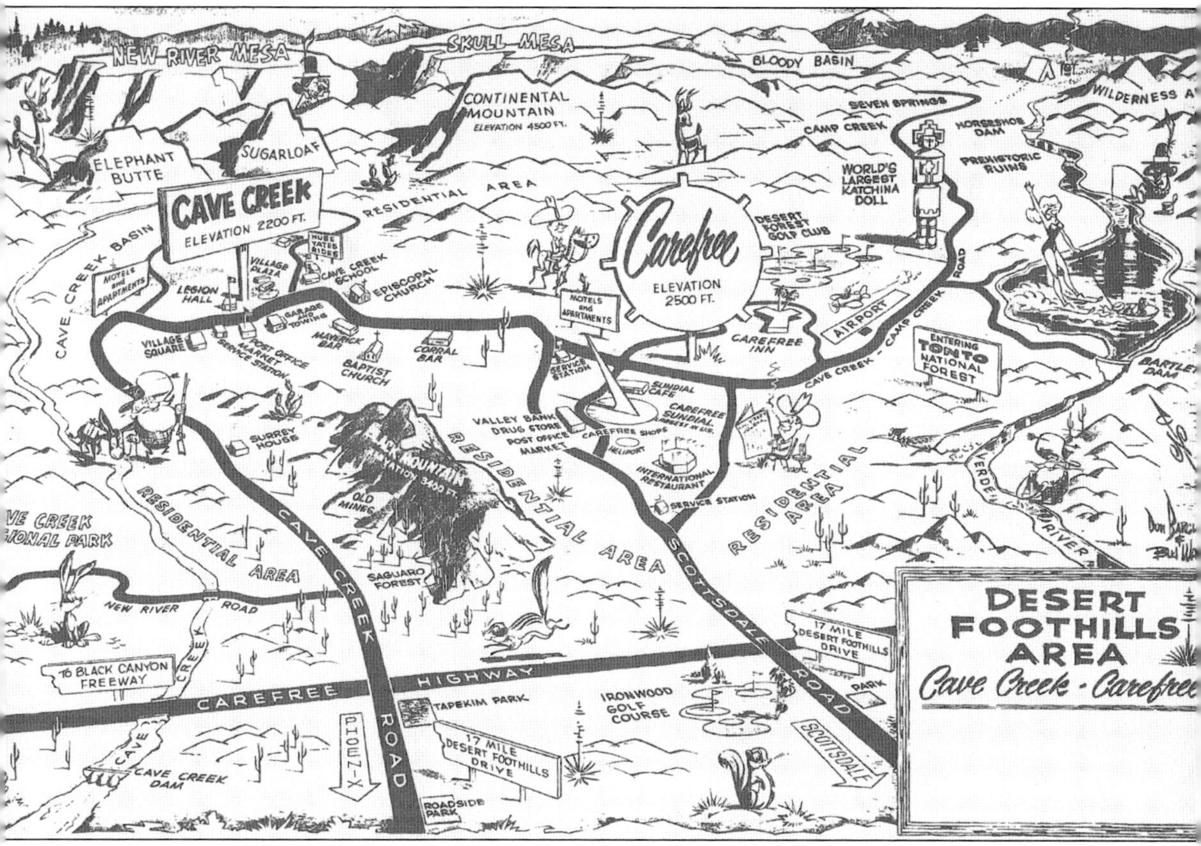

This busy brochure map of early Cave Creek and Carefree shows visitors many attractions. The natural beauty and the many amenities offered in the early 1960s continue today. (Courtesy of the Cave Creek Museum.)

On the Cover: This photograph shows wash day at Cave Creek around 1920. Frances Newman Houck, the second wife of James Houck, sits in her chair while a visitor identified as Nellie uses a washing board. Martha Houck Lee, the daughter of James Houck and his first wife, Beatrice, recalled that women washed beside the irrigation ditch that flowed from the pond to the fields. (Courtesy of the Cave Creek Museum.)

IMAGES
of America

CAVE CREEK AND CAREFREE

Patrick Grady and
the Cave Creek Museum

ARCADIA
PUBLISHING

ISBN 978-1-4671-3039-4

Published by Arcadia Publishing
Charleston, South Carolina

Printed in the United States of America

Library of Congress Control Number: 2013932919

For all general information, please contact Arcadia Publishing:
Telephone 843-853-2070
Fax 843-853-0044
E-mail sales@arcadiapublishing.com
For customer service and orders:
Toll-Free 1-888-313-2665

Visit us on the Internet at www.arcadiapublishing.com

Dedicated to the founders, volunteers, members, and staff of the Cave Creek Museum

Contents

ACKNOWLEDGMENTS

This local history is the product of a wonderful partnership with the Cave Creek Museum. Its invaluable digitized photograph collection was utilized to make this book possible and accounts for the majority of photographs in the book. Audrey Beaubien Woodward also shared her personal photograph collection of her times at Spur Cross Ranch.

A special recognition to Frances Carlson is warranted. Her collection of early-1900s photographs of Cave Creek taken by teenager Dulcy Houck is priceless. Much of Carlson's careful research from her book *Cave Creek and Carefree* is evident in many chapter introductions and photograph captions. The Cartwright family has also continued the museum's efforts to collect images of the ranching era, and Sue Mueller, Nancy Zeno, Stephanie Bradley, and Ron Roberts provided photographs from their personal collections.

We were able to gather information from a number of museum board members and volunteers to collaborate on this project. There were a number of "cooks in the kitchen." Thanks for everyone's thoughtfulness, enthusiasm, and patience. Thanks to Nancy Zeno, Bob Cook, Charlie Connell, Ron Roberts, Kraig Nelson, Stephanie Bradley, and Susan Vanik for their chapter contributions. We owe you a debt of gratitude. We hope you enjoy the final product. Stephanie also served admirably as our final editor.

Sue Mueller contributed in so many ways, particularly with the photograph research and the book layout, as well as technical coordination with Arcadia Publishing. Her attention to myriad details was both time-consuming and remarkable. Evelyn Johnson, the museum director, was the catalyst for moving the museum forward on this project. She contributed to many facets of the work. Thanks for your trust in us.

Finally, much thanks to Alyssa Jones of Arcadia Publishing for her ready assistance throughout the publishing process.

As the principal author and historical watchdog, I thoroughly enjoyed working with all of you. The Cave Creek Museum is a treasure to the desert foothills community. Thanks to all of the volunteers who devote thousands of hours to the museum and its many educational activities. Through their commitment, the connection to the heritage of our past is preserved for us all today and for future generations.

Unless otherwise specified, all images are courtesy of the Cave Creek Museum.

INTRODUCTION

The towns of Cave Creek and Carefree are nestled in the lush landscape of the desert foothills of the Sonoran Desert, 35 miles north of Phoenix. Black Mountain, rising nearly 4,000 feet and visible for miles, is the spectacular natural portal to both towns. The area is home to a plethora of archaeological ruins, reminders of a once thriving Hohokam presence. The creek itself, a marvelous riparian ecosystem, journeys from its headwaters at Seven Springs to Carefree Highway and south.

Early settlement owes its existence to the creek and the military road, built in 1870, which linked Fort McDowell, along the Verde River, to Fort Whipple, on Granite Creek near Prescott. Faint trail signs are still evident in both towns, with the remains of the Cavalry Remount Station visible on private property along the creek. The growth of Phoenix along the Salt River, coupled with the cessation of Apache raids, led William Hellings, an enterprising flour mill owner, to build a road from Phoenix to the creek in 1873. The lure of gold, ever present in Arizona territorial history, attracted prospectors who flocked to the springs, washes, ravines, and canyons of the surrounding mountains in the mid-1870s and beyond. Early gold strikes at Gold Hill, the Phoenix Mine, and the Golden Reef solidified the area's reputation.

Mining activity led to the first stage station, which was settled along Cave Creek by Jeriah Wood in 1877. The station soon passed into the hands of the Hoskin family, who resided there from 1881 to 1900. It then bustled under its next owners, James and Beatrice Houck, who established a successful sheepshearing operation in 1900, along with a post office, stage stop, saloon, boardinghouse, and general store. The one-room schoolhouse, built in 1886, also stood on the Houck ranch.

At the same time, the gramma grass growing on the mesas, along the creek, and in expansive desert valleys to the south drew cattle ranchers. Beginning with Jeriah Wood, and then the Hoskins, Cartwrights, and Logan Morris in the 1880s, cattle ranches stretched from the New River across Cave Creek and east to the Verde River. The Cartwright Ranch at Seven Springs was a historic Arizona ranch, lasting until 1980.

In the 1920s and 1930s, Cave Creek experienced population growth largely due to homesteading around all sides of Black Mountain. In addition, tuberculosis patients, seeking relief from their lung ailments, came to the desert. Cave Creek offered both sanitariums and individual cabins. Tourists and home seekers alike were lured to the area's bucolic setting.

Following World War II, dude ranches offered the Western experience to visitors from around the globe. Small subdivisions laid out on old homesteaded property began to appear. The Cave Creek Improvement Association was formed to spearhead improved roads, electricity, phone service, and water for the area. The town core moved from the creek to Cave Creek Road, north of Black Mountain.

The beauty of the foothills area to the east of Black Mountain seized the imagination of Kenyon Turner "K.T." Palmer and Tom Darlington, two real estate entrepreneurs from Scottsdale. In 1955, the two formed the Carefree Development Corporation with a vision to create a unique, master-planned community. By 1959, town development was under way.

The desert foothills towns of Cave Creek and Carefree continued to grow in the second half of the 20th century, with each legally incorporating as a town in the 1980s under the threat of annexation by the neighboring cities of Phoenix and Scottsdale. Both communities are committed to planning for a sustainable future, respecting the fragile nature of the desert foothills.

Carefree, a town of 3,363 residents in 2010, is noted for its distinctive, semirural residential community and vibrant town center, with its unique collection of shops, galleries, and restaurants. The Carefree Desert Garden and amphitheater provide a dynamic setting for art events and community gatherings. The town has a notable resort, a golf course, and even a private airport. This unique, master-planned small town fosters neighborhoods that blend into the natural terrain and are sensitive to the native vegetation and wildlife.

Cave Creek, a historic town whose 2010 population was 5,015, has endeavored to maintain its rural development pattern and an eclectic lifestyle that reflects its western, equestrian heritage and its reputation as a haven for artists. Its town core, along Cave Creek Road, is a major tourist attraction in the "Valley of the Sun," with historical buildings blended with new venues, all with dramatic desert views. Galleries and other retail offerings abound. From high-end eateries to relaxed western bars and restaurants that offer dancing and bull-riding events, Cave Creek provides a wide range of dining and entertainment choices. The town features a striking golf course on a former ranch site, significant amounts of open space, wildlife habitat areas, the Spur Cross Ranch Conservation Area along Cave Creek with its myriad hiking trails, as well as horseback riding and cycling events.

The historical legacy of Cave Creek and Carefree remains a vital link to the present. Understanding the past provides a sense of place. Early town leaders, residents, and even local characters imbued a certain pioneering spirit and unique slant on life that pervades both towns today.

The Cave Creek Museum captures this shared community past with its outstanding collection of prehistoric and historical exhibits, both indoor and outdoor.

This volume of stories and images presents a greater understanding of the special people and places that have led to the towns of Cave Creek and Carefree.

One

First Inhabitants

The Cave Creek area of the desert foothills, north of the Phoenix Basin, is an oasis in the Sonoran Desert that was used by Native Americans for thousands of years. The elevation is higher, which brings increased precipitation, resulting in greater abundance of plant and animal resources.

In and around Cave Creek and Carefree are the remains of dwellings and artifacts from an ancient way of life. Pit houses were built in the low-lying areas from about 700 to 1100 AD. Fragments of Hohokam pottery, both plain and figured, abound. From about 1100 to 1300 AD, stone-walled dwellings were built in the highlands. The figured Hohokam pots became less common.

Traces of fertile fields have been found near the creek, where corn, beans, squash, and cotton were grown. The creek ran year-round, making irrigation canals feasible. Cotton and irrigation are further signs of the influence of Hohokam culture.

On the slopes, semidomesticated agaves were grown for their fleshy hearts, then harvested and roasted in large pits. Saguaro fruit was collected in season, another bounty of the Sonoran Desert.

When Europeans entered the area, the prehistoric settlements were in ruins. The O'odham peoples, who claim the Hohokam as ancestors, were living in the Hohokam heartland of the Gila and Salt Rivers. The Tonto Apache and Yavapai tribes were using the Cave Creek area for hunting, gathering, and small-scale agriculture. Their simple, temporary dwellings made little or no impact on the landscape. By the 1870s, these tribes had been removed from Cave Creek.

As miners searched the desert foothills for riches and ranchers soon followed, the search for artifacts among the ruins became a fascinating pastime for cowboys and visitors. However, it was not until the late 1900s that serious efforts were made to study the Cave Creek area's prehistory. Today, archaeologists continue to use local volunteer help for this effort. The Desert Foothills Chapter of the Arizona Archaeological Society is an active group that has contributed much to the knowledge of ancient Cave Creek.

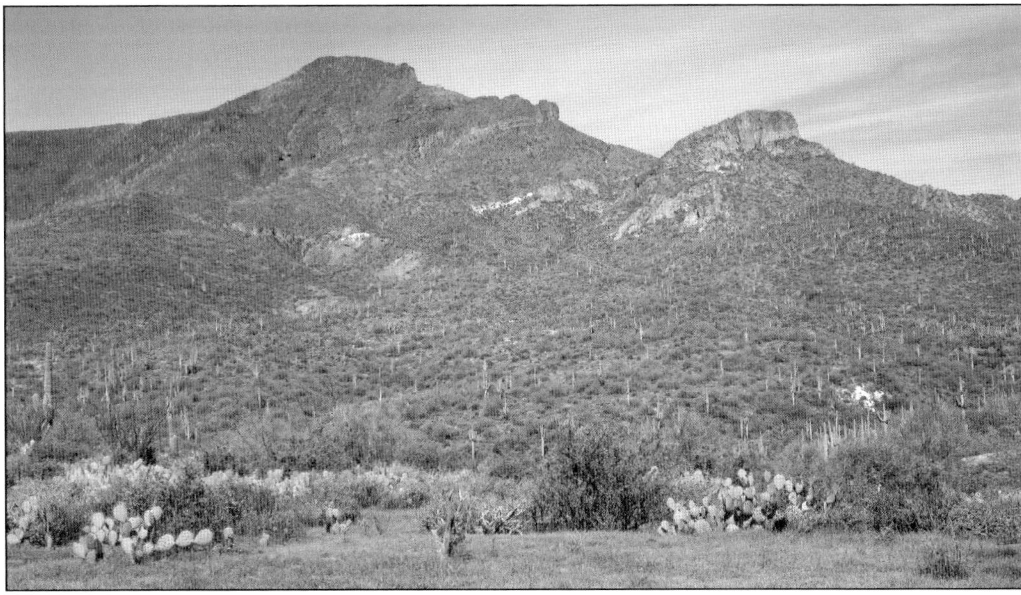

Cave Creek's northern skyline is dominated by Elephant Mountain, in the Spur Cross Ranch Conservation Area. Many visitors take a strenuous, guided hike to the prominent butte, in the center right of this photograph, where they discover, hidden by the vertical cliff, the remains of a prehistoric hilltop fort.

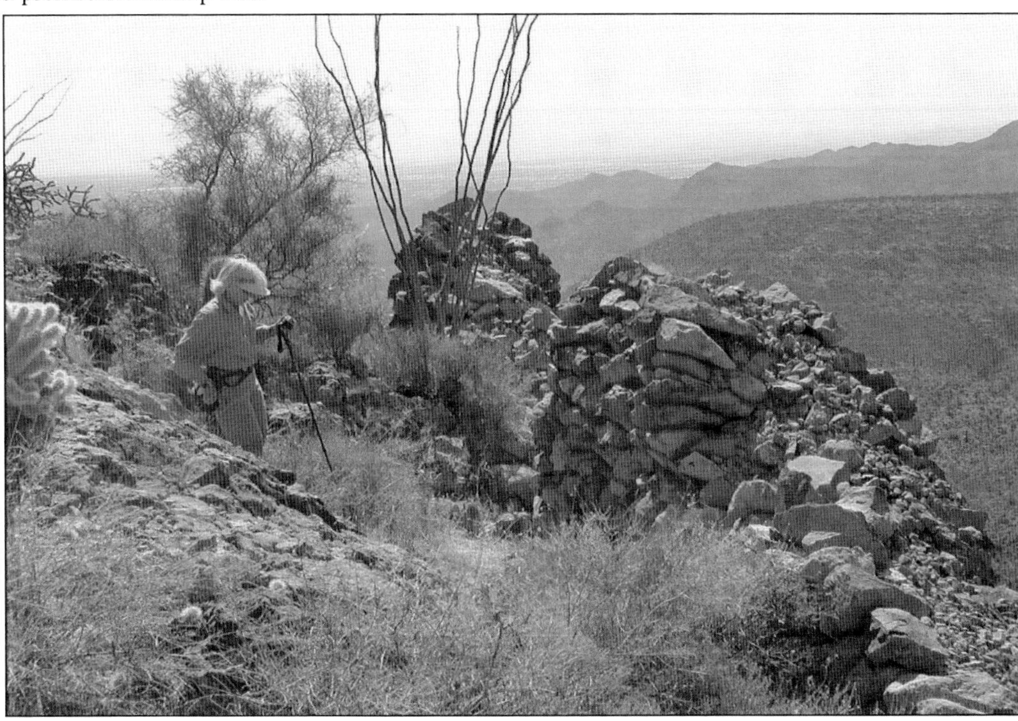

On Elephant Mountain, the undulating remains of the hilltop fort's walls can be seen. There are window openings that could have been used to view the approaches. The fort is also in the line of sight of a least two additional hilltop forts, all part of a regional system of similar structures. (Courtesy of Tom McGuire.)

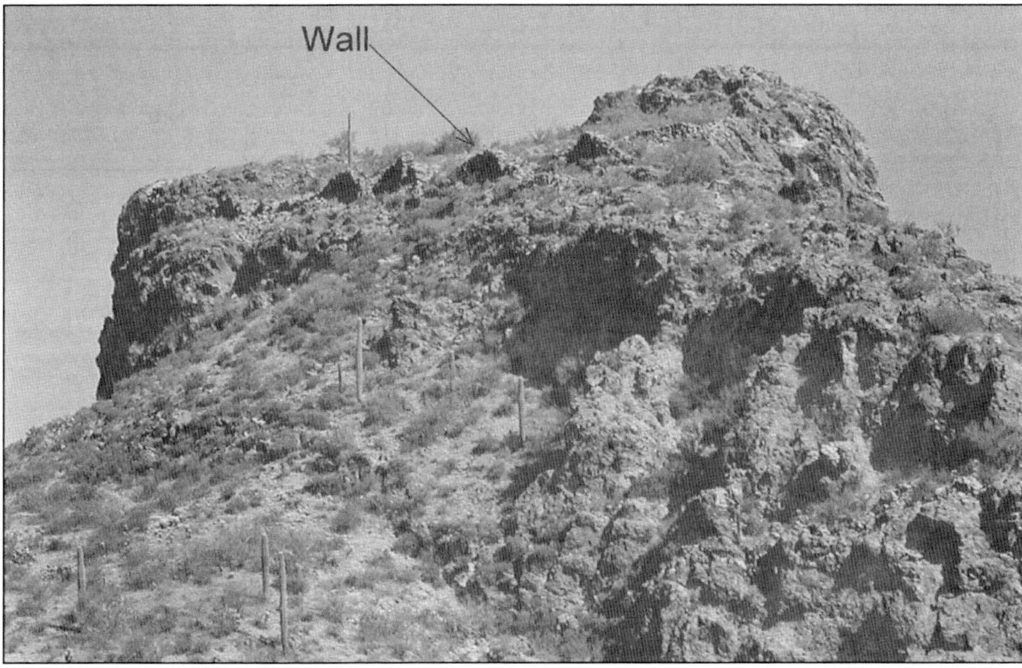

In this photograph, the hilltop fort ruins on Elephant Mountain are a distinct linear feature. From the site, views extend for miles beyond Black Mountain and the town of Cave Creek. The structure probably dates to between 1050 and 1200 AD. A tall lone saguaro is on top of the butte. (Courtesy of Kevin Smith.)

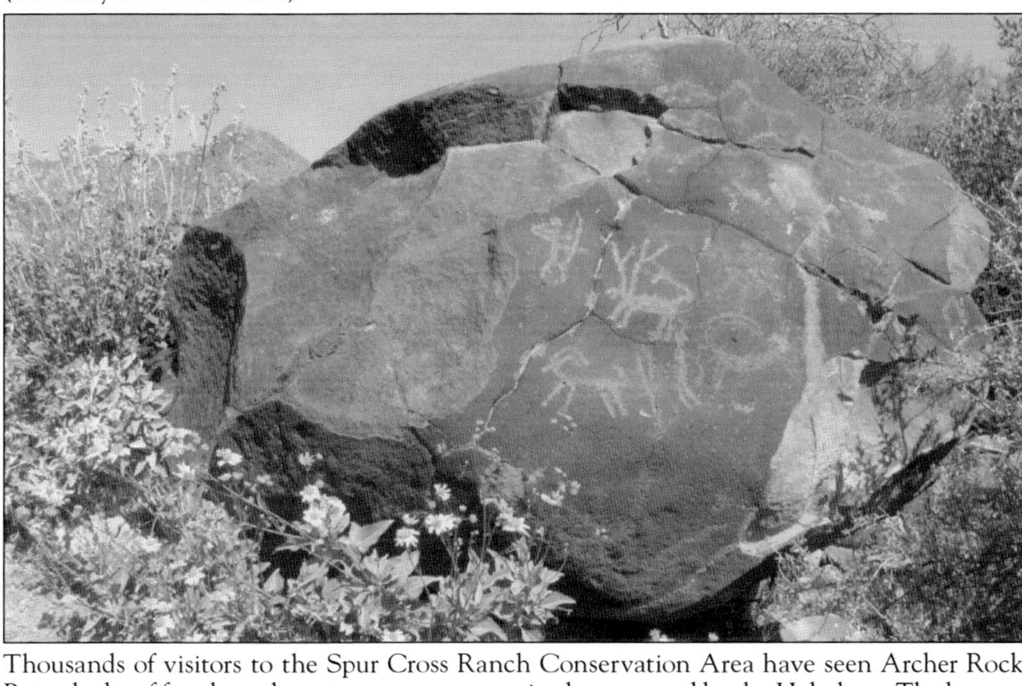

Thousands of visitors to the Spur Cross Ranch Conservation Area have seen Archer Rock. Petroglyphs of four-legged creatures are common in the area used by the Hohokam. The human-like figure with a bow and arrow is rare, however. No one knows exactly when the bow and arrow began to supplement or replace spears and atlatls.

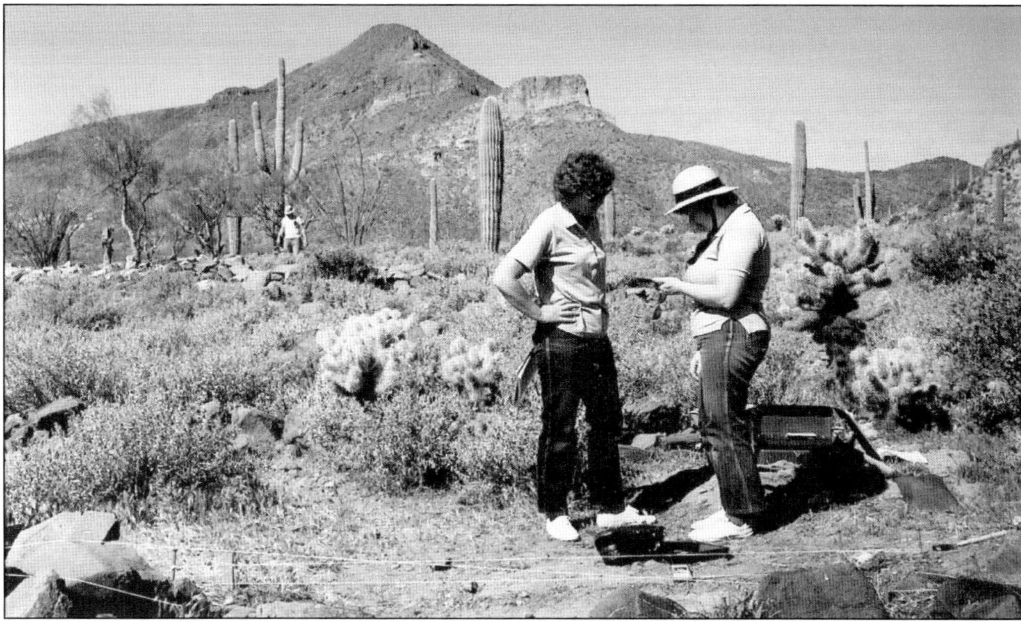

Volunteers from the Desert Foothills Chapter of the Arizona Archaeological Society prepare to excavate part of the First Mesa ruin in the Spur Cross Ranch Conservation Area in the mid-1980s. Strings mark the excavation units. Elephant Mountain and its butte are in the background.

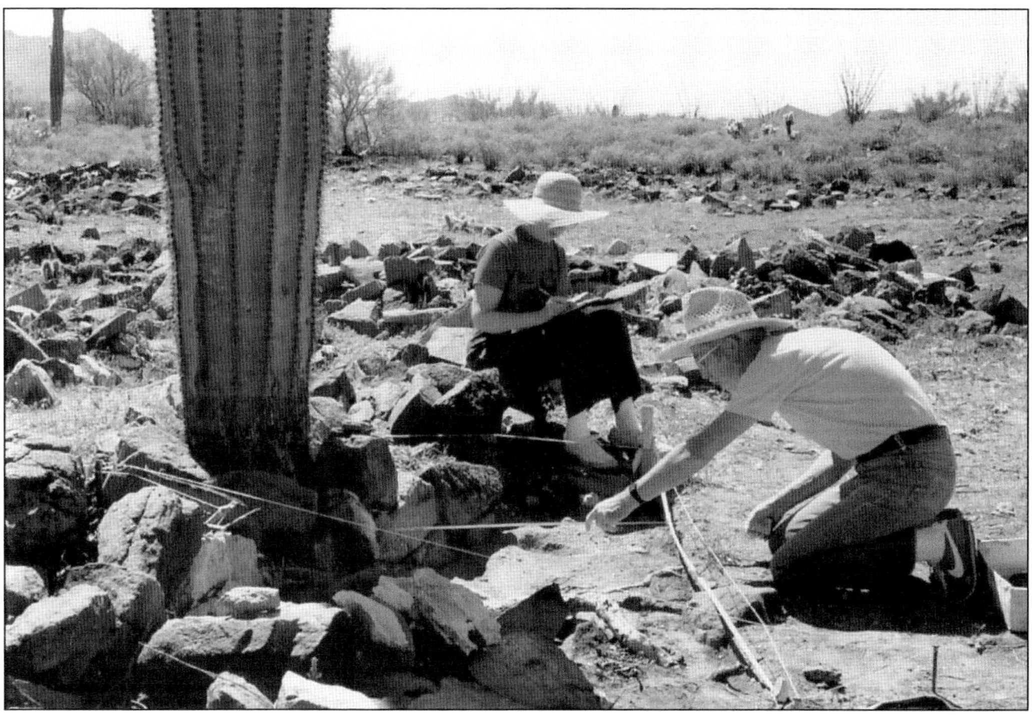

Working carefully to preserve a large saguaro, volunteers excavate a unit on the First Mesa, keeping detailed records of their finds. Excavators, who included students from Arizona State University, moved tons of fallen rock by hand to locate the bases of the walls and the dirt floors, which were below the current ground level by a foot or more.

Dr. Charles Redman of Arizona State University, with his baby on his back, inspects a student's excavation unit on the First Mesa ruin. The typical unit was a meter square, less than half the size of a typical room. It looks like many rocks will have to be moved.

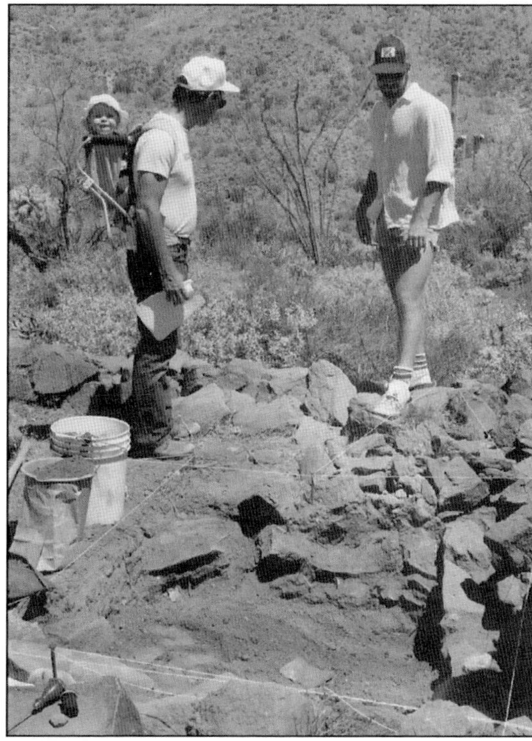

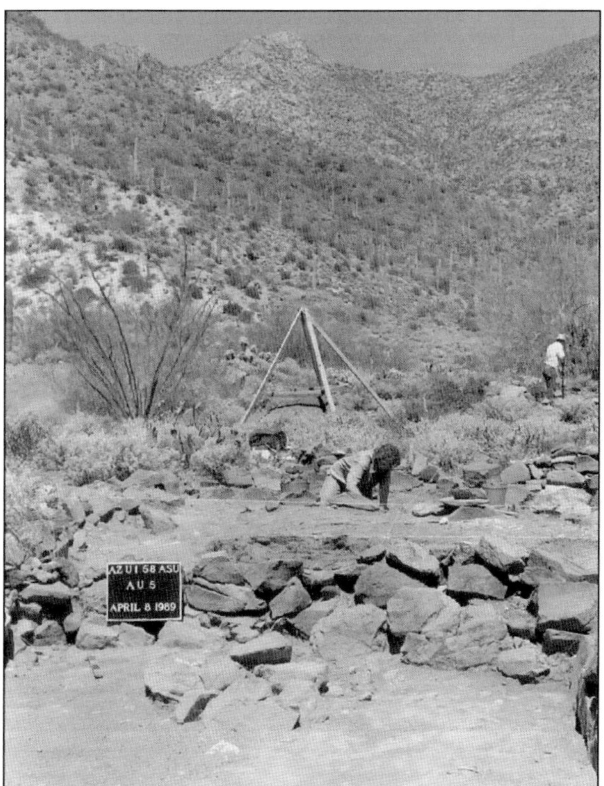

Volunteers worked in 1989 to excavate a small ruin of several dwellings, while Arizona State University students worked on the large ruin on Second Mesa. Many of the archaeological sites in the Spur Cross Ranch Conservation Area have been mapped, but few have been excavated.

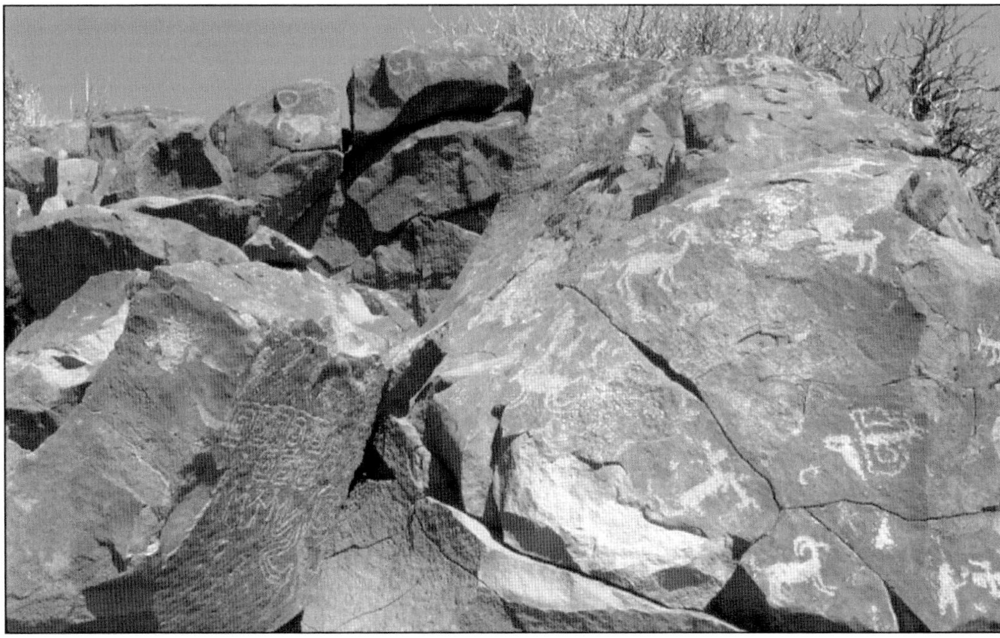

Skull Mesa, across Cave Creek from Spur Cross Ranch, is in the Tonto National Forest. Hardy hikers will be rewarded by its treasure trove of petroglyphs. Among the motifs common in the region are birds, several kinds of animal figures, possible humans, and abstract geometrics. (Courtesy of Kevin Smith.)

This close-up of part of the petroglyph gallery above shows figures standing hand-in-hand. The long-necked water birds at the top are similar to motifs found in some red-on-buff Hohokam pottery made 1,000 years ago or more. Petroglyphs cannot truly be dated, but such similarities can suggest a possible time period. (Courtesy of Kevin Smith.)

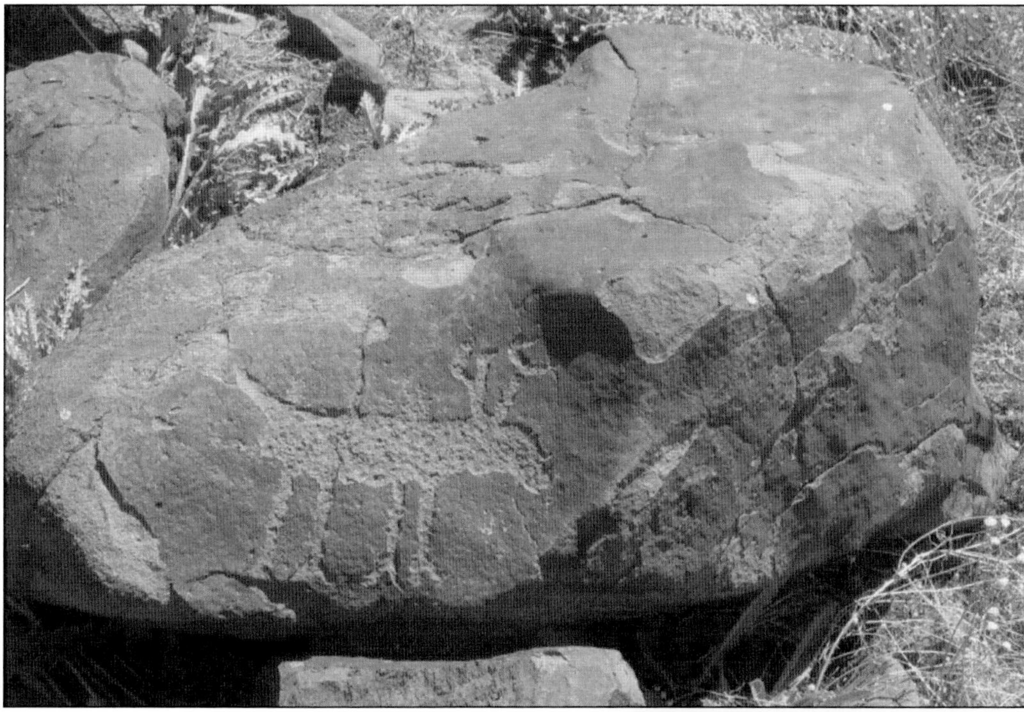

Deer-like figures, such as the stag figure seen above on Skull Mesa, are common petroglyph subjects found in and around the Cave Creek watershed. (Courtesy of Kevin Smith.)

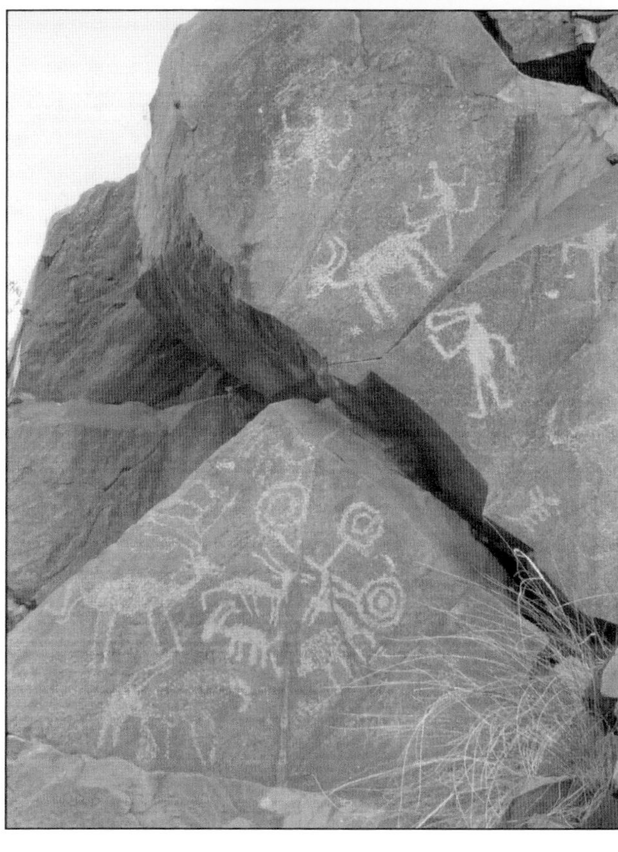

Another petroglyph gallery, this time from Grapevine Wash, is on private property along Carefree's northern border. The debate on the meaning of petroglyphs is never-ending. Knowledge of their true meaning, however, remains with the culture that made them. (Courtesy of the Desert Foothills Land Trust.)

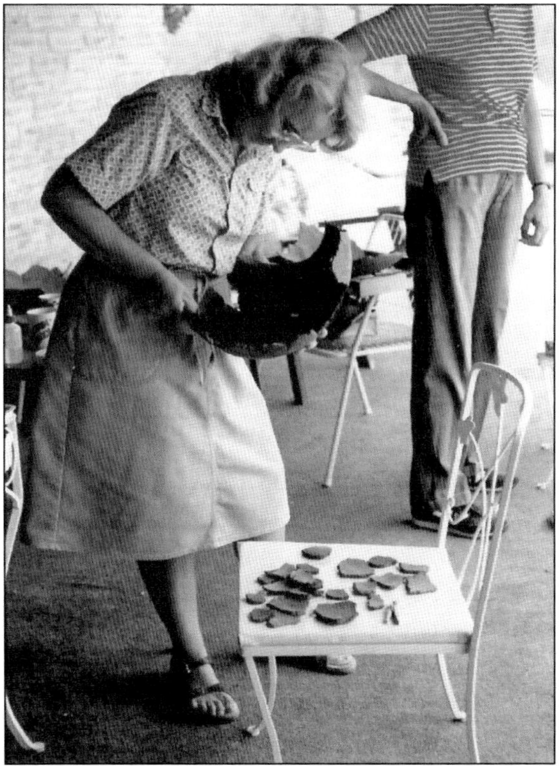

In 1985, the Livingston family found a Hohokam-style pit house while excavating for a pool not far from Carefree Highway and Cave Creek Road. Members of the Arizona Archaeology Society, professionally supervised, excavated the dwelling and pieced together some of the broken pots.

The half of a plain-ware vessel below is from the Livingston site. The storage jar, or olla, is about 19 inches across and 18 inches high. Many pots this large and larger have been found at local sites. They were made without a potter's wheel.

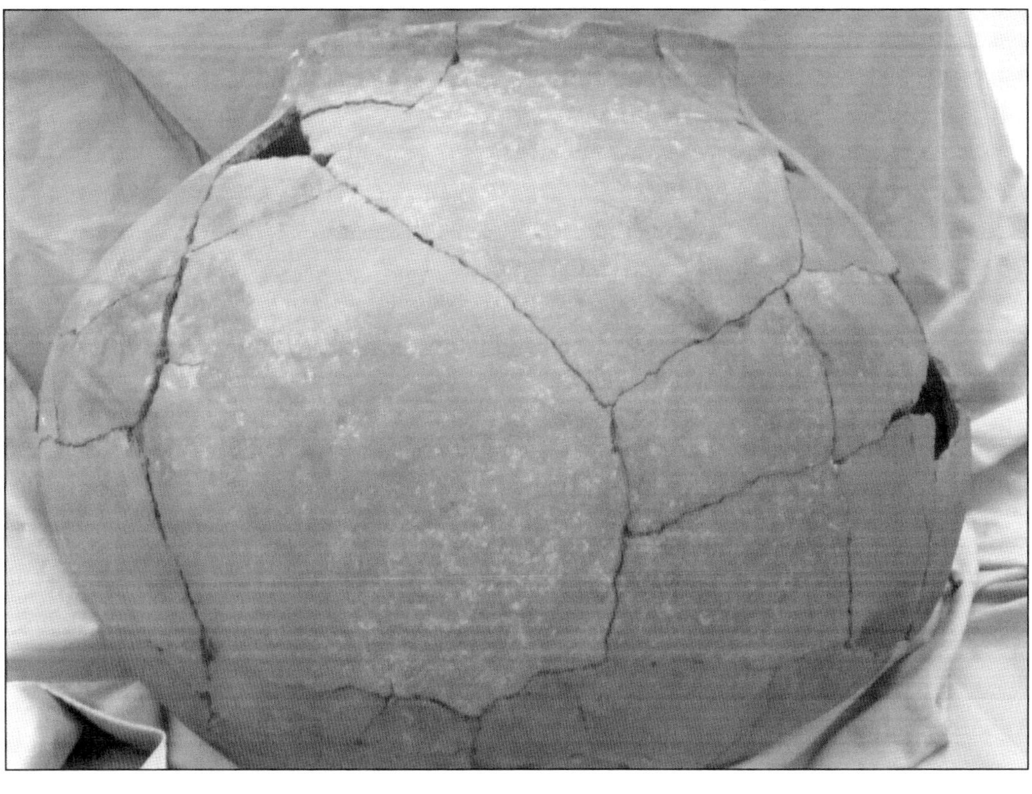

Many Cave Creek residents have found artifacts in their backyards, sometimes just a few pottery sherds or stone tool pieces and sometimes whole sites. A few have invited the public to tour their finds, such as these artifacts from the Patterson site. The owners carefully pieced together several Hohokam vessels, showing the skills of the ancient potters. (Courtesy of the Desert Foothills Chapter of the Arizona Archaeological Society.)

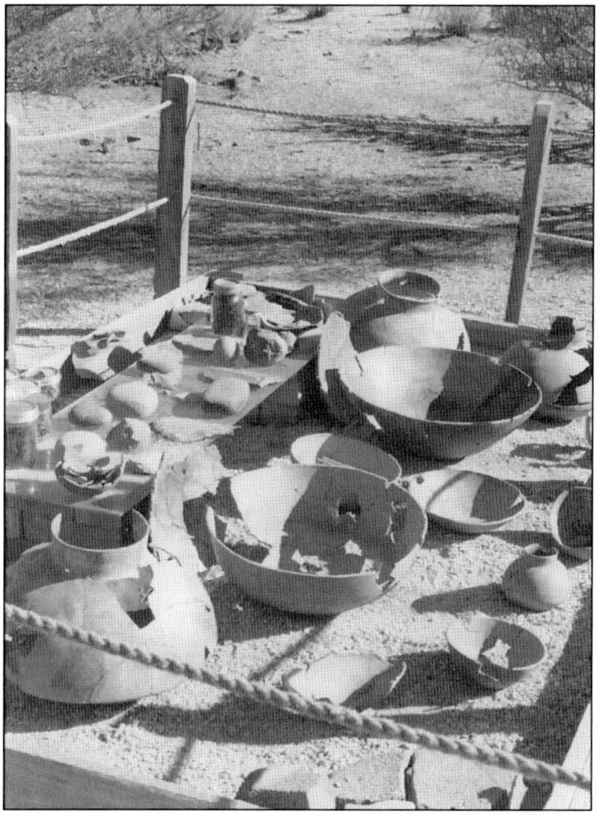

The excavated dwelling floor below, at the Mueller site in Cave Creek, shows a typical Hohokam pit house structure: two large center support posts and smaller posts around the perimeter. The wood has disintegrated but postholes remain. Between the door opening (center top) and the large postholes is a clay-lined hearth. A second hearth was in the entryway. An archaeologist supervised the excavation and conducted a field school at the site.

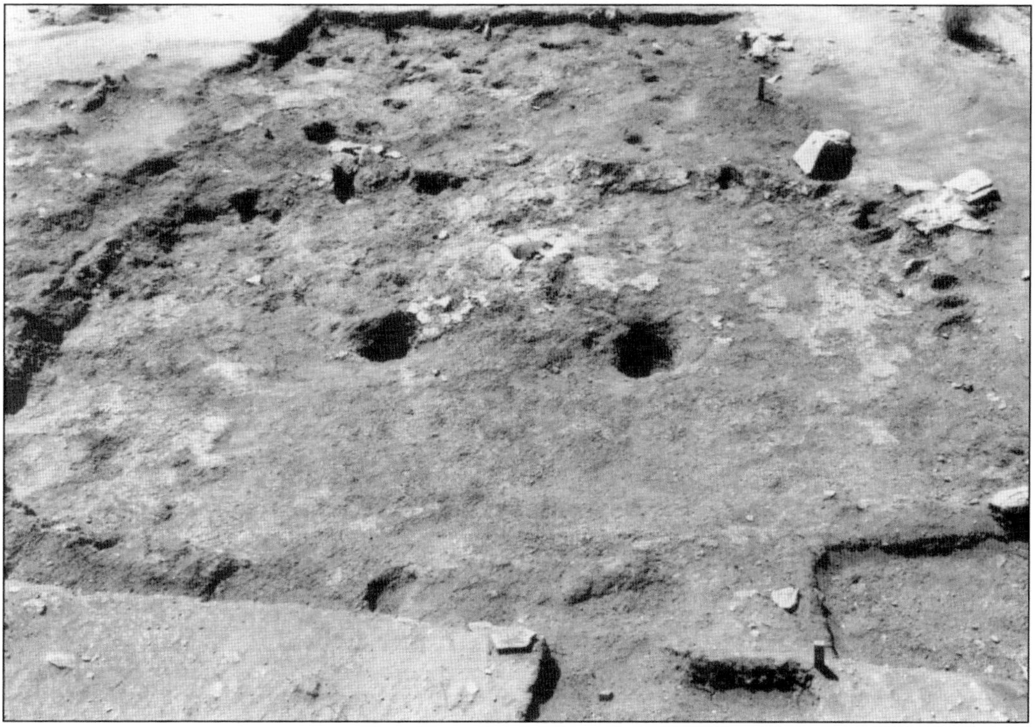

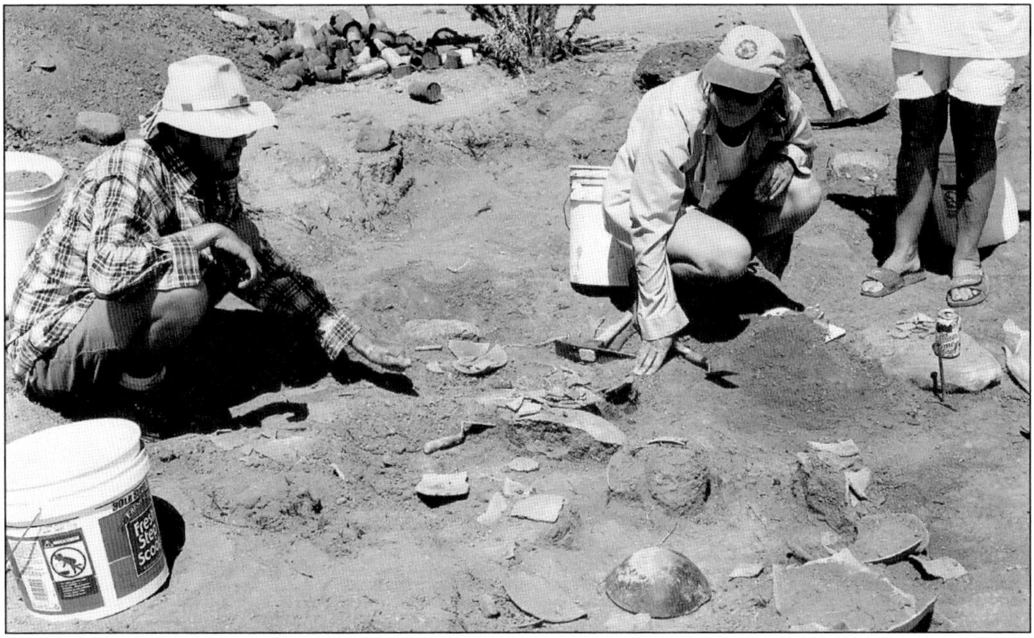

Several pit houses were excavated in 1999 in the Estado de Cholla subdivision on Carefree Highway. Archaeologists, assisted by local volunteers, determined that the dwellings were occupied in approximately 1000 AD by people who grew corn, cotton, and other crops in fields nearby.

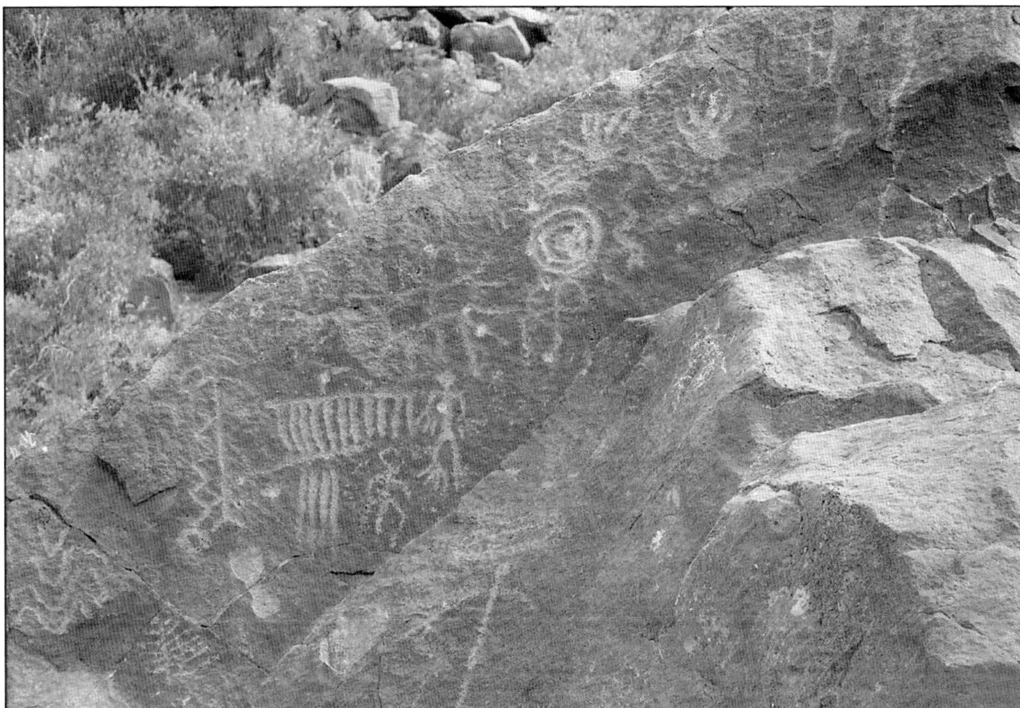

Nearly 100 years ago, the Lewis brothers homesteaded the 6L Ranch on upper Cave Creek. Today, little remains of the ranch, which is surrounded by the Tonto National Forest. The area is better known for its boulders like these, covered with typical Hohokam petroglyphs.

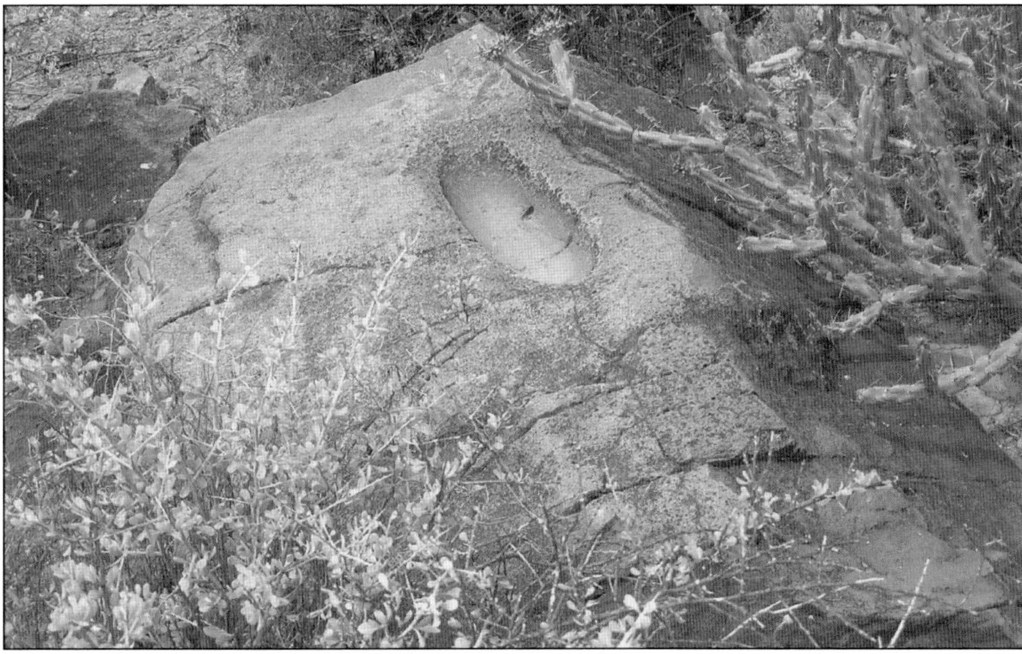

Many metates, or grinding stones, have been found in the desert foothills of Cave Creek. They were used to grind corn, seeds, and other tough foods using manos, which are stones held in the hand. The Cave Creek Museum has numerous examples of metates and manos. Some metates, like this one at 6L Ranch, remain in the bedrock.

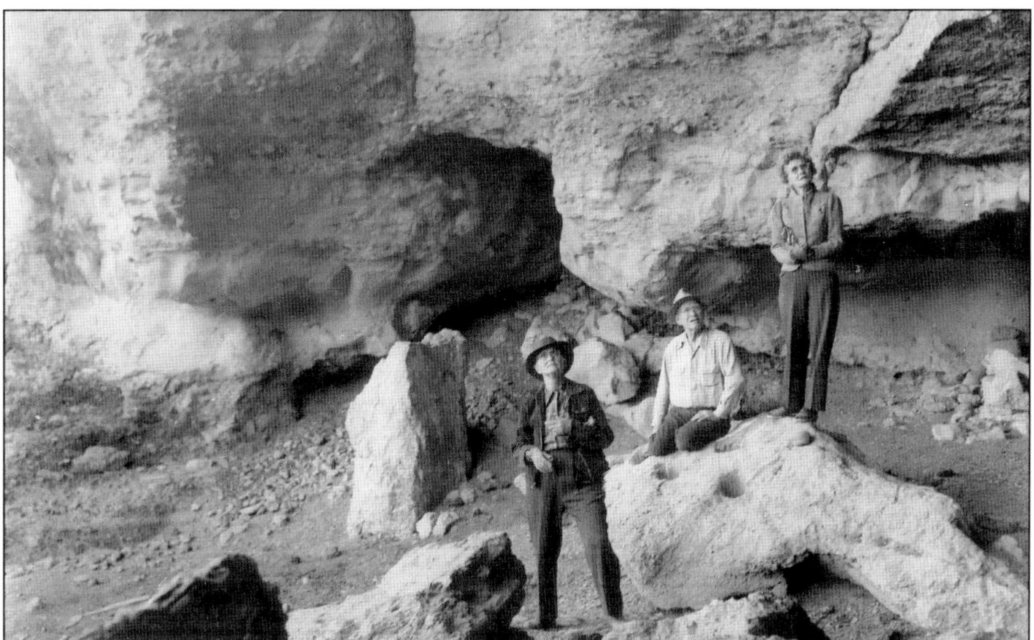

Inside Cave Creek's cave, prehistoric remnants such as these mortar holes can be found. The site also includes petroglyphs and a few small pictographs (rock paintings) as well as historical graffiti. The cave was the location of a bloody fight between the United States 5th Cavalry and the Tonto Apaches in 1873.

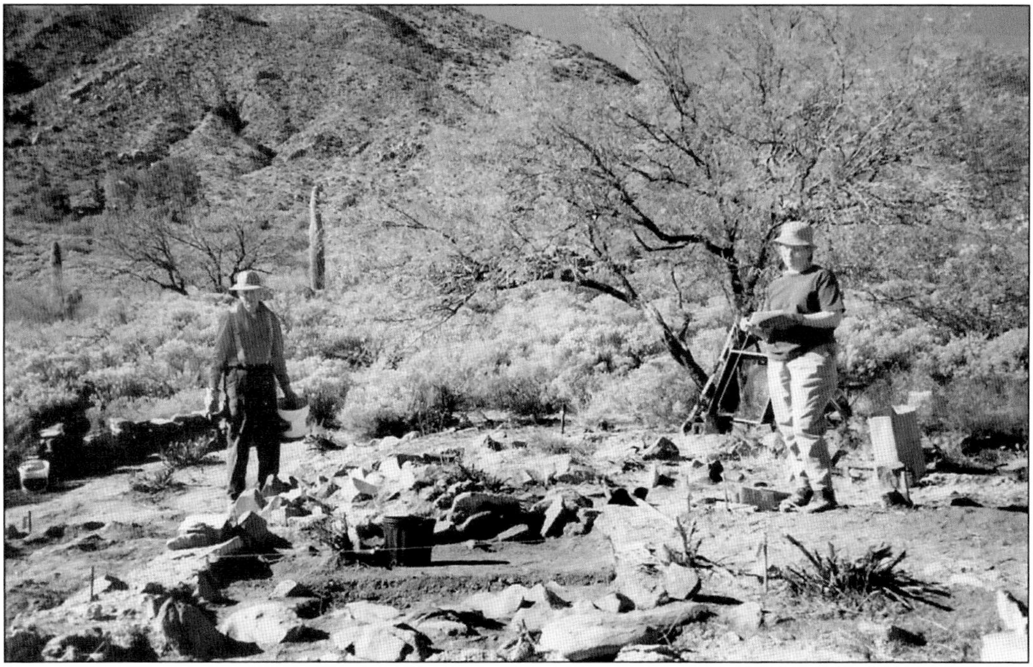

Frank Casanova (left) supervised the excavation of the Blue Wash ruin on his property in Tonto Hills, northeast of Carefree, with the help of volunteers like this one from the Arizona Archaeological Society.

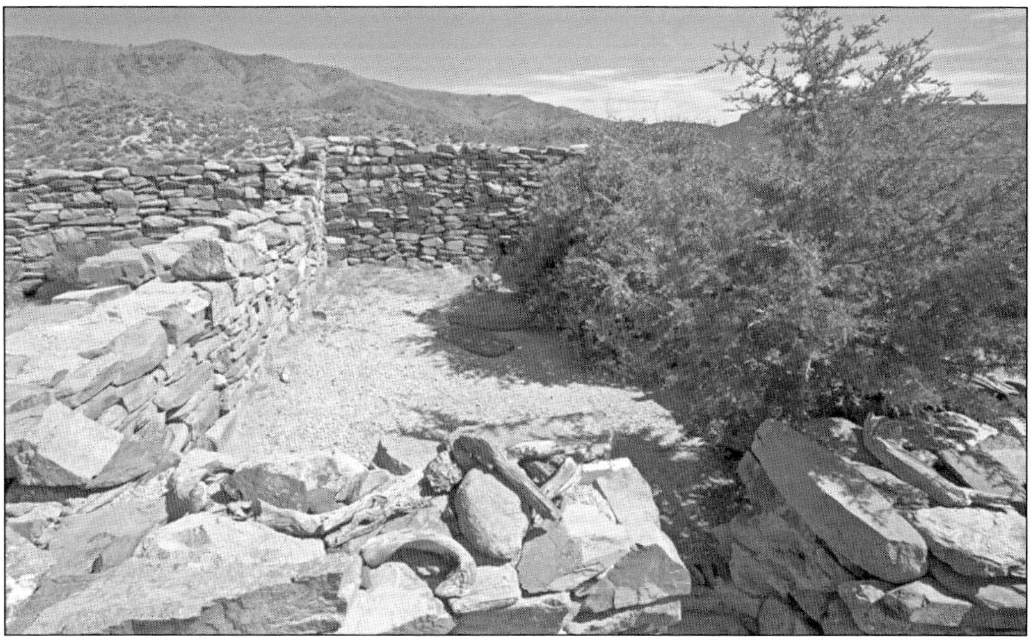

This is a partially rebuilt room of the Blue Wash ruin on the Casanova property. Frank Casanova rebuilt part of the small pueblo to resemble the rock-walled rooms of the area dating from approximately 1200–1300 AD. Sears-Kay ruin, nearby in the Tonto National Forest, is another pueblo from that era. An interpretive replica of the Sears-Kay ruin is on exhibit at the Cave Creek Museum. (Courtesy of Larry Morehouse.)

Two

The Military Road

With the end of the Civil War, the occupation and settlement of the West resumed, which included the recently created Arizona Territory.

In the late 1860s, the US Army was ordered to subdue and remove all Native Americans to reservations. In central Arizona, Fort Whipple, Camp Verde, and Fort McDowell were established as bases of operations, primarily against the Tonto Apache. These highly mobile, fierce warriors fought to keep their territory. In 1870, this territory included the Cave Creek watershed and the New River Mountains.

Distribution of supplies and communication between posts was a problem, so the construction of roads capable of travel by small escort wagons became a priority. In October 1870, Gen. George Stoneman and a small troop of cavalry left Fort McDowell to explore a possible route to Fort Whipple. Their first objective was to locate "Bubbling Springs," a source of water and forage on Cave Creek near what became Rancho Mañana. From this location, the troops continued up the east bank of the creek, crossing it once they were clear of Go John Mountain. They then proceeded northwest to the New River and up Black Canyon to Fort Whipple. After the survey, work began to construct the Military Road. Several years later, the route was changed to go south of Go John Mountain in order to accommodate larger wagons.

Not far from where the road crossed the creek is the large cave that is the town's namesake. Troops from Fort McDowell on a scouting patrol discovered an Apache rancheria near the cave. In a deceptive move, the troops made a show of returning to the fort on the Military Road. However, a smaller contingent secretly remained behind, including famous scout Al Sieber. The soldiers then attacked the rancheria on Christmas Eve 1873, killing nine warriors, including the war chief Nanotz. The area then became safe for settlement, with prospectors being the first to arrive in 1874.

There are still faint reminders of the Military Road through Carefree near the private airport, before it winds its way along the north side of Black Mountain. There are fascinating ruins at the Cavalry Remount Station, located near where the Military Road crosses the creek. Both military and historical artifacts have been recovered at the site. Local historians continue to explore and document the route of the historic Military Road.

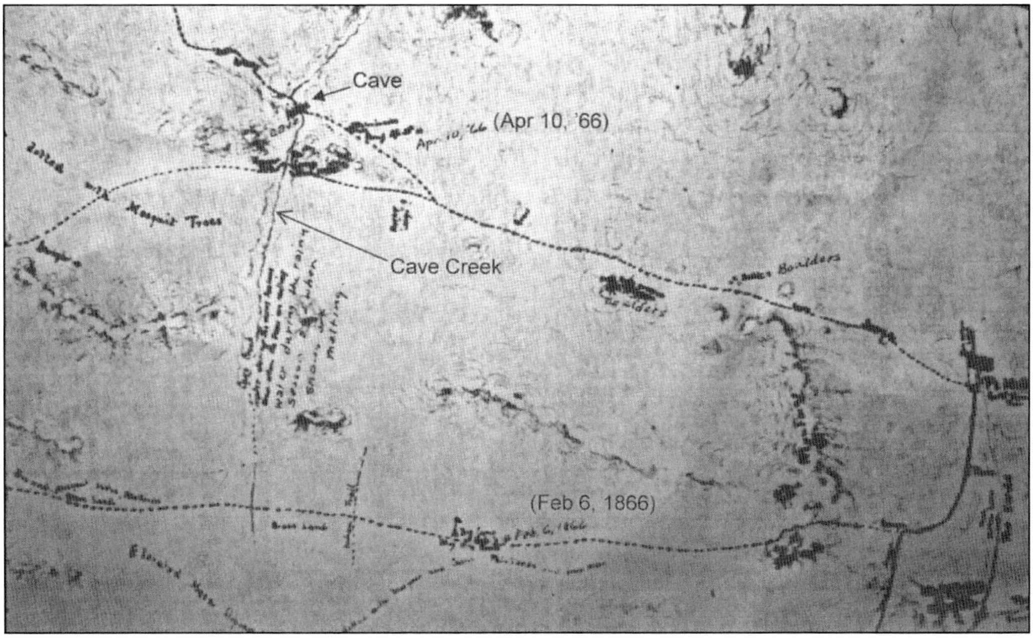

This portion of an 1866 military map shows the Indian trails in the Cave Creek area. These Indian trails became the basis of the Military Road in 1870. (Courtesy of the Arizona Historical Foundation, Arizona State University.)

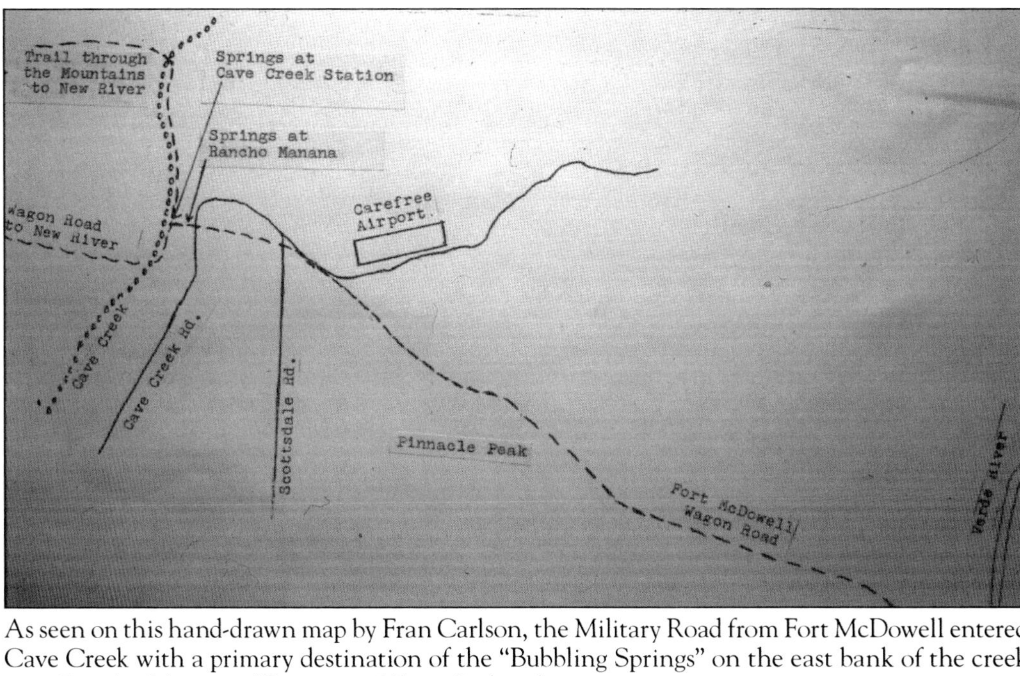

As seen on this hand-drawn map by Fran Carlson, the Military Road from Fort McDowell entered Cave Creek with a primary destination of the "Bubbling Springs" on the east bank of the creek near Rancho Mañana. (Courtesy of Fran Carlson.)

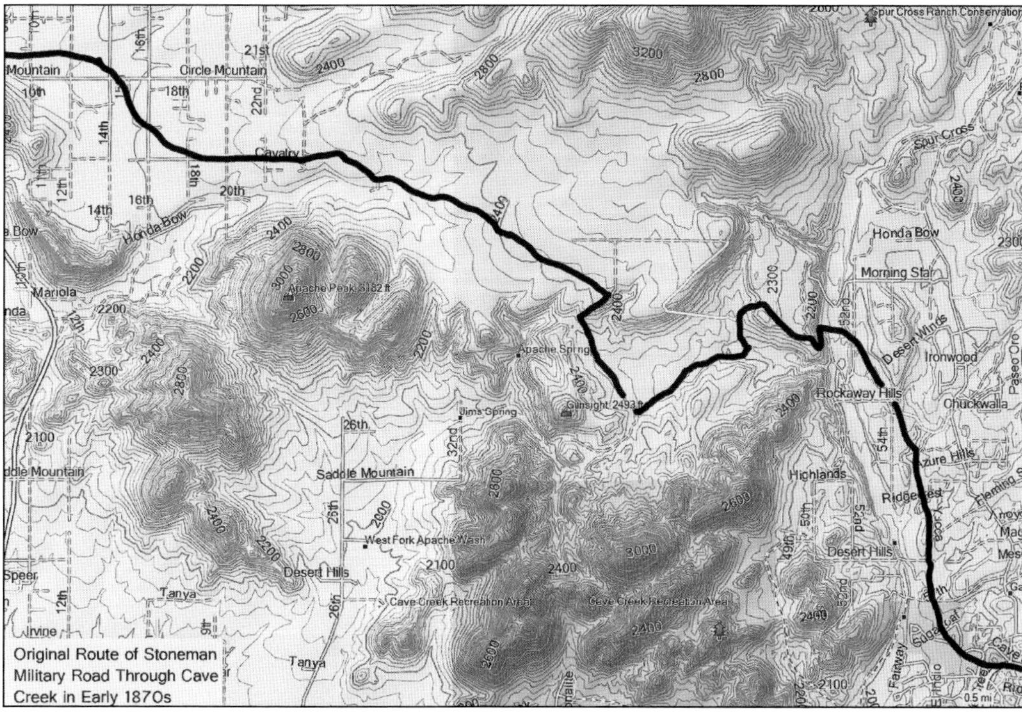

The Military Road continued up the east bank of Cave Creek, crossing north of Go John Mountain, and then went northwest between Apache Peak and New River Mesa. (Courtesy of Bob Cook.)

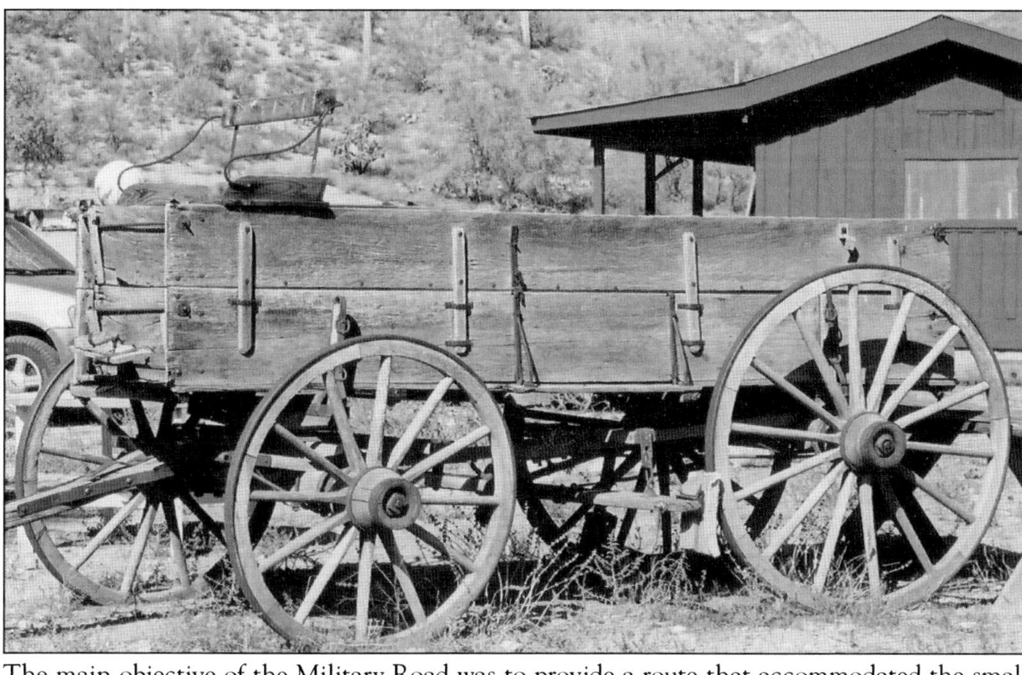

The main objective of the Military Road was to provide a route that accommodated the small escorts or ambulance wagons similar to the one seen here. Supplies and medical support were critical to the Army's field operation.

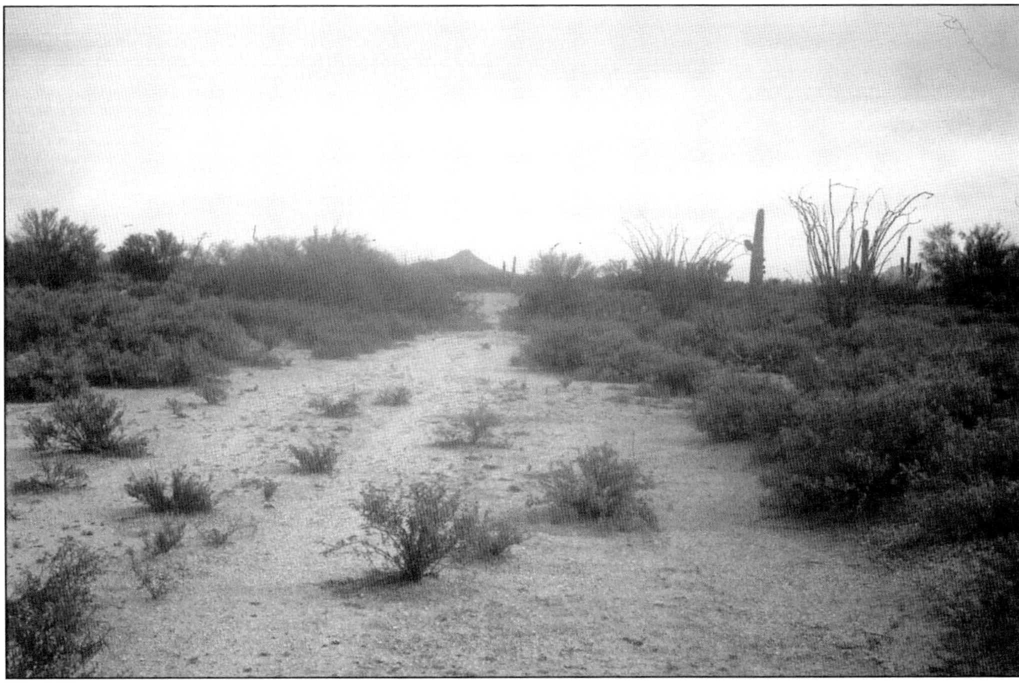

A distinct segment of the Military Road remains near today's Carefree Airport. Its southeast/northwest axis clearly points to the creek and New River. Goldie Brown Mountain is in the center background.

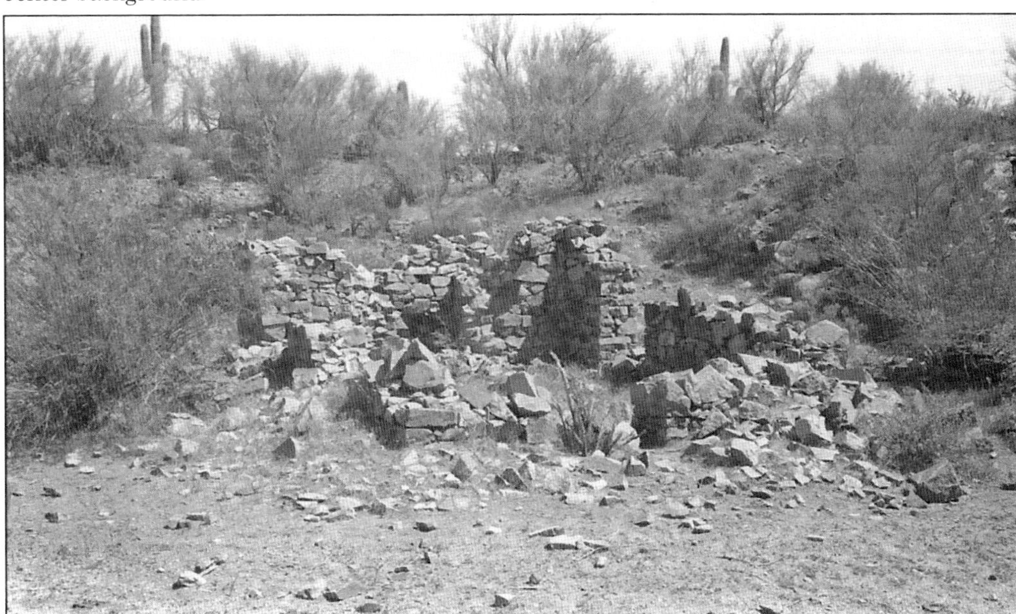

North of the "Bubbling Springs" on the creek are the ruins of several small buildings that were on the Military Road. Called the Cavalry Remount Station, this location has been identified by local historians as a stopover and supply post for the military. The structure had two rooms, one with a fireplace that may have served as a kitchen. Archaeological excavations and surveys have recovered many military artifacts from the site.

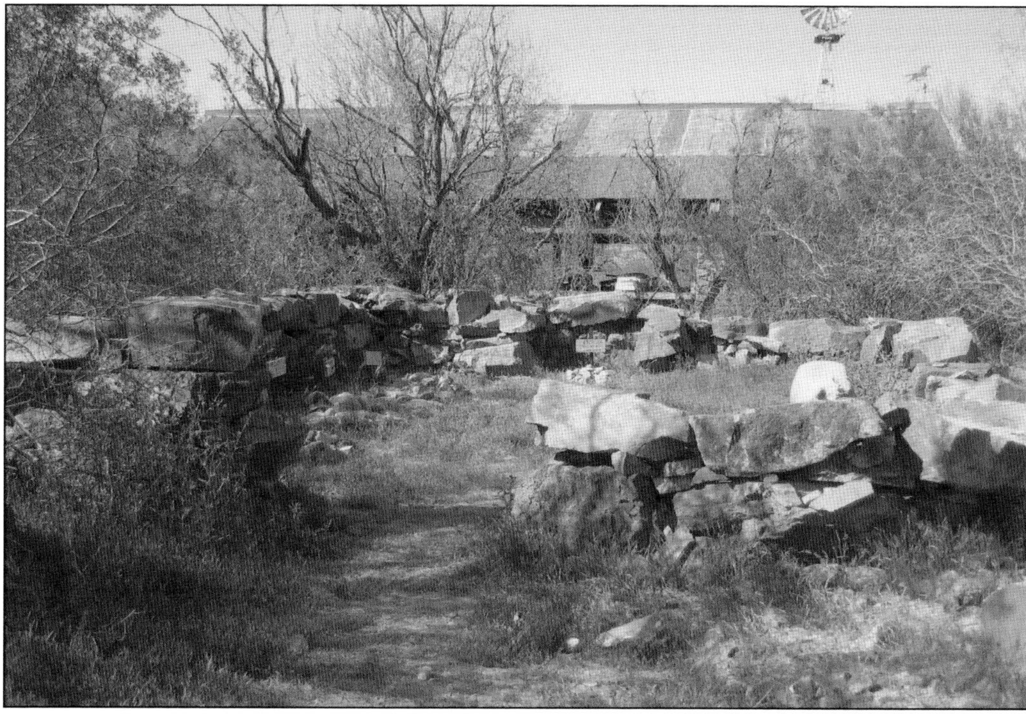

A larger one-room structure at the Cavalry Remount Station has a fireplace and may have been used as a barracks. After the end of the military operations in the 1870s and 1880s, there is a report that the site operated as a general store and saloon, servicing the miners in the area. (Courtesy of Bob Cook.)

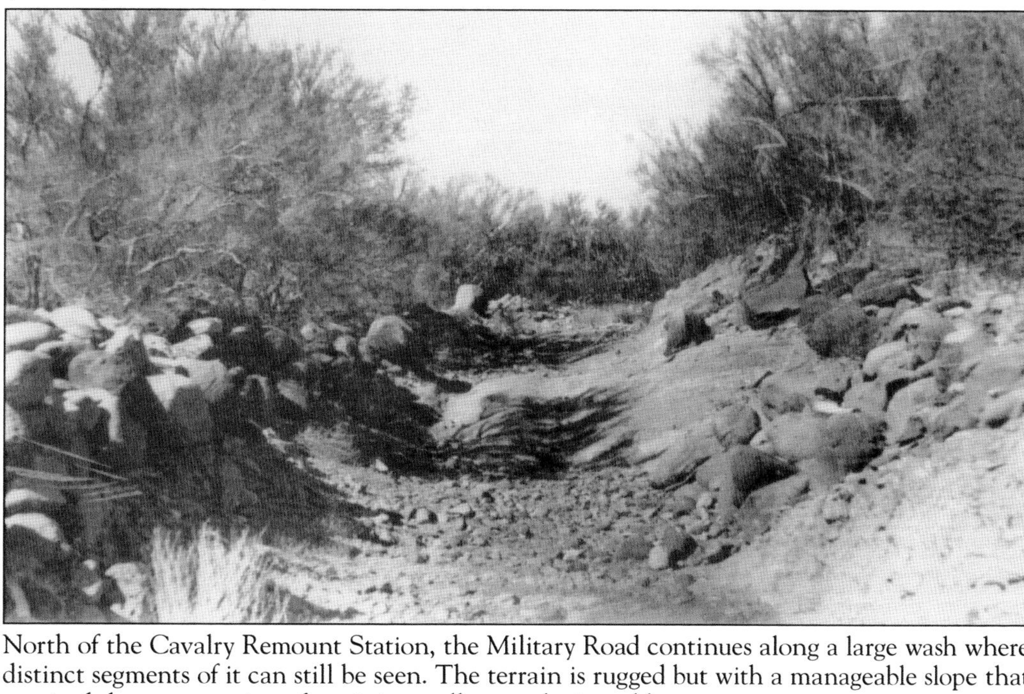

North of the Cavalry Remount Station, the Military Road continues along a large wash where distinct segments of it can still be seen. The terrain is rugged but with a manageable slope that required the construction of retaining walls to make it usable.

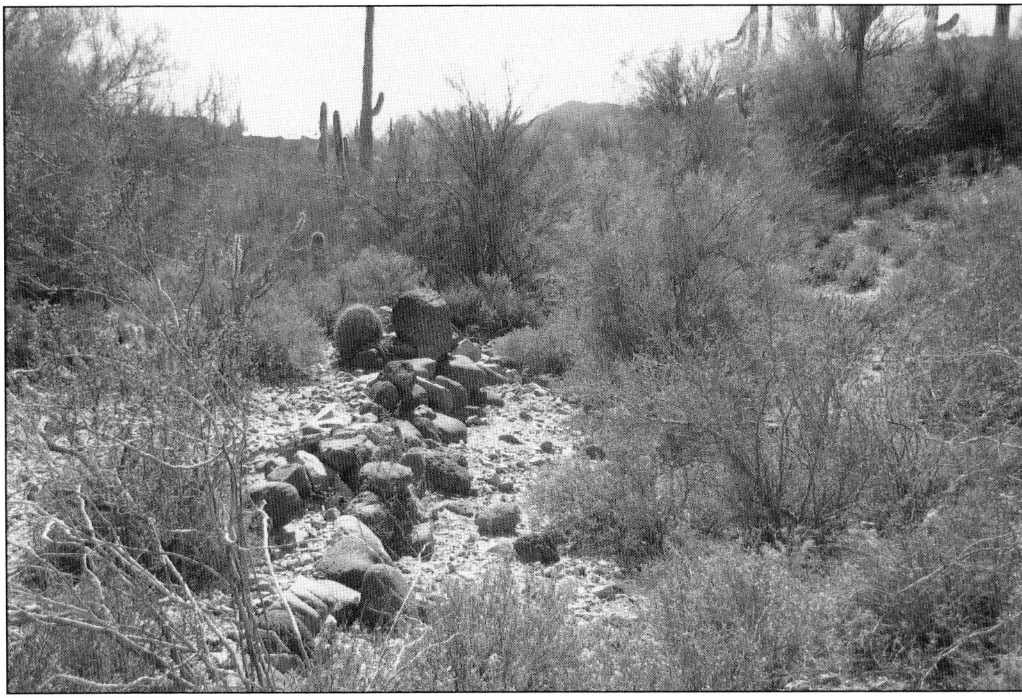

The photograph above shows how the Military Road was built into the side of the wash using large boulders to create the roadbed. The view looks southwest. (Courtesy of Bob Cook.)

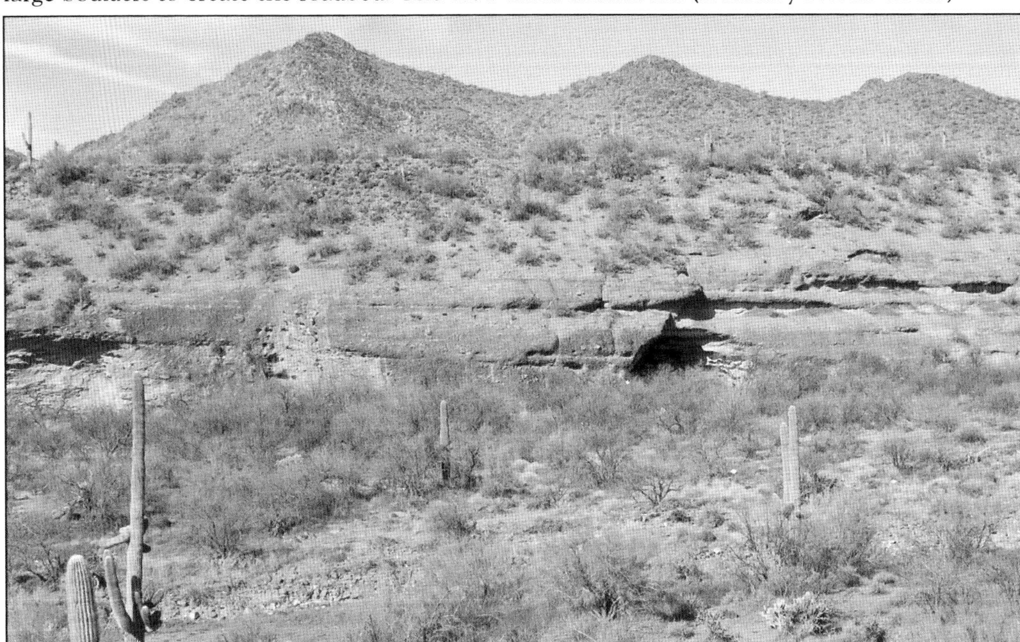

Cave Creek's namesake, this large, recessive rock shelter, is a prominent feature of the creek as it drains south from the mountains. Now on private property, the cave has been used by wildlife and Native Americans for thousands of years as well as by cavalry troops. (Courtesy of Desert Foothills Land Trust.)

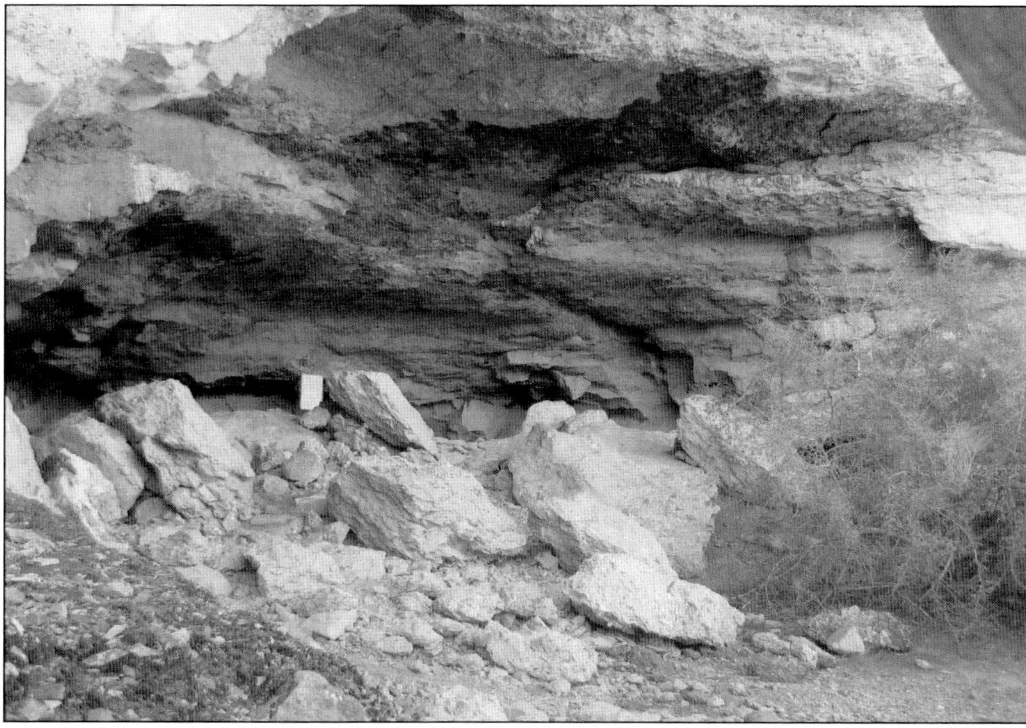

The cave is a large erosional feature cut into the embankment. The overhang has provided shelter from the elements and from danger for many. Army reports from the Christmas Eve 1873 attack note that there were 11 Apache wikiups, or shelters, in and around the cave. The total Apache casualties during that attack are unknown, but nine warriors were killed.

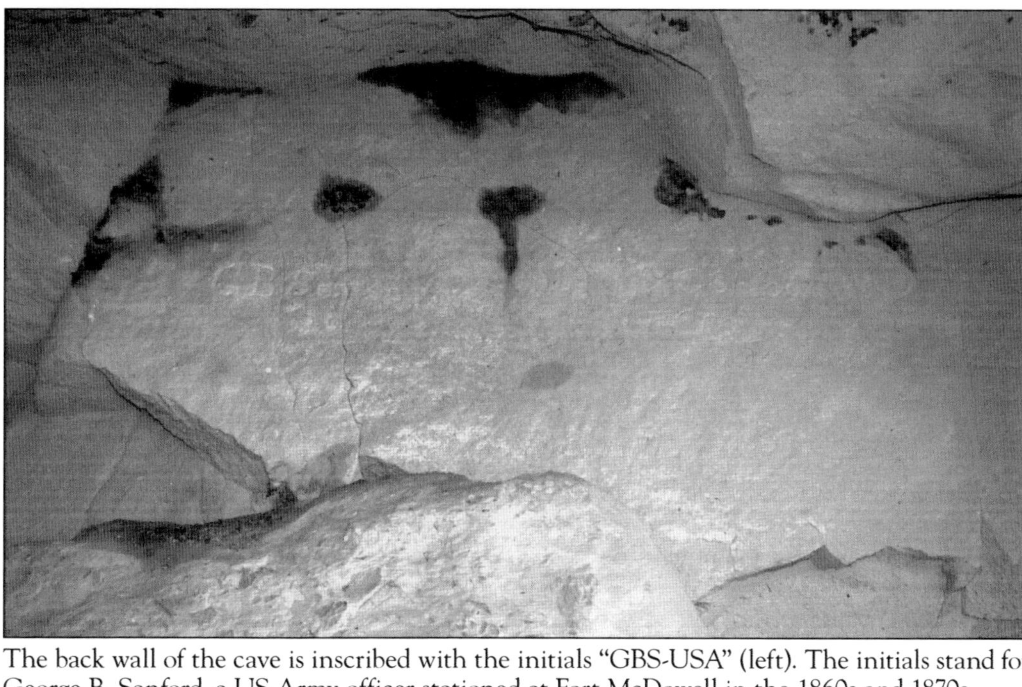

The back wall of the cave is inscribed with the initials "GBS-USA" (left). The initials stand for George B. Sanford, a US Army officer stationed at Fort McDowell in the 1860s and 1870s.

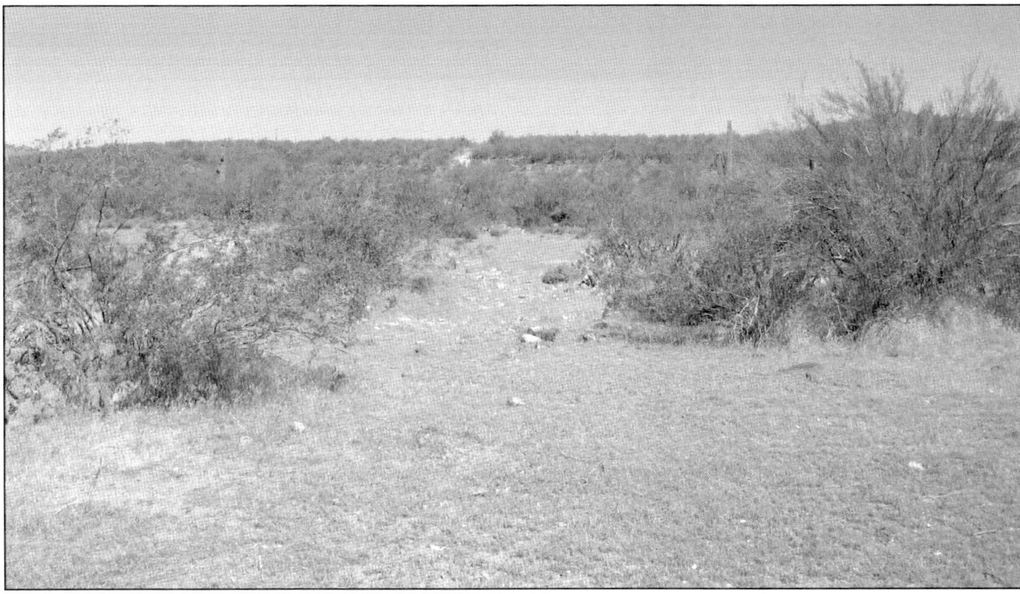

Remnants of the Military Road can be seen clearly today on the route from the creek northwest to New River. The terrain is primarily soil over caliche, or hardpan. This soil wore away quickly from use and has never grown back. (Courtesy of Bob Cook.)

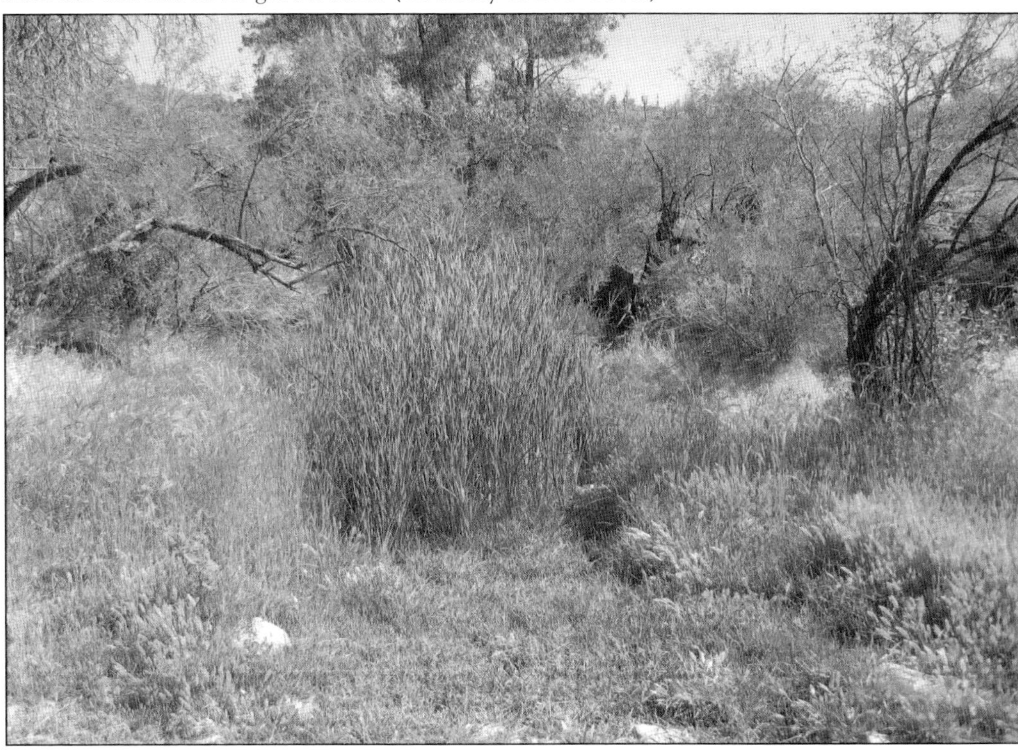

Near the Military Road at the north end of Apache Peak lies a historical spring that was used occasionally by the military as a bivouac area or a water source. Apache Spring is generally dependable as a year-round water source and has been used by game and human travelers for centuries. (Courtesy of Bob Cook.)

Three

Cave Creek Mining District

Following the cessation of skirmishes with the Apaches in the early 1870s, the area opened up to prospectors and miners. The 144-square-mile Cave Creek Mining District extended into the Continental Mountains and supported at least 126 mining claims over the years. The majority of the productive mines yielded gold, silver, and copper. Additionally, lead, tungsten, jasper, and onyx were mined. The mining process was laborious. Ore was crushed in rock arrastres, with mules supplying power.

William Rowe, a rancher along the Salt River, made the first major gold discovery in 1874. Originally the Lyon Mine, the area soon became known as Gold Hill.

Other early noteworthy mining claims included the Golden Star Mine, founded by William Hellings, which had a 10-stamp mill powered by local firewood. The mine folded within two years. Charles Philes came from Phoenix to work for Hellings and stayed until 1913, filing his last mining claim at the age of 84. Charles Fleming arrived in 1876 and mined on the southwest side of Continental Mountain until his death in 1903. Farther east, Edward Cave, known as Old Rackensack, claimed the Red Rover Mine in 1880.

In 1878, three settlers from Phoenix discovered gold in their claim, the Phoenix Mine. They sold it to a New York stockbroker two years later. By 1887, with a 10-stamp mill in place, the small mining camp of Liscum materialized with both a post office and a school. The Panic of 1893 doomed the venture.

A half mile to the southwest was the Maricopa Mine. It and the Phoenix Mine are reported to have been the largest gold-producing mines, perhaps accounting for $250,000 of annual revenue until 1900, by which time the Cave Creek mining boom was largely over.

The Mormon Girl Mine, on Black Mountain's southwest flank, drew the popular Taylor family to dig from the mid-1880s until 1899, when their stash of gold was stolen. Subsequent owners tried their luck through the 1960s.

Mining activity in the 1900s was sporadic, although many local ranchers continued to work small claims. The Great Depression drew some hard-luck prospectors to the area. The Red Rover Mine found some new life for a time, but the desert has reclaimed most mining sites.

The Cave Creek Museum has moved the historical Golden Reef stamp mill to its grounds and restored it. The stamp mill is a magnificent reminder of an important chapter of Cave Creek history.

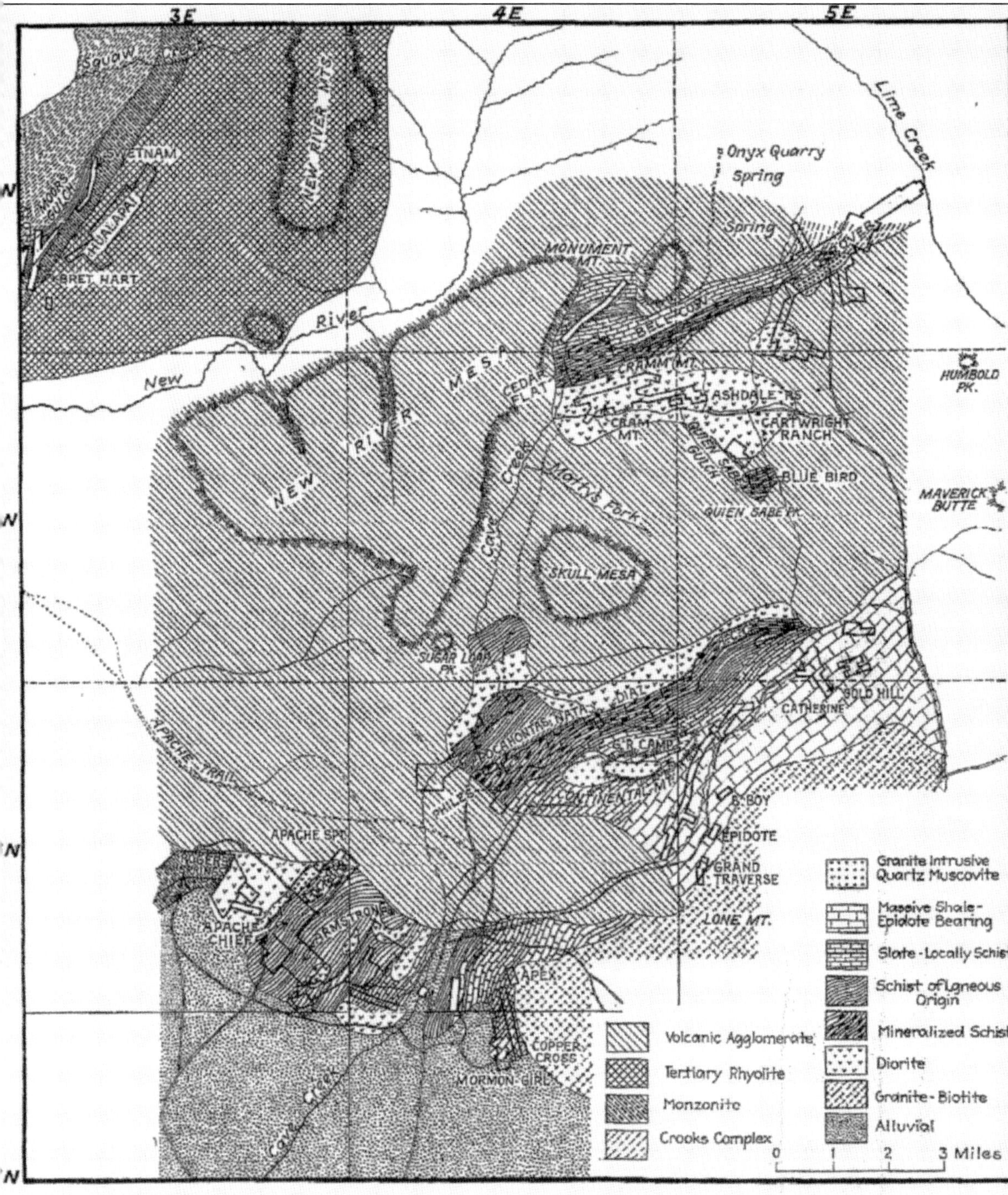

This map shows the Cave Creek Mining District, as published in the *Engineering and Mining Journal* (Volume 110, No. 14) on October 2, 1920. The district covers the Red Rover in the north, Gold Hill to the east, the Mormon Girl Mine in the south, and the Daisy claim on the west side. There were at least 126 claims documented in the Cave Creek Mining District.

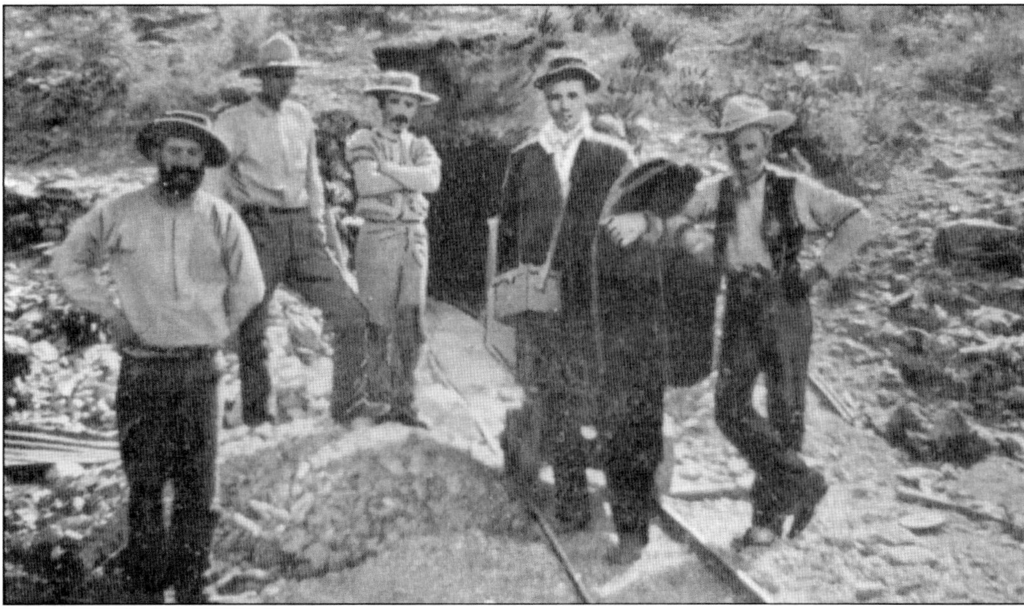

The Mormon Girl Mine produced lode gold, copper, silver, lead, zinc, and silicon. Colorful chrysocolla, a green mineral attesting to the presence of copper, is common near the mine.

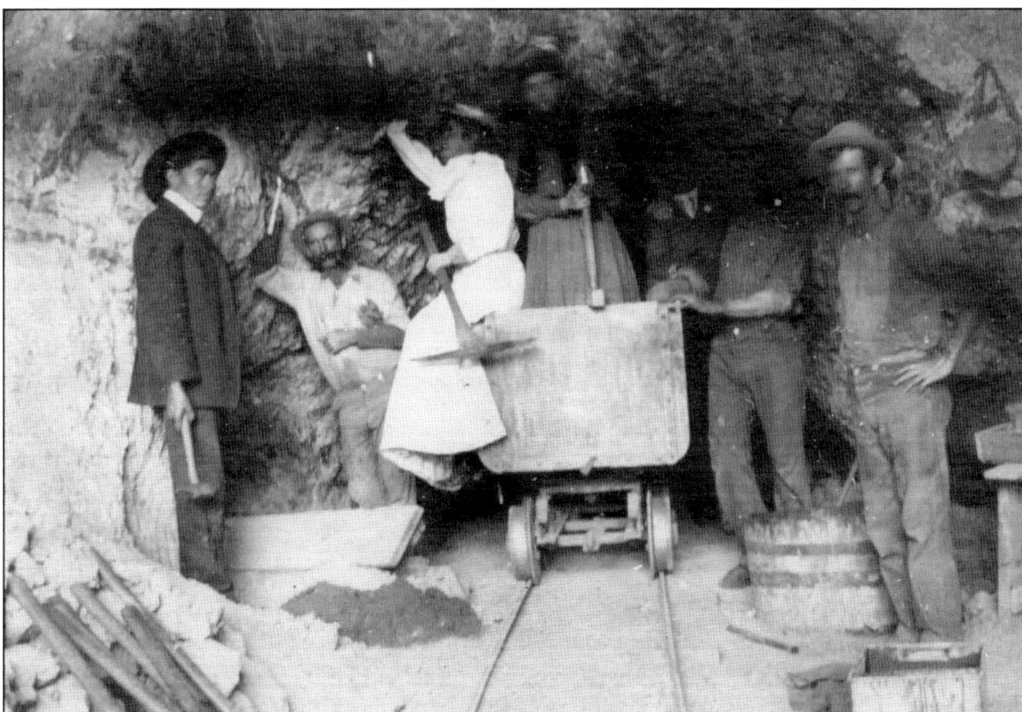

The Mormon Girl Mine was a Taylor family affair. Three brothers, Edward, Frank, and Samuel Taylor, along with their father, Isaac, built a stamp mill for their operation a mile from the mine at the creek. The Taylors were active in the little community, holding parties and picnics, participating in the debating society, and even creating a little newspaper. By 1910, most of the Taylor clan had moved to Norwalk, California.

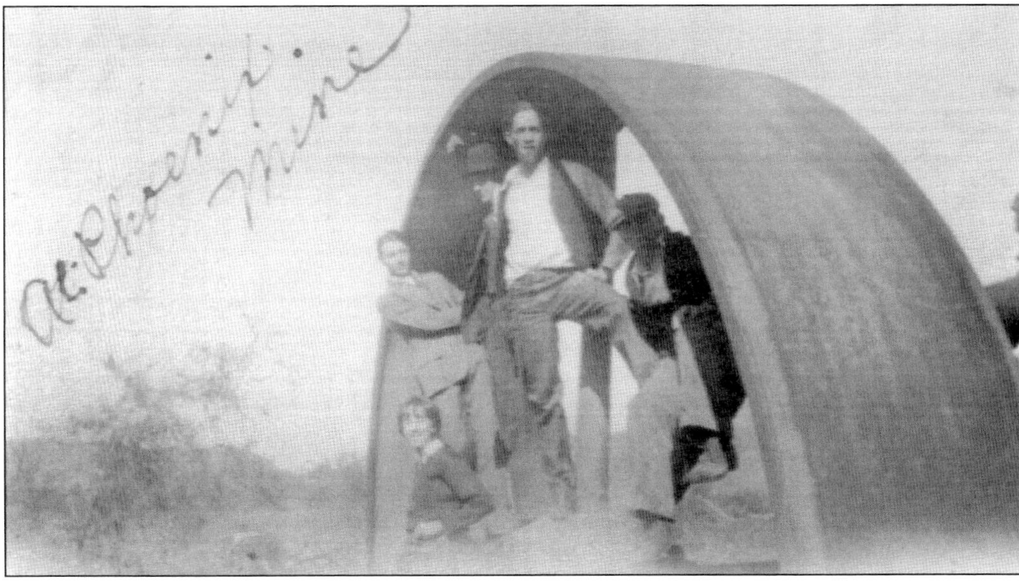

Several men stand comfortably in this giant flywheel of a 250-horsepower Corliss steam engine. Located at the Phoenix Mine, the massive engine supplied power to as many as 100 stamps, each weighing 950 pounds. Stamps were mighty metal shafts that crushed the ore down to the consistency of fine sand.

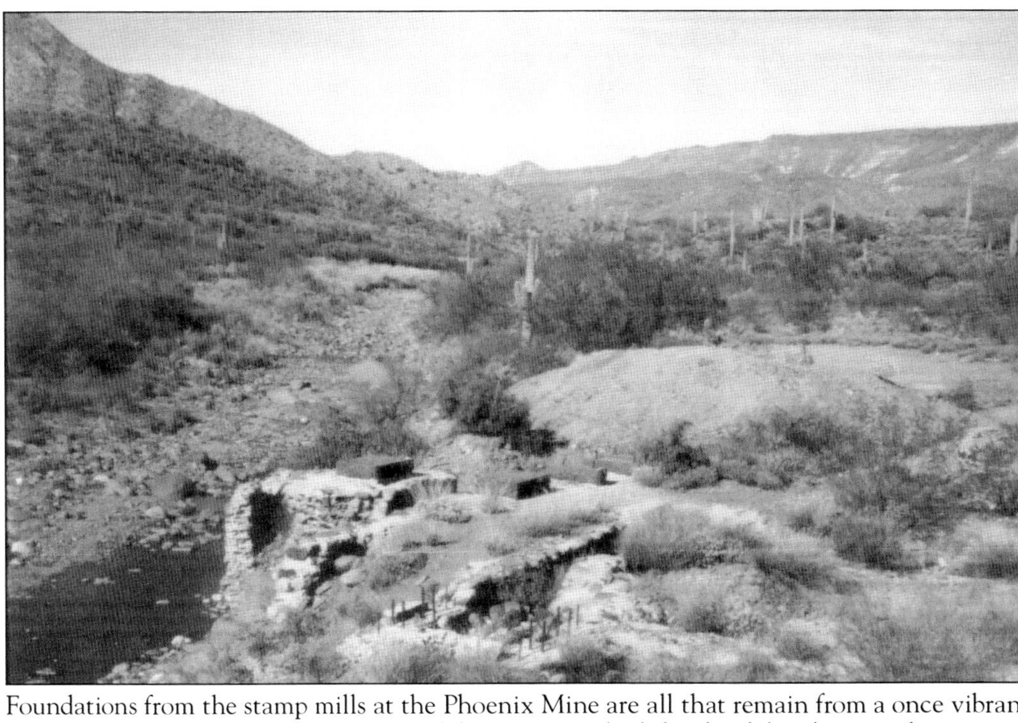

Foundations from the stamp mills at the Phoenix Mine are all that remain from a once vibrant industry. Cave Creek flows at the base of the ruins, on the left side of the photograph.

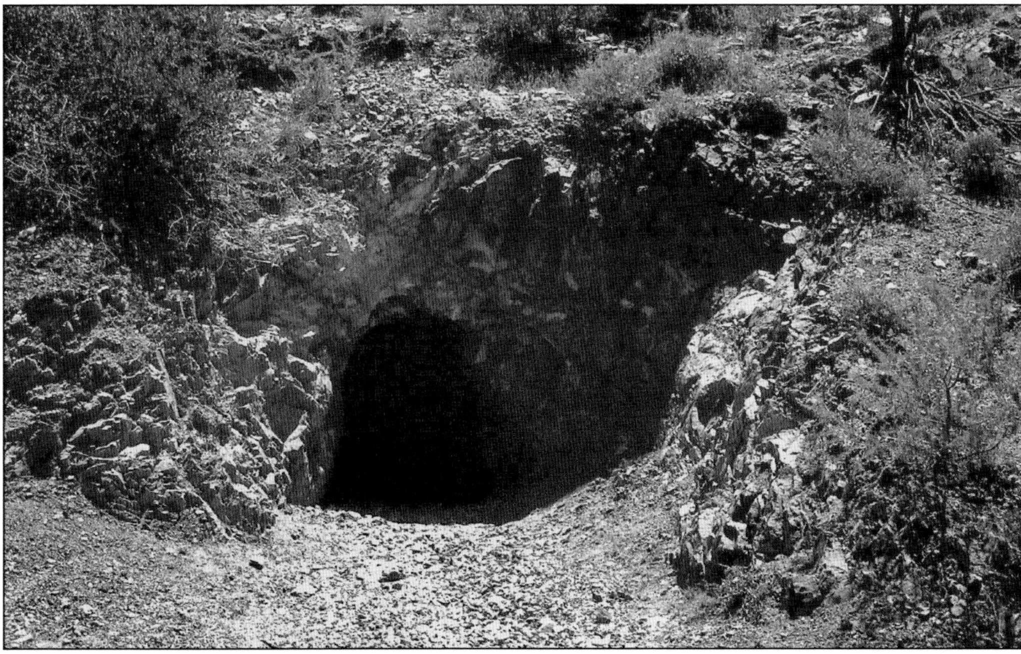

The Maricopa Mine, one of the largest early-day gold producers, yielded lode gold, molybdenum, vanadium, iron sulfide, and lead sulfide. It was just a few miles north of the Cave Creek Post Office, joining the Phoenix Mine on the south end. Prior to 1900, it produced about 5,000 tons of $15 ore.

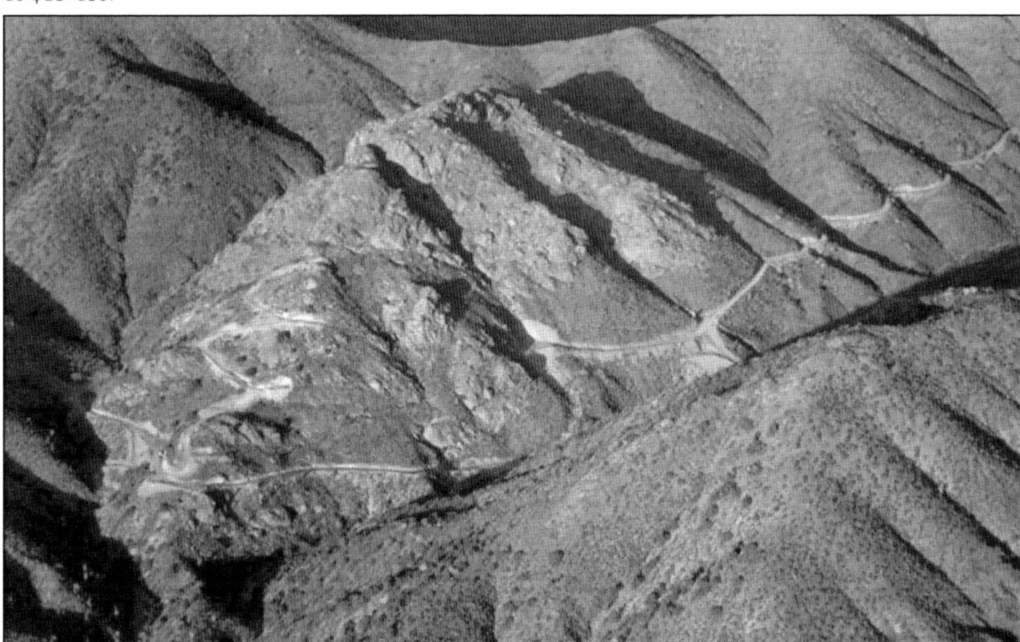

Gold Hill is part of the Portmanteau group of mines, which produced gold, silver, and copper over the years. There were several other mines that were associated with this group, including the Raven, Davis, Fairview, Legal Tender, and Lyon claims. This aerial view shows the extensive acreage covered by the Gold Hill Mine site. (Courtesy of Preston Westmoreland.)

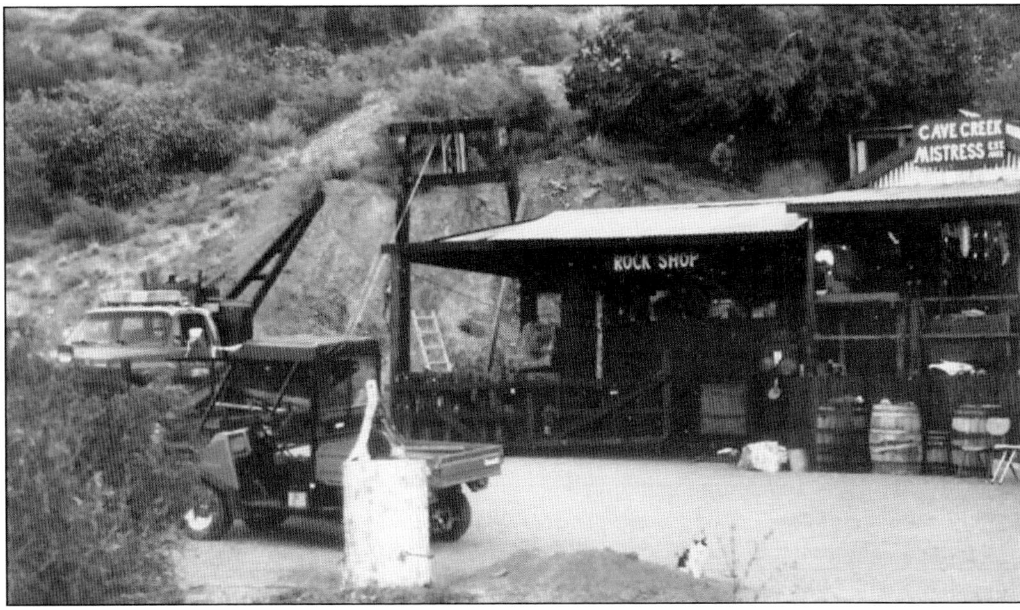

The Mistress Mine was on the Steineggar/Surprise patent claims, which were established in 1896. The intent of the project was to establish an original mine site to capture the mining mystique of the area for visitors to see. The original excavation was more of a pit than a shaft. This photograph shows an installed headframe over the vertical shaft and adit below. (Courtesy of Pete Incardona.)

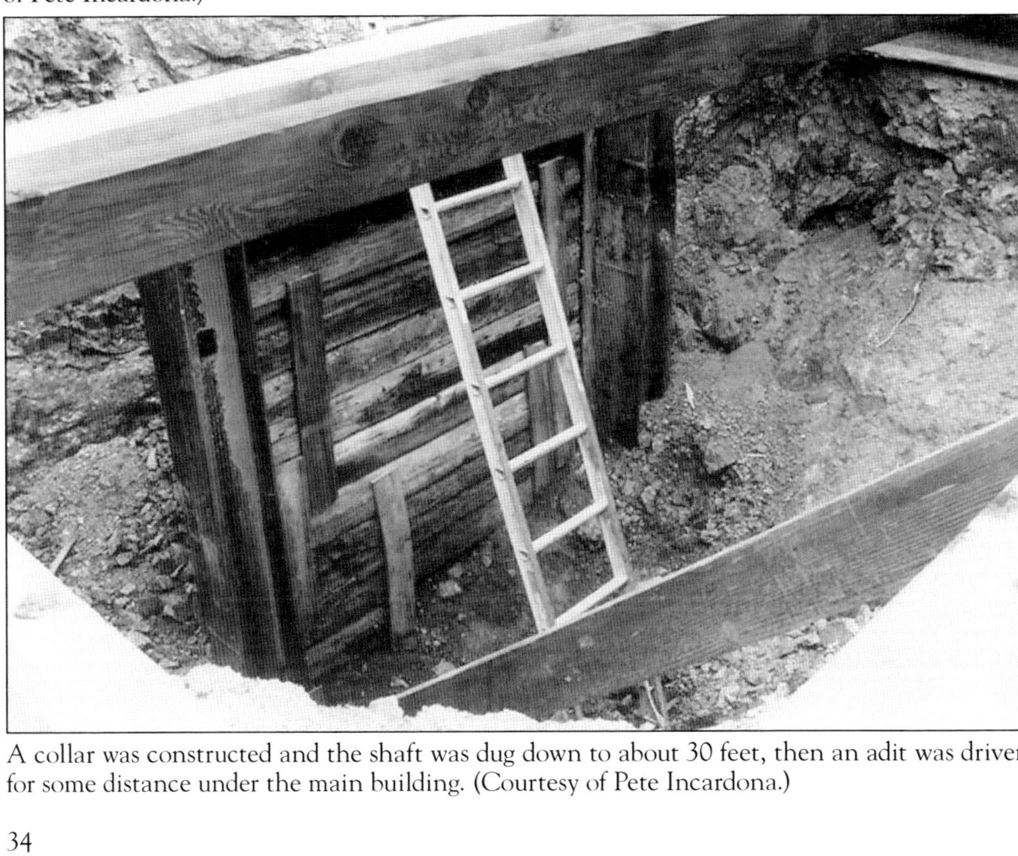

A collar was constructed and the shaft was dug down to about 30 feet, then an adit was driven for some distance under the main building. (Courtesy of Pete Incardona.)

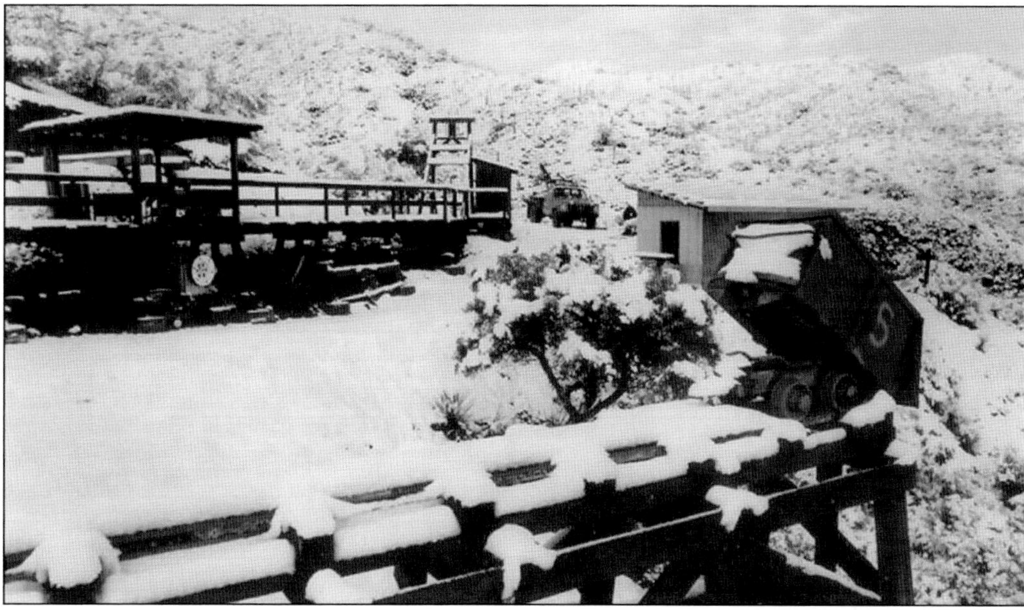

This photograph shows a rare snowfall at the Mistress Mine. (Courtesy of Pete Incardona.)

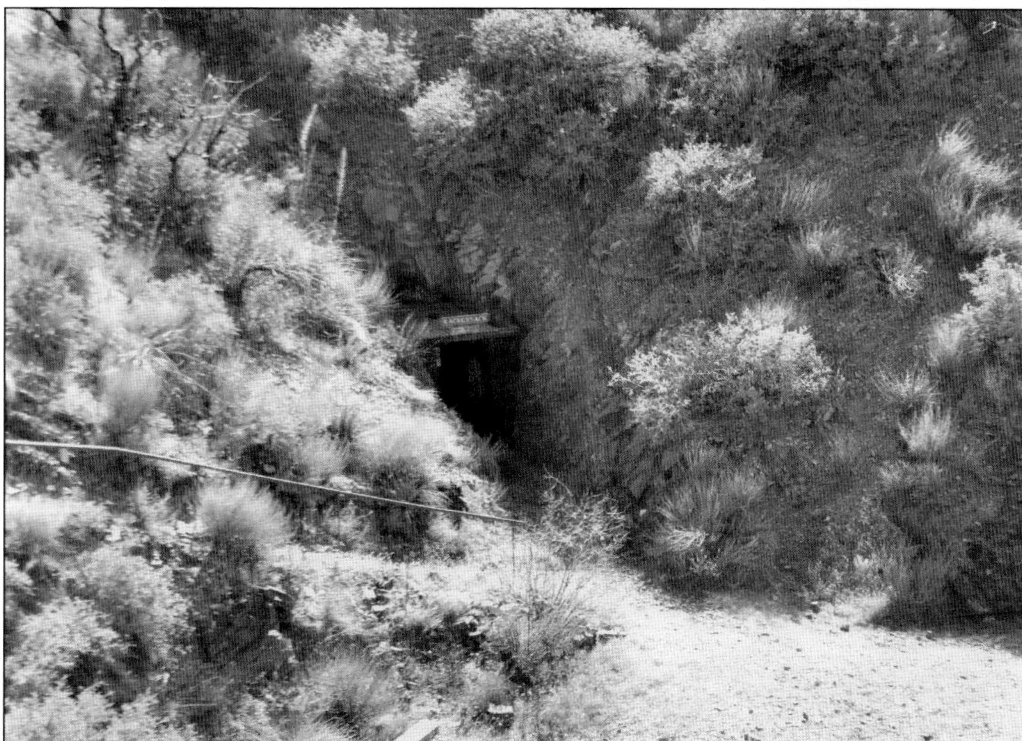

The Rackensack group consisted of three claims: the Dallas, the El Paso, and the Fort Worth. Like many of the other mines in the area, gold, silver, and copper were the commodities found there. This photograph shows the portal to the Upper Fort Worth Mine, which was dug between 1880 and 1908 with hand tools. It extends about 85 feet to a split that branches about 90 feet in each direction. (Courtesy of Charles Connell.)

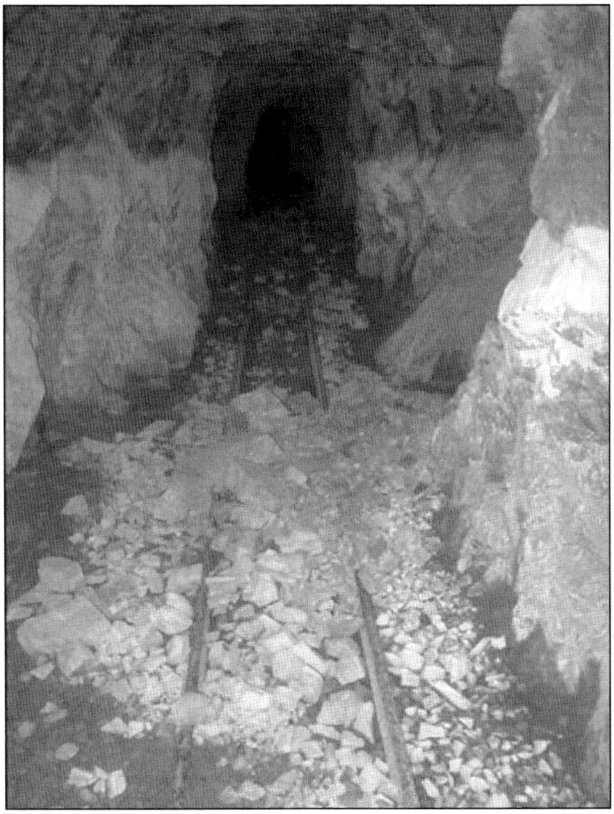

The Lower Fort Worth Mine goes back and intersects with a vertical shaft from the Upper Fort Worth Mine about 200 feet above these workings. After 1908, this mine was worked using machinery. Note the rails that were used to transport the ore in ore carts from the mine. (Courtesy of Charles Underwood.)

Below, at Rackensack claim No. 1, rotary drilling for water took place in front of the No. 5 Toothpick adit. This supplied water for the operations to run the trammel and the shaker table. The adit was named because of the size of the timbers used for support. They were four-inch-by-four-inch timbers, not the usual eight-inch-by-eight-inch ones. (Courtesy of the Tonto National Forest Service.)

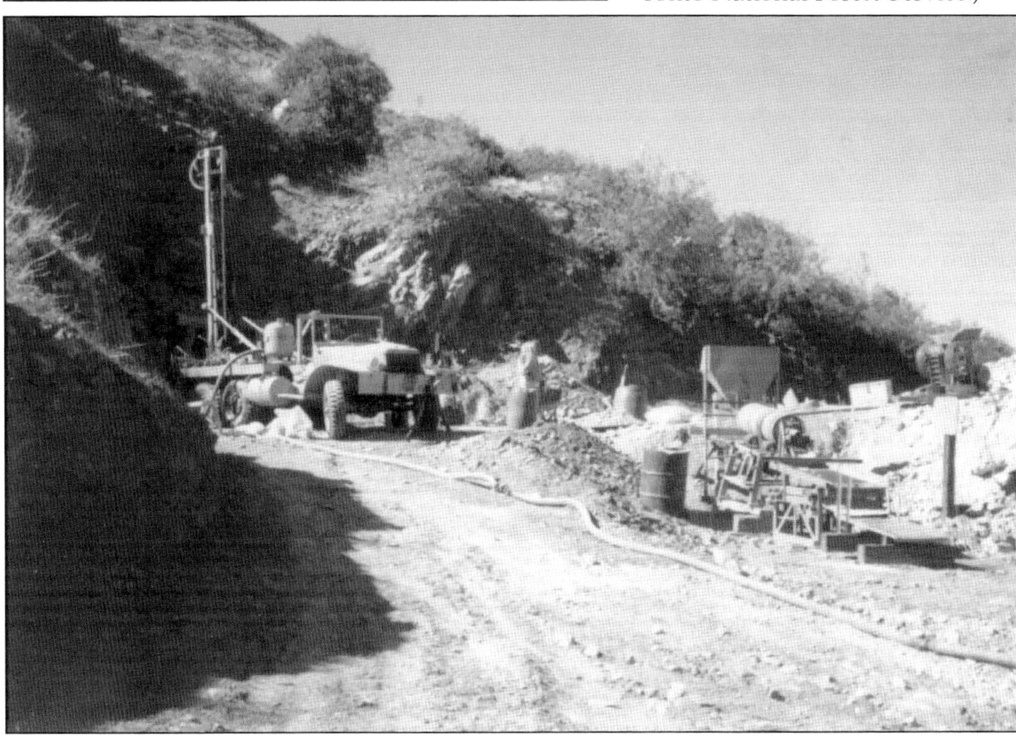

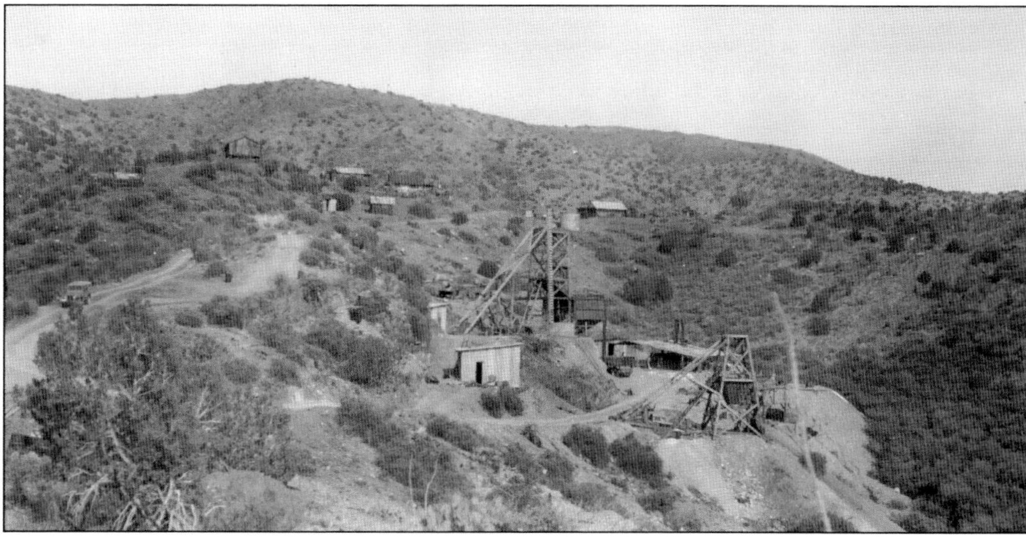

These two photographs show the same view of the Red Rover Mine taken about 50 years apart. The picture above was taken in the 1950s and the second in 1996, showing a marked decline in the site. Just above the headframe, which is in the middle of the photograph above, are a water tank and a house that are visible in both pictures. (Both, courtesy of Arizona Geological Survey.)

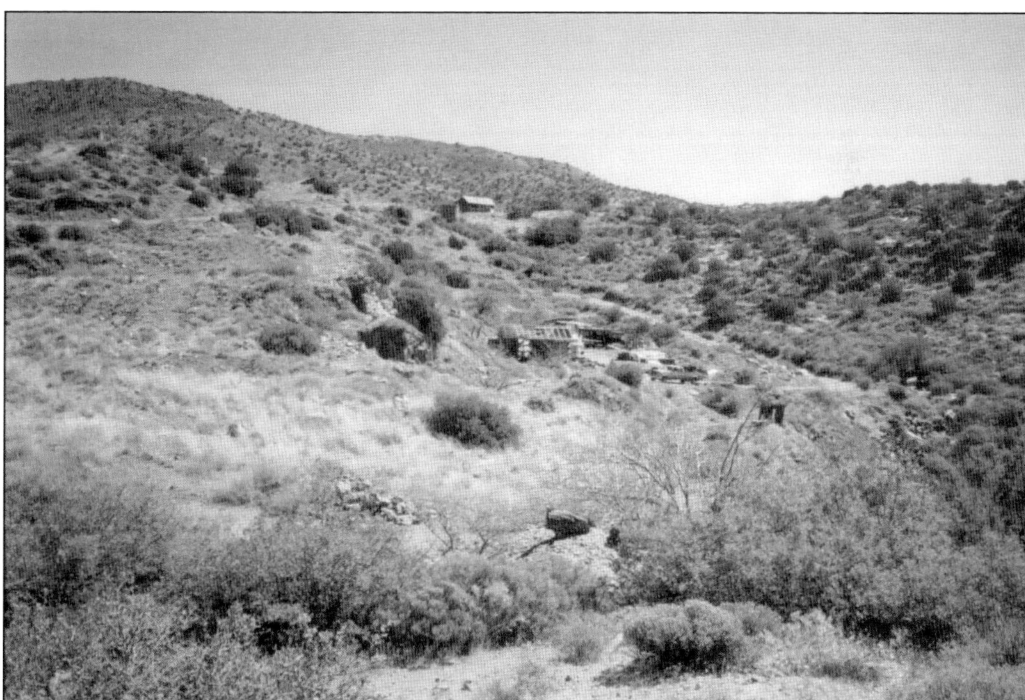

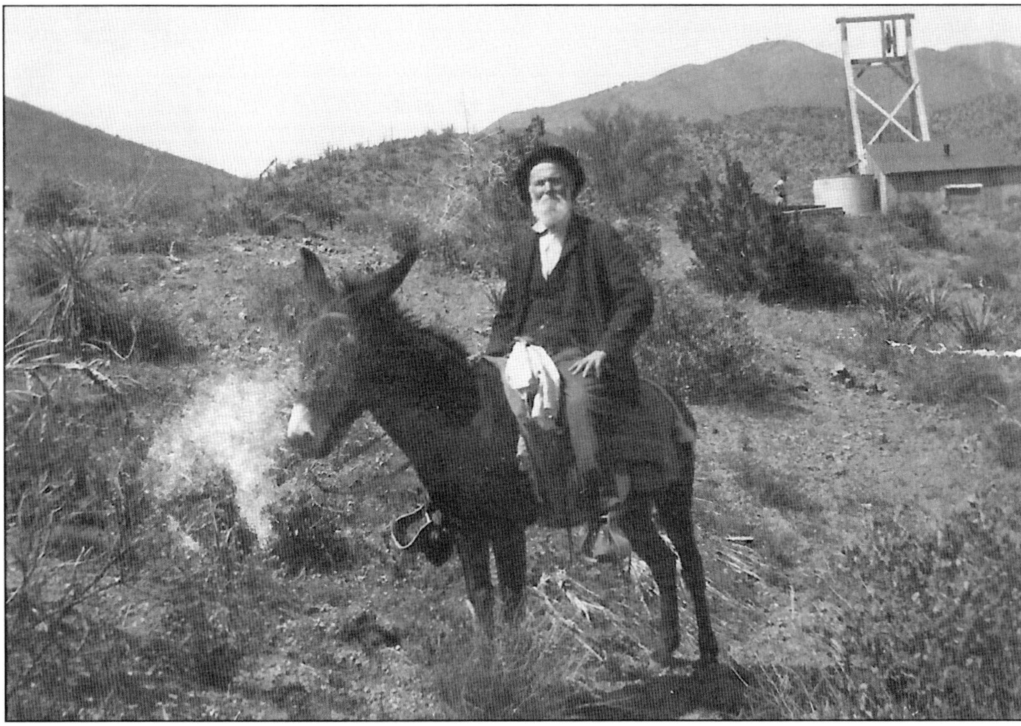

Charles Fleming (above) came from Texas in 1876 to claim a mine and mill site with a natural spring on Continental Mountain, near the end of what is now Fleming Springs Road. His oasis included a rock home (below), fruit trees, and a vegetable garden. Fleming did all the mining himself. The grinding of ore was accomplished with a handmade *arrastre* and mules and later with waterpower from the spring. Fleming died in 1903 and is buried on the mountain that provided his livelihood and his home for three decades.

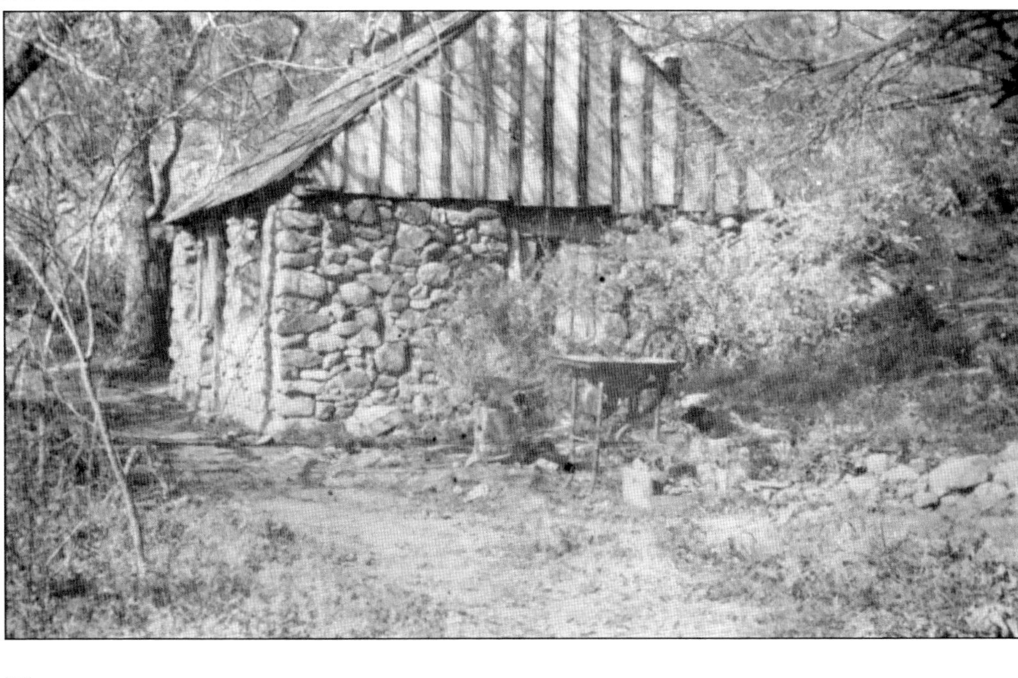

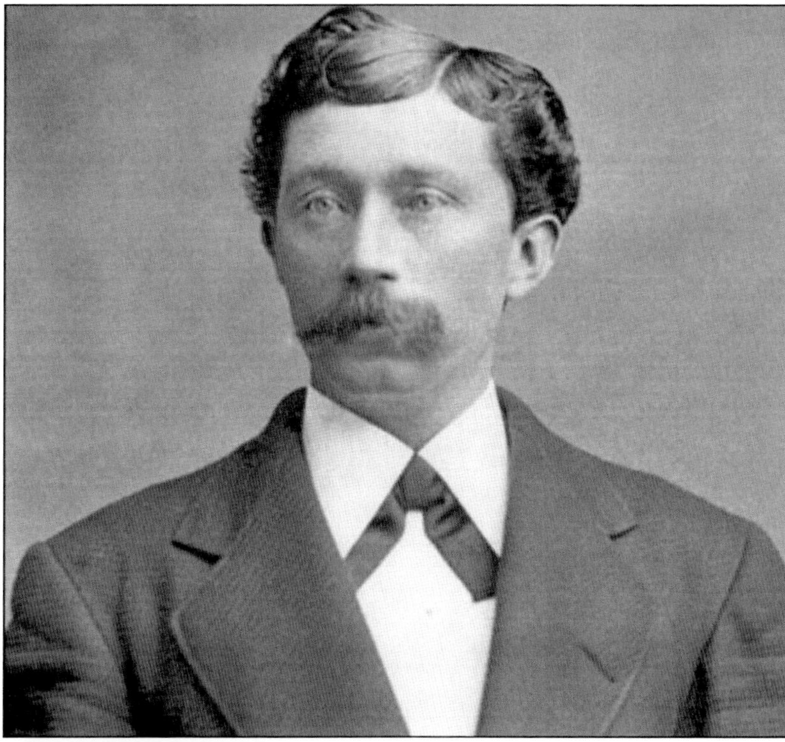

Following a stint as post sutler at Fort McDowell, William Hellings, seen here, and his brother started a flour mill and store in Phoenix in 1871. In 1876, Hellings acquired a claim on Continental Mountain, the Golden Star, later renamed the Golden Reef. By the end of 1880, his dream had collapsed, and he moved his mining interests to Globe. He died in San Francisco in 1913, still engaged in mining.

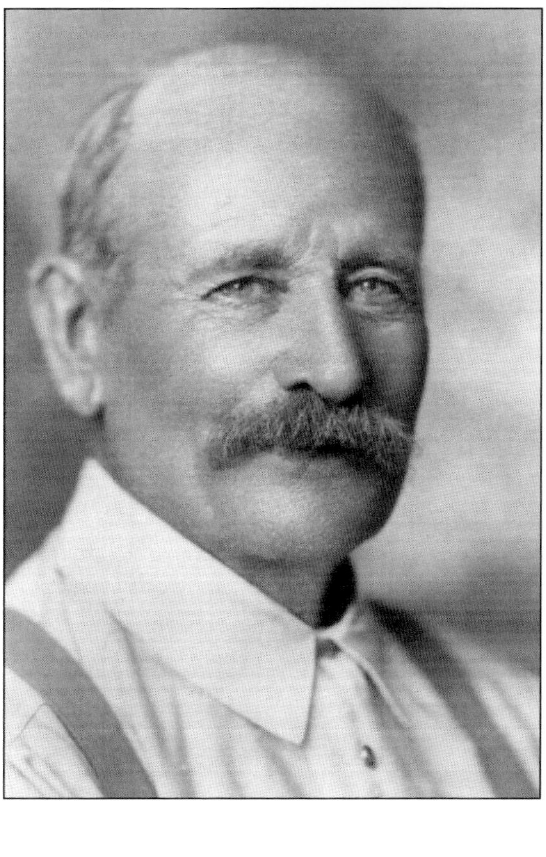

Charles Philes, seen here, worked for Hellings. He claimed his own mill site next to the springs that would later bear his name, on the future site of the Sierra Vista dude ranch. He married his young wife, Florence, in 1894 in California, bringing her back to Cave Creek to his "dugout" camp. He filed his last claim in 1919 at the age of 84 and died three years later in Phoenix.

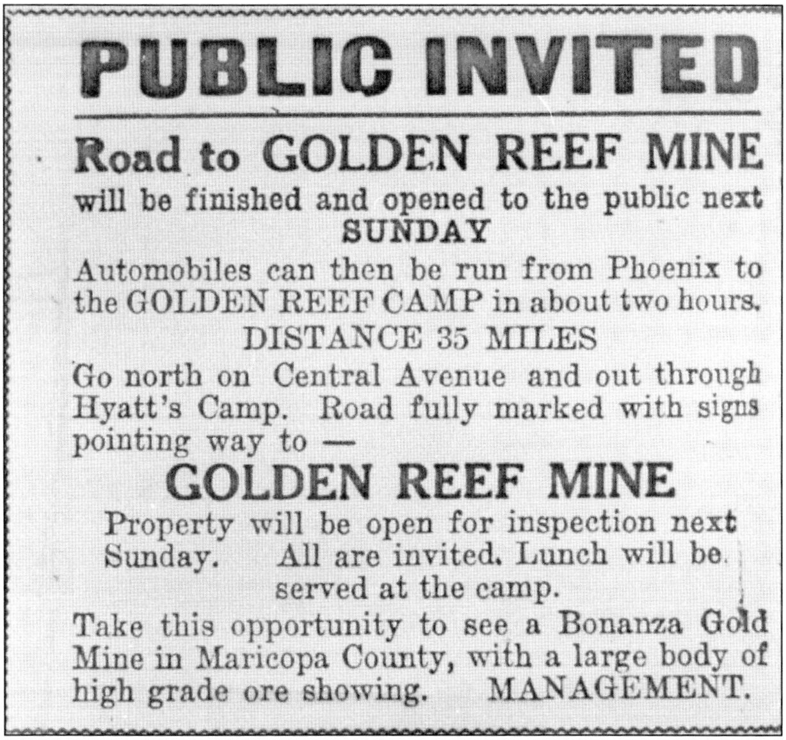

PUBLIC INVITED

Road to GOLDEN REEF MINE

will be finished and opened to the public next
SUNDAY

Automobiles can then be run from Phoenix to the GOLDEN REEF CAMP in about two hours.

DISTANCE 35 MILES

Go north on Central Avenue and out through Hyatt's Camp. Road fully marked with signs pointing way to —

GOLDEN REEF MINE

Property will be open for inspection next Sunday. All are invited. Lunch will be served at the camp.

Take this opportunity to see a Bonanza Gold Mine in Maricopa County, with a large body of high grade ore showing. MANAGEMENT.

Lunch was a meager enticement to draw people to see the Golden Reef Mine, as travel was over rutted dirt roads that coursed up and down, following the contour of the land. This undated advertisement was likely a hopeful invitation to investors.

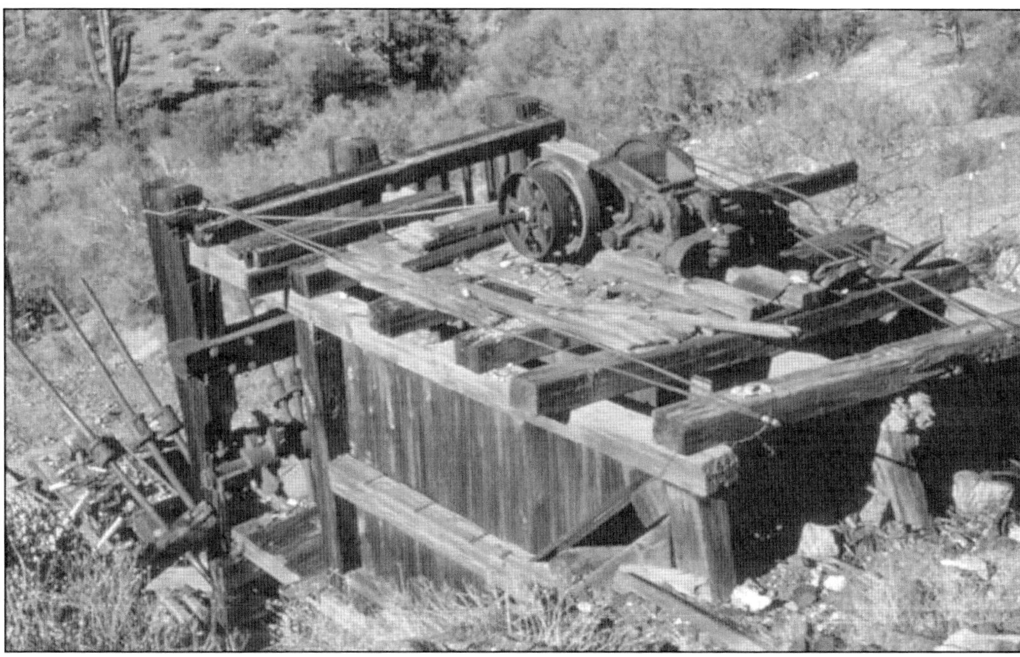

There were no photographs of the Golden Reef Mine, stamp mill, or tram towers in the early days, but photographs taken in the 1980s show a fallen-down mill, weathered tram towers, and a caved-in mine entrance. The primary crusher is seen here on top of the ore bin. Ore was transported via the tram system and fed into the crusher, dropping the residue into the large ore bin under it. (Courtesy of Rudy Fowler.)

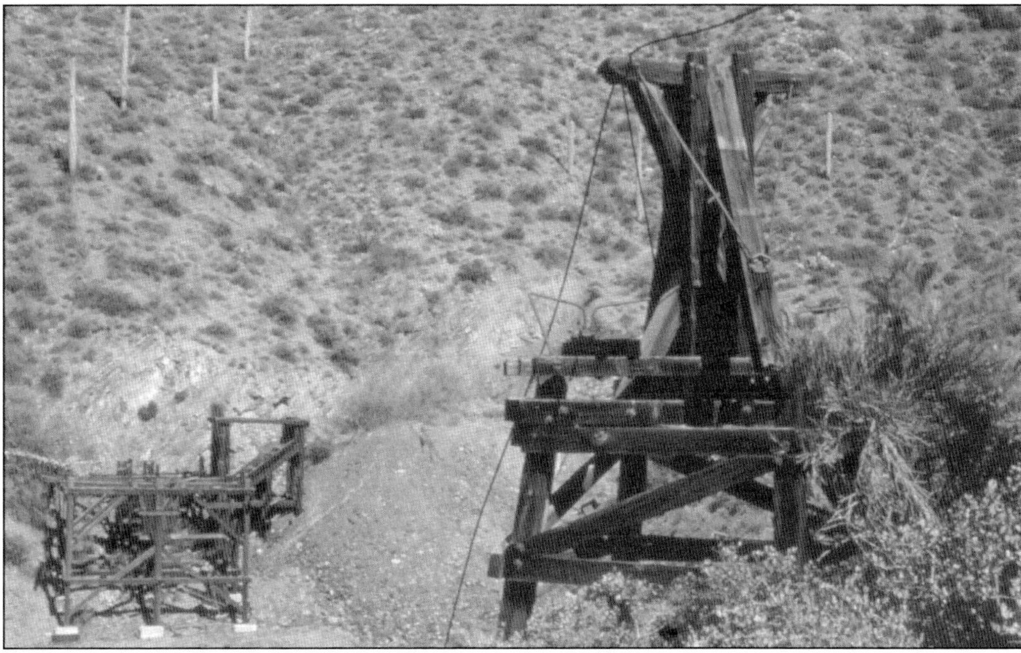

This photograph shows one of the eight tram towers still standing, in the right foreground. In the lower left is the tram station, where ore was loaded into the buckets and returned to the mill, 2,000 feet from the mine. The fine-grained gray material between the station and the tower are mining tailings. (Courtesy of Rudy Fowler.)

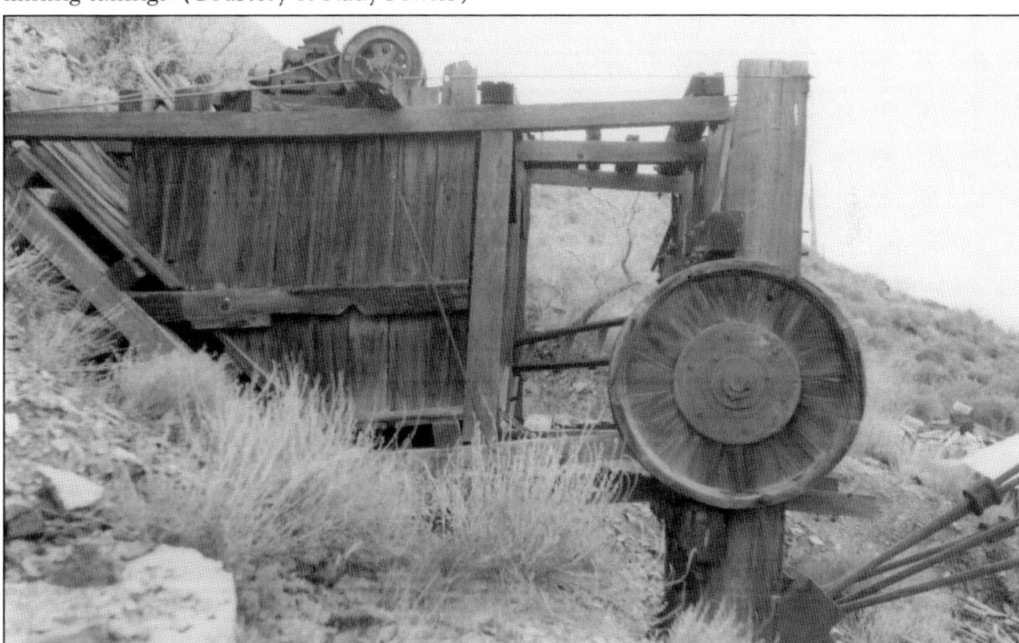

The Golden Reef 10-stamp mill is seen here in its original location. The long rods, or stamps, that splay out (lower right) crushed ore that went into the mortar box, under the stamps. The ore bin fed two-inch-sized material into the mortar boxes, and the stamps would then crush the ore down to 20 mesh, or holes, per inch. The gold would be extracted from the concentrates.

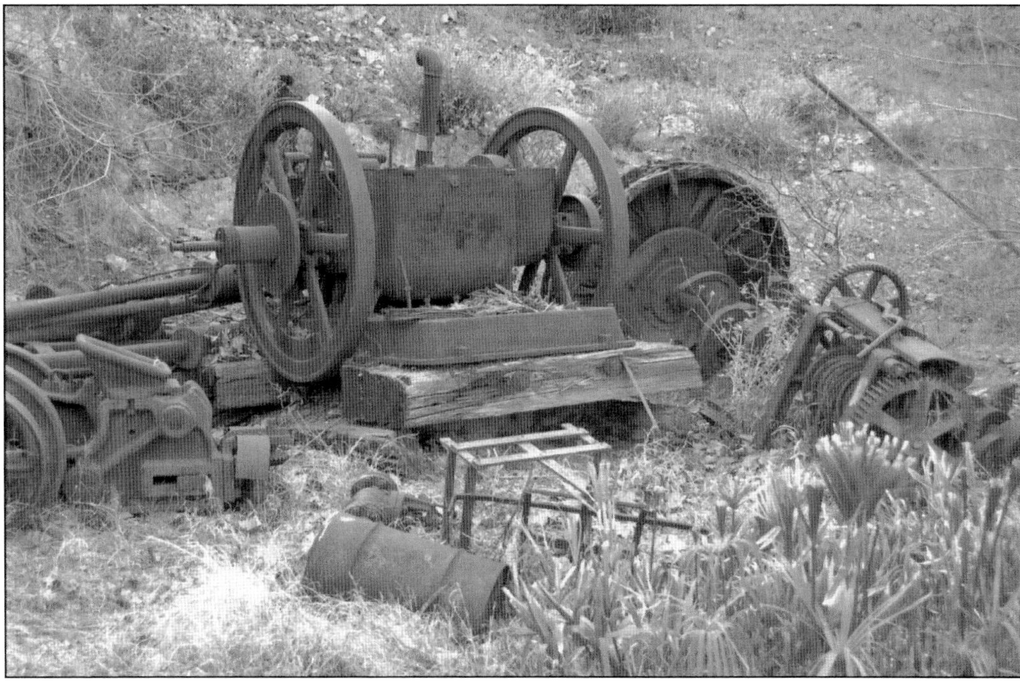

The major parts of the stamp mill remaining in situ on Continental Mountain included the primary driver, a Rumley engine (center), the primary ore crusher, and the bull wheel, the large circular piece to the right of center. (Courtesy of Charles Connell.)

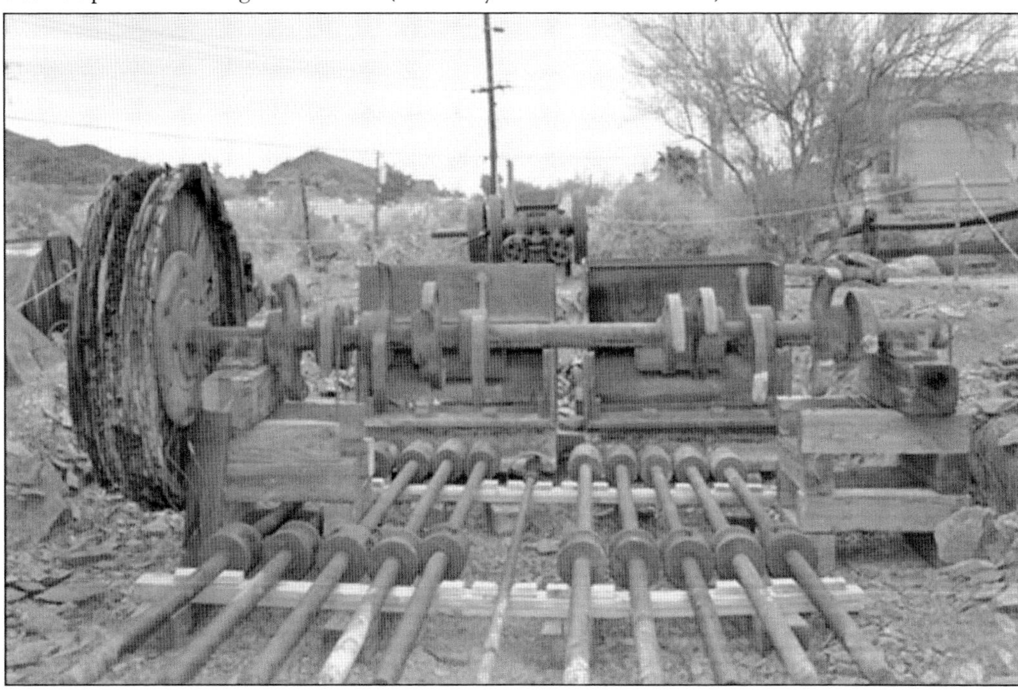

This photograph shows the parts of the mill that were put together at the Cave Creek Museum right after the move from Continental Mountain. The parts include the bull wheel and camshaft, 10 stamps, two mortar boxes, and the primary crusher, in the background. (Courtesy of Charles Connell.)

Four

Early Settlement

The discovery of gold in the 1870s led to Cave Creek's first settlement. William Hellings built a road out from Phoenix in 1873. Jeriah Wood came to the Cave Creek area in 1877, settling along the creek near the springs that Gen. George Stoneman's troops had discovered in 1870. Wood brought his 16-year-old bride up from Phoenix in 1880 to start their lives together in a one-room adobe dwelling. In addition to cattle ranching, Wood set up a stage station to meet the needs of miners and freighters. The stage road ran along the east side of the creek through his property. A post office, called Overton, was also established.

By 1881, Jedder and Jennie Hoskin left Phoenix to take over the station, which soon became known as Cave Creek Station. Jedder also ran cattle and operated the stage line to transport mail, passengers, and freight back and forth to Phoenix. By the 1890s, Cave Creek Station was a lively village made up of the Hoskins, Burris, Taylor, and Linville families. A.J. and Malinda Linville homesteaded south of the Hoskinses on the west side of the creek in 1891, raising cattle and, later, goats. Both of their adult sons and their families later joined them. A one-room schoolhouse opened in 1886. Church services were held there, and Jedder and Jennie Hoskin taught Sunday school. The village even had a literary society. Christmas festivities and year-end school recitals were significant community gatherings.

With a continuing drought in the 1890s and a decline in mining, many families left. By 1900, only 97 people remained in the town. The Linvilles and the Houcks, the new owners of Cave Creek Station, became the nucleus of the small village. Later, Ed Howard and his parents moved to the area. James Houck, a Civil War veteran and a participant in the Pleasant Valley War, built a successful sheepshearing operation. His ranch continued to be the center of community life, with a post office, a stage stop, a boardinghouse, a general store, a schoolhouse, and a saloon. Thanksgiving and Fourth of July celebrations were traditional local events.

In 1921, after his ranch had been in decline for several years, James Houck took his own life. A year later, Jeriah Wood died in Phoenix and Jedder Hoskin passed away in California. A.J. and Malinda Linville were already deceased by that time. The real pioneer era of Cave Creek was over.

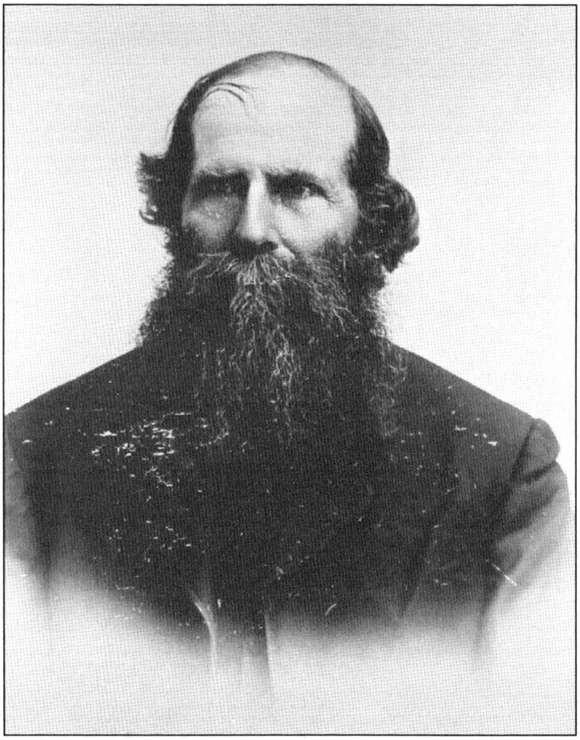

Andrew J. Linville of Missouri was Cave Creek's first homesteader, locating along the west bank of the creek in 1891. His sons and their families later joined him, making a total of 15 Linvilles living in two frame houses. They farmed, raised cattle, and tried their hand at goats. Andrew died on the ranch in 1906. Most of the family left a few years later due to the ongoing drought.

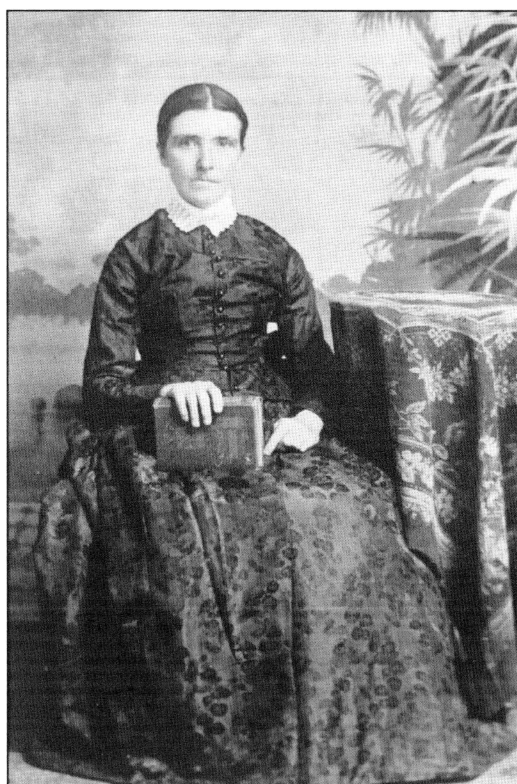

Malinda Linville, Andrew's wife, had the pioneer spirit. She refused to move from their 240-acre farm to Phoenix after her husband's death. By 1915, the well had fallen in, although she still somehow kept a small garden. She died in Phoenix in 1918.

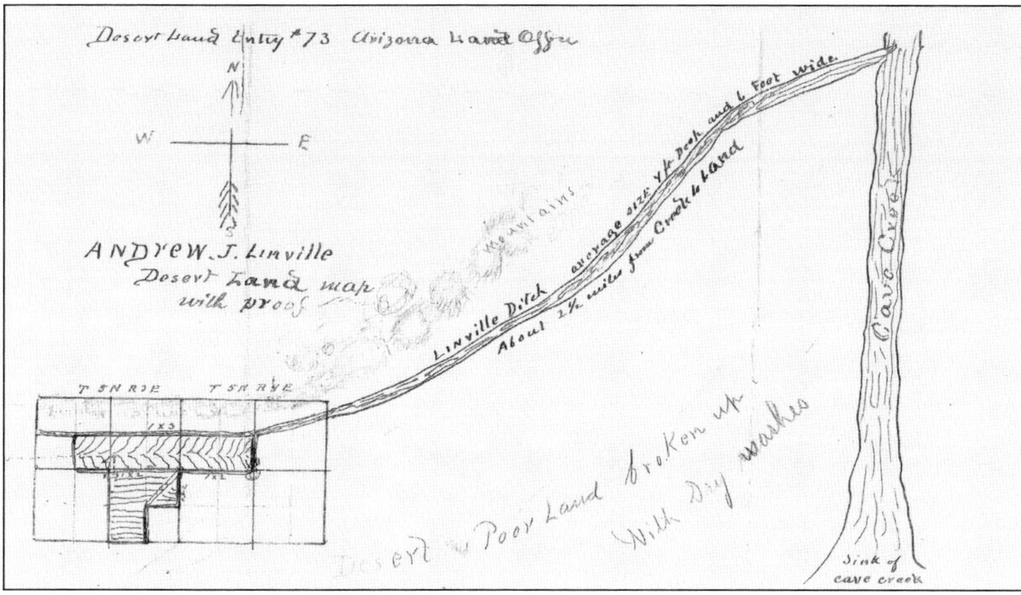

The key to survival was access to water. The Linvilles filed a water claim in 1891, building a four-foot-wide, six-foot-deep ditch from the creek to the farm. Their irrigation plan was augmented by flumes and smaller lateral ditches. The canal pathway followed a prehistoric Hohokam canal.

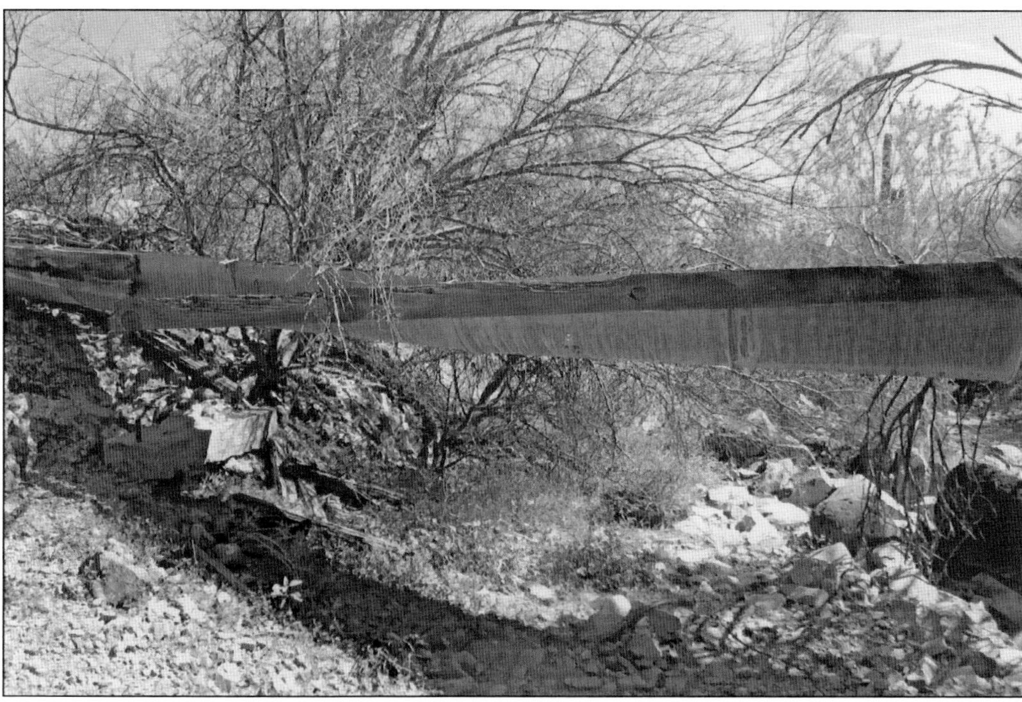

This contemporary photograph of the Linvilles' flume shows the ruins of the ingenious flume system. Andrew Linville noted in his homestead file, "It has been a great hard work." Homer Smith later repaired and improved the irrigation channels in the 1940s for the headquarters of his cattle ranch. (Courtesy of Bob Flach.)

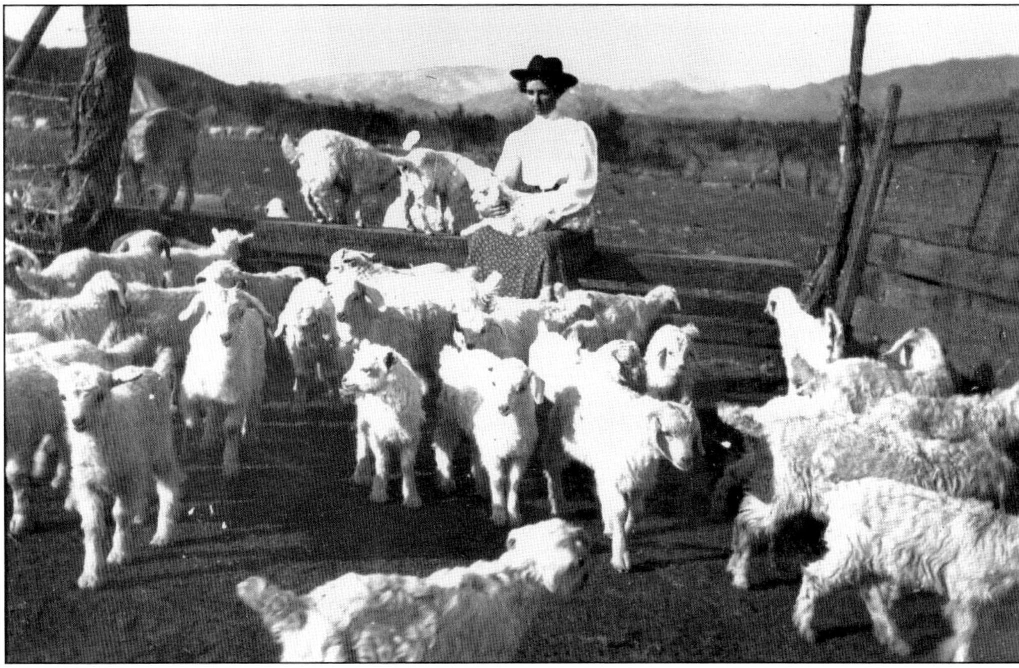

With a kid on her lap, one of the Linville women sits on the fence of an Angora goat pen. The Linvilles hoped that the goats would do better than cattle during the drought, as goats ate tougher forage and required less water. Unfortunately, this option did not prove successful. By 1910, all of the Linvilles, except Malinda, had left the ranch for Phoenix and other employment.

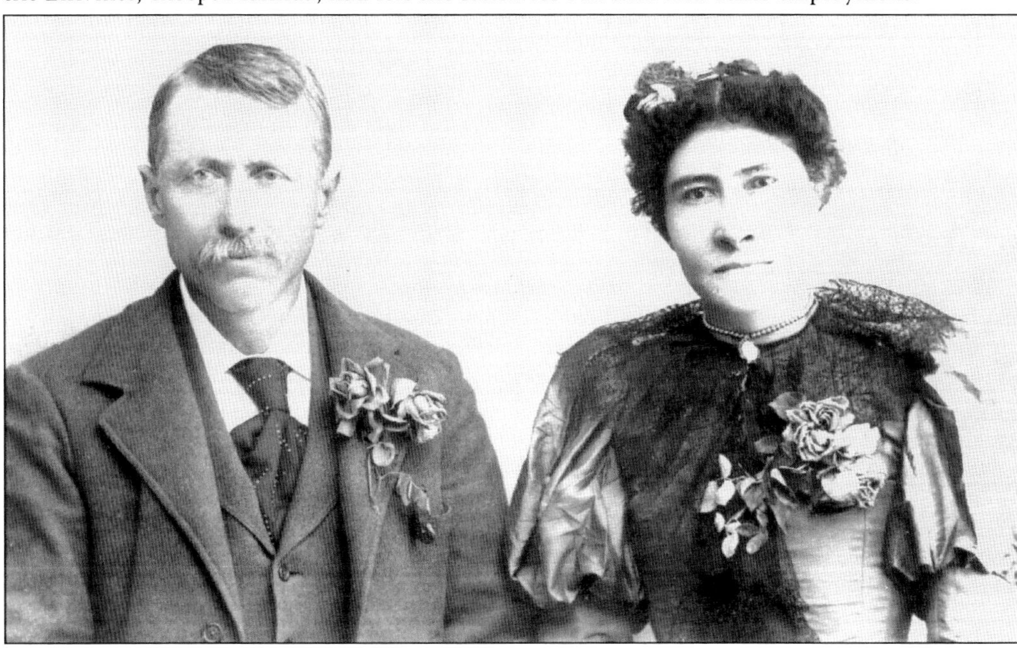

James and Beatrice Houck were married in 1880 at Fort Wingate, New Mexico. James was 34 and Beatrice was 14. By 1900, they and their six children owned Cave Creek Station, formerly occupied by the Woods and Hoskins families. The Houcks divorced in 1913. Later, Beatrice ran a boardinghouse in Ray, Arizona.

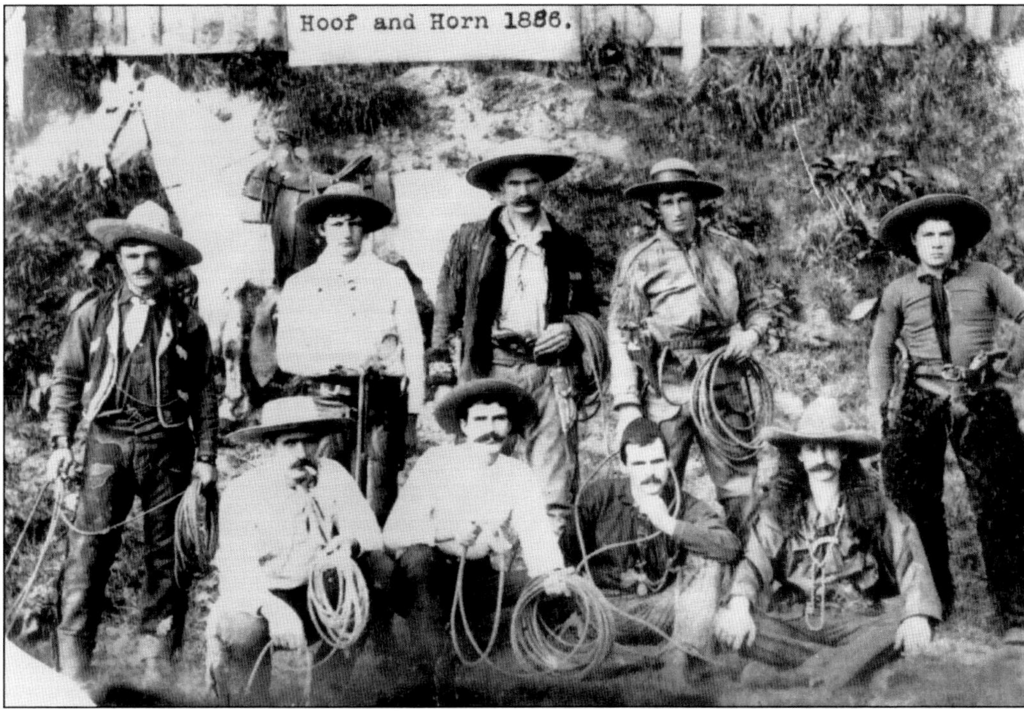

James Houck (seated, far right) is seen here with the Tewksbury family, important sheep ranchers in the area. Houck fought in the Pleasant Valley War against the Graham cattle-ranching family. He was also involved in the vigilante hanging of three cowboys and the killing of Billy Graham. The last of the original Graham faction was murdered in Tempe in 1902. Edwin Tewksbury, the defendant in that murder, was acquitted.

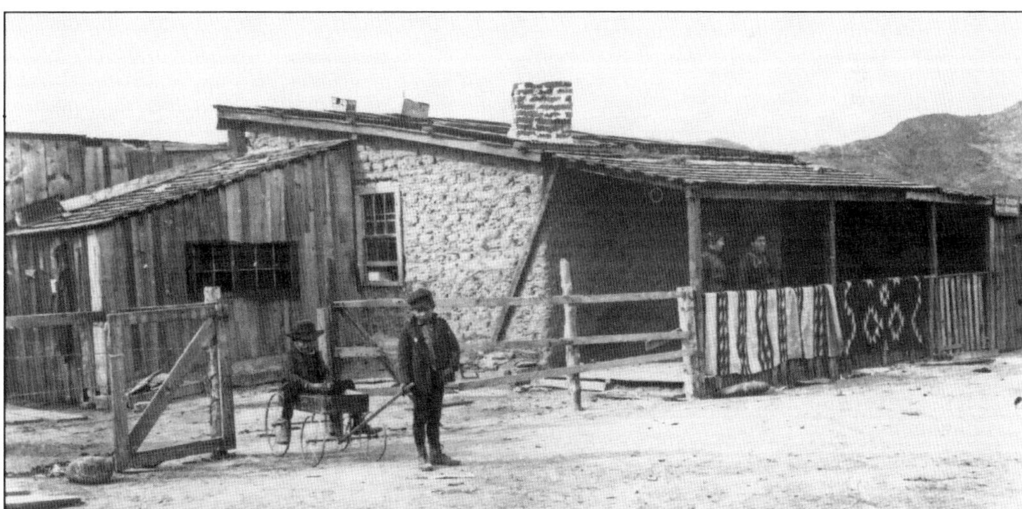

The adobe portion of the Houck ranch at Cave Creek Station dates to 1877 and was built by Jeriah Wood. The Houcks erected several wood-frame additions. The Navajo rugs on the front porch are reminders of Houck's trading post days in northern Arizona in the 1870s. The early post office was to the right.

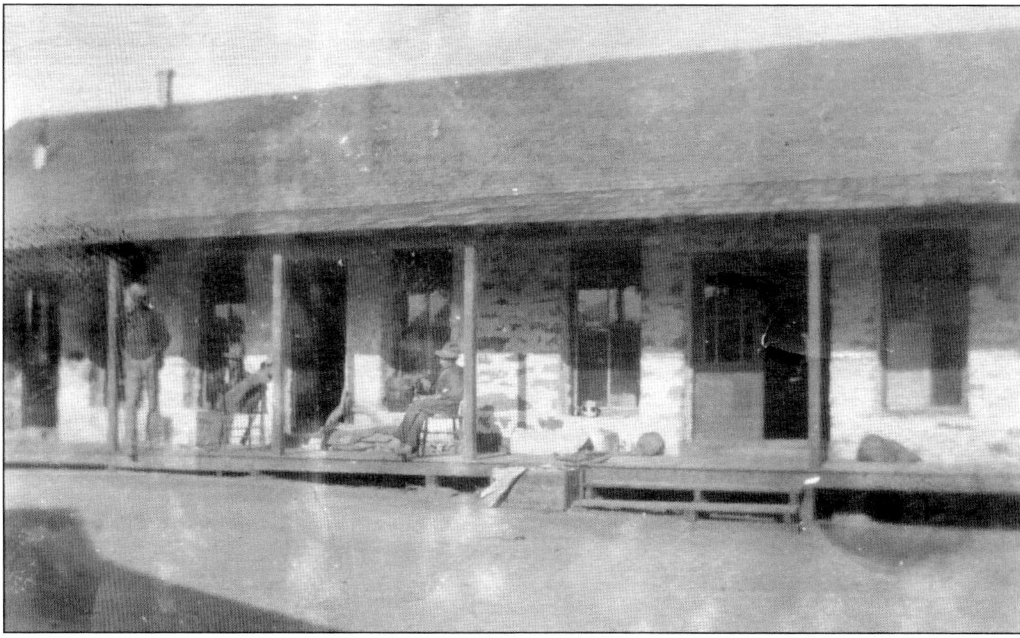

This rock building was constructed by James Houck and two of his sons. Facing the stage road, which ran along the east bank of the creek from Phoenix and a little south of the Houck house, this building included a general store, a post office, and a saloon. It was the true community center for more than two decades.

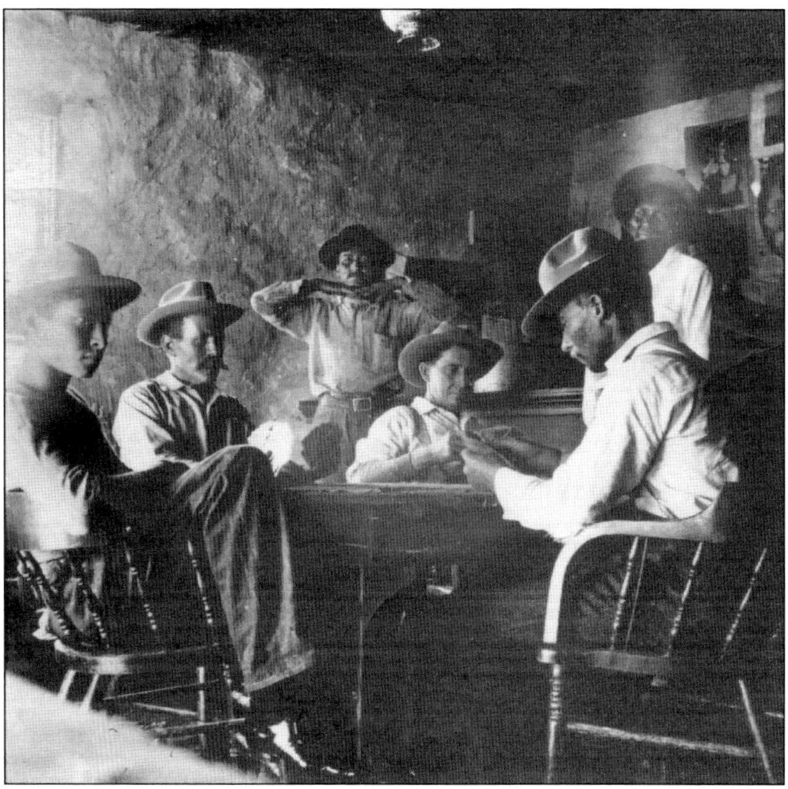

The saloon was a favorite for local miners and ranchers. Seen here around the card table are John Lewis (second from left) and Ed Howard (right). The saloon hosted many a dance on Saturday nights, with John and William Lewis playing the fiddle and the guitar, joined by Houck's sons. The saloon was especially popular during sheepshearing season, with its influx of boarders.

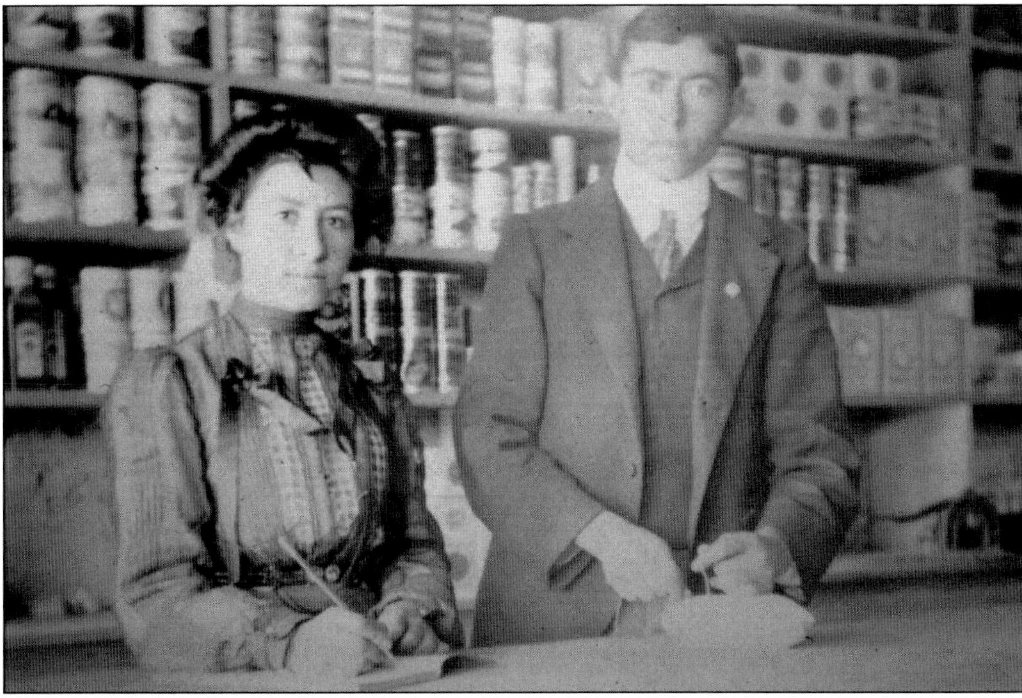

Offering provisions for miners and ranchers, James Houck described his general store as "a small commissary." A 1921 record shows that the store also carried overalls, shoes, shirts, supplies, rifles, mousetraps, hammers, and nails for the small village of 109. Here, his daughter Dulcy and son Tom assist customers. In the 1920 census, Houck called himself a truck farmer.

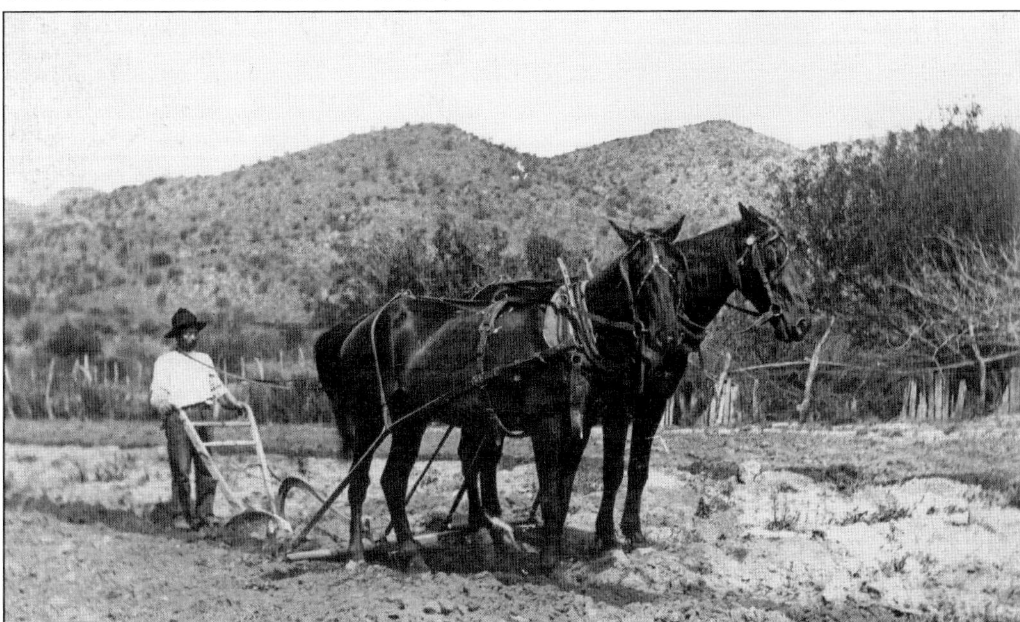

Life on the ranch also involved a small amount of farming, perhaps up to eight acres. The fields at one time were planted with wheat, barley, alfalfa, and garden produce. The Japanese gardener, seen here, provided assistance in the fields and the rose garden.

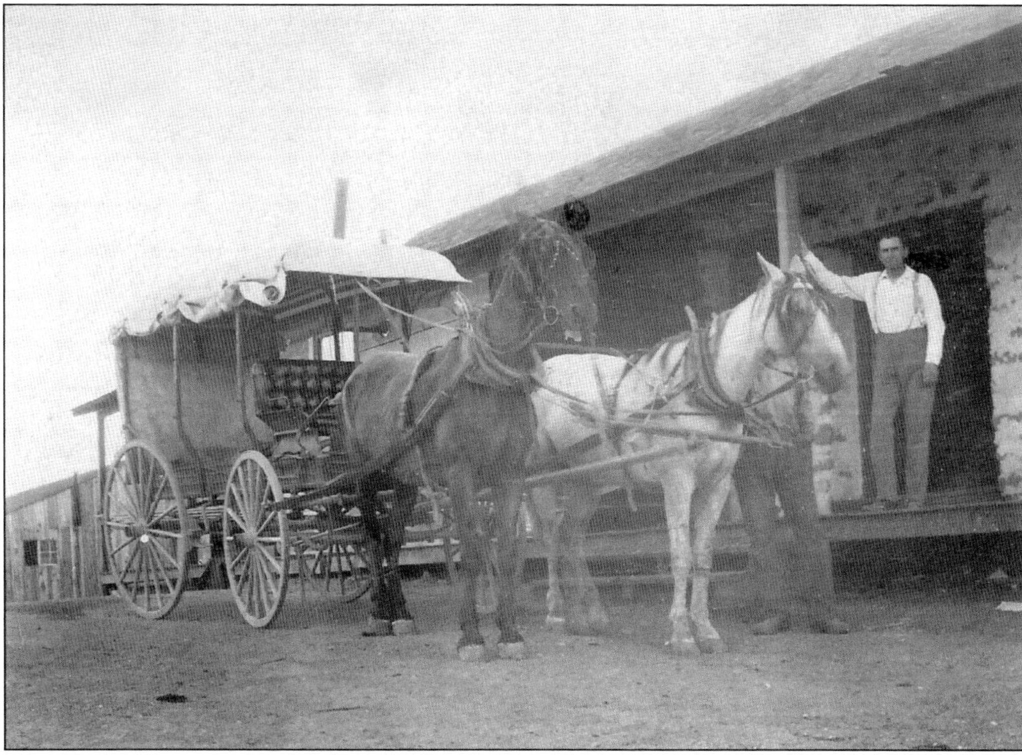

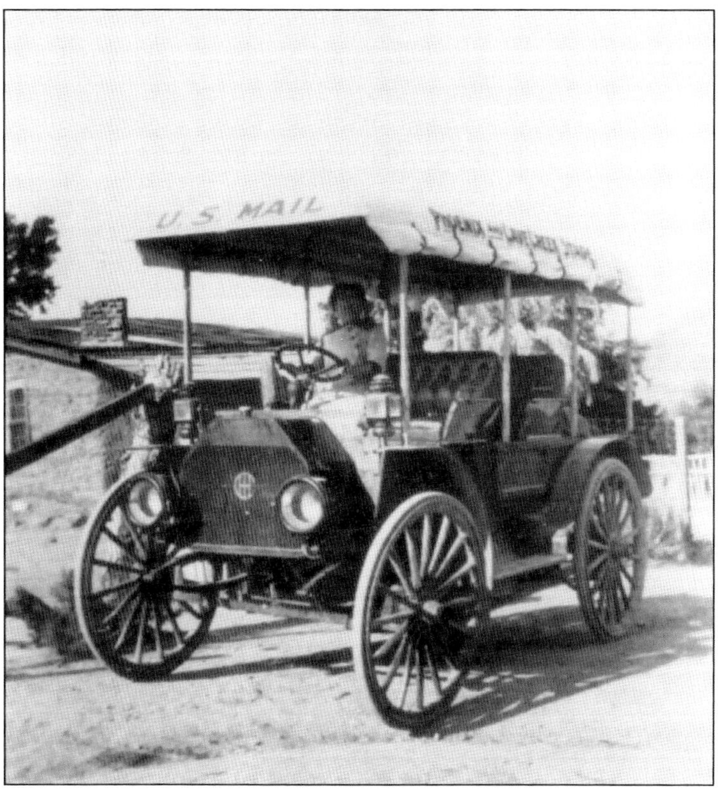

The horses pulling the buggy above carried the mail and passengers between Cave Creek and Phoenix, running three times a week. The dusty trip to Phoenix took all day. James Houck's son Tom was the primary driver. Later, the Houcks purchased one of the first International trucks, pictured at left. By 1915, the Houcks had lost the mail contract to their neighbor Ed Howard.

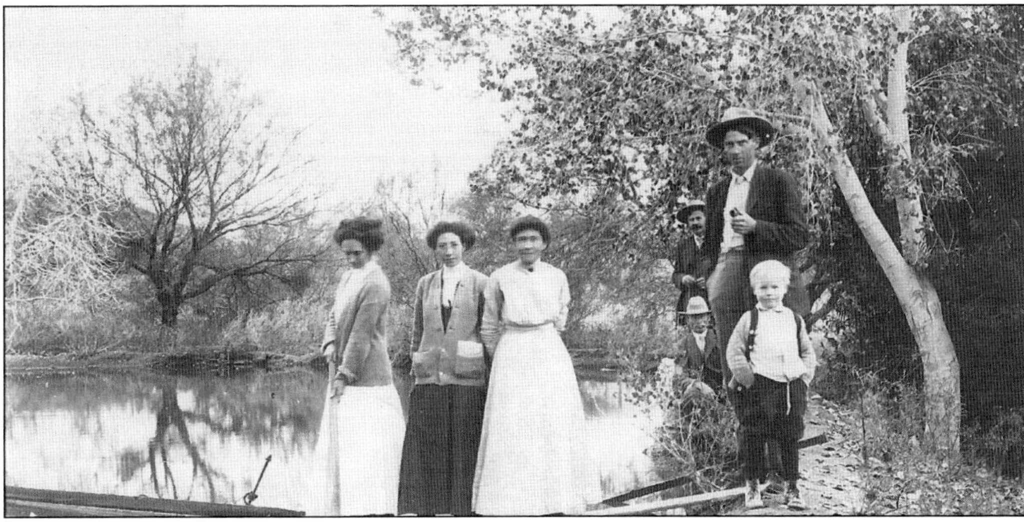

This spring-fed pond was just east of the Houck house. This marvel in the desert was a wonderful place for social gatherings and picnics, as seen in this photograph from the early 1900s. Several children from 1930s-era Cave Creek recalled the times they visited Frances Newman Houck, James Houck's second wife, and swam in the pond.

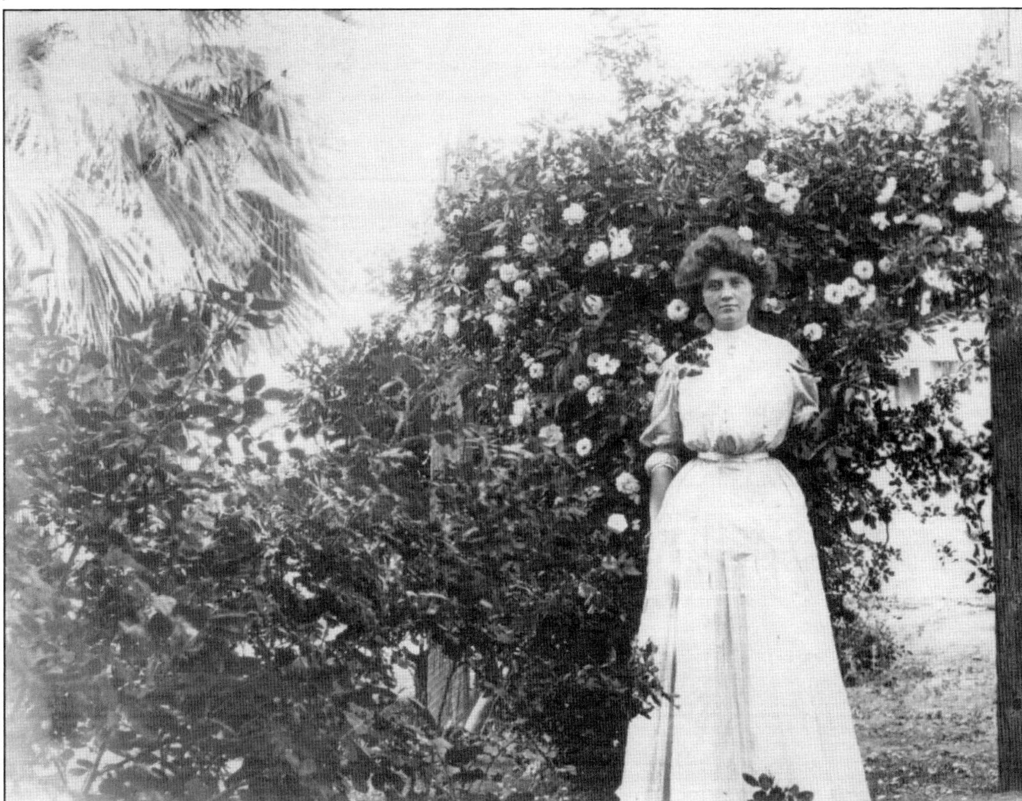

The rose garden next to the pond was begun by Jennie Hoskin in the 1890s. Such delicate beauty and delightful scent must have brought quiet respite in the middle of the desert on a hot summer day.

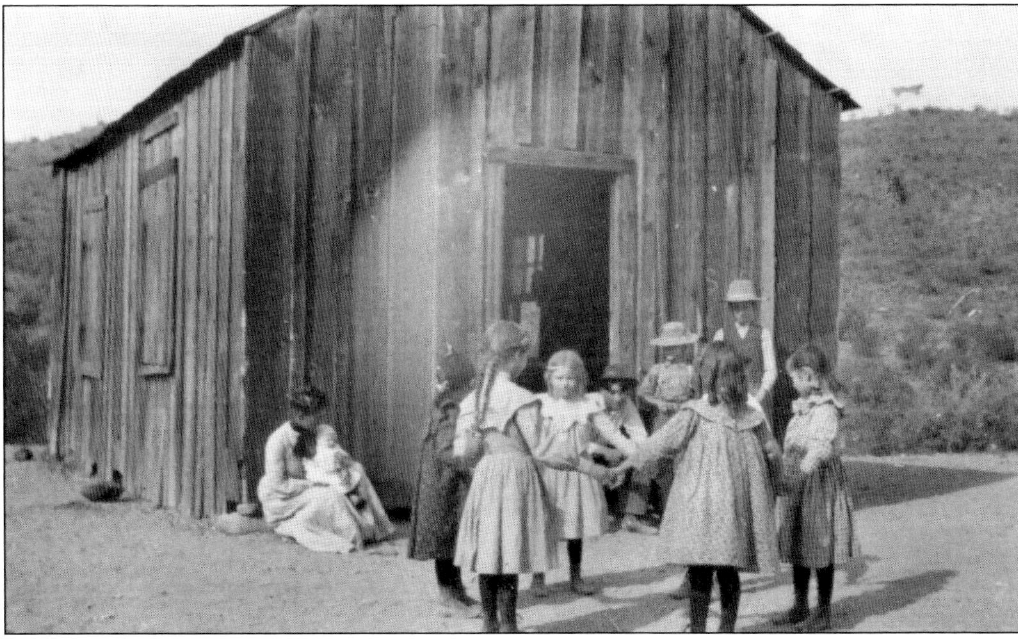

The one-room schoolhouse, built in 1886, also hosted church services and Sunday school. Christmas festivities and year-end school programs were held there. It was also the meeting place for the Cave Creek Literary Society. By 1913, with the Linville and Houck children gone, the school closed. The Houcks sent their daughters to Tempe Normal School (later Arizona State University), while the boys went to Phoenix for high school and then to technical training schools.

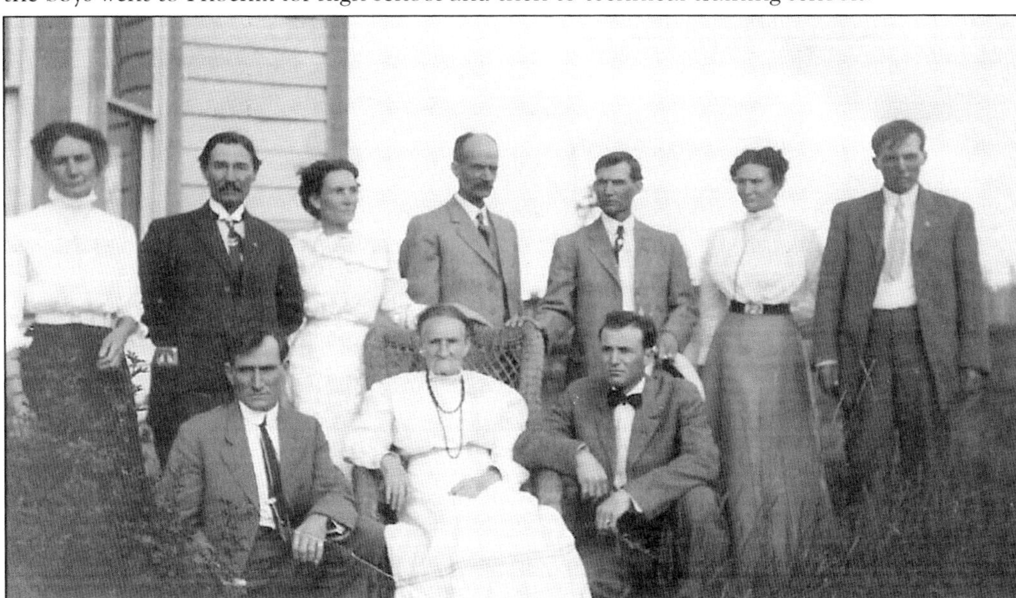

In 1914, Houck married his second wife, Frances Newman Houck (standing, far left). After James Houck's suicide in 1921, Frances expanded the ranch, homesteading an additional 520 acres. In 1927, she built a two-room, 10-foot-by-20-foot house, where she lived, without electricity or indoor plumbing, throughout the Depression. She later sold off portions of the ranch and moved to Phoenix. The ranch eventually became known as Andora Hills.

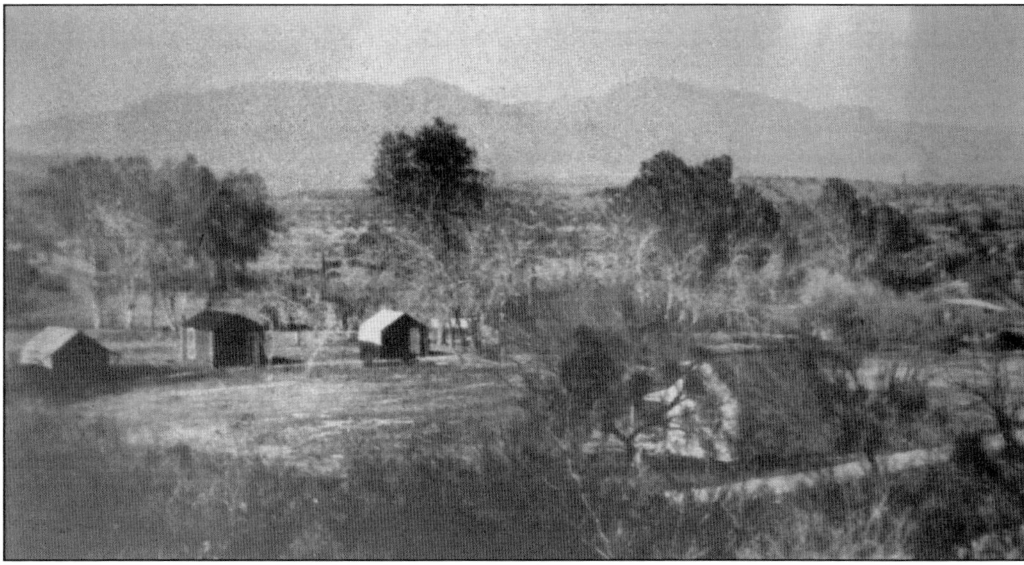

The Howard Ranch, purchased by Ed Howard's parents in 1904, had its own dairy and egg supply as well as ample springwater for irrigating their small farm of barley, vegetables, grapes, figs, and other fruit trees. They also operated a cottage resort for "health seekers." By 1915, the Howards had the post office contract. The extended family lived in the two frame houses on the ranch.

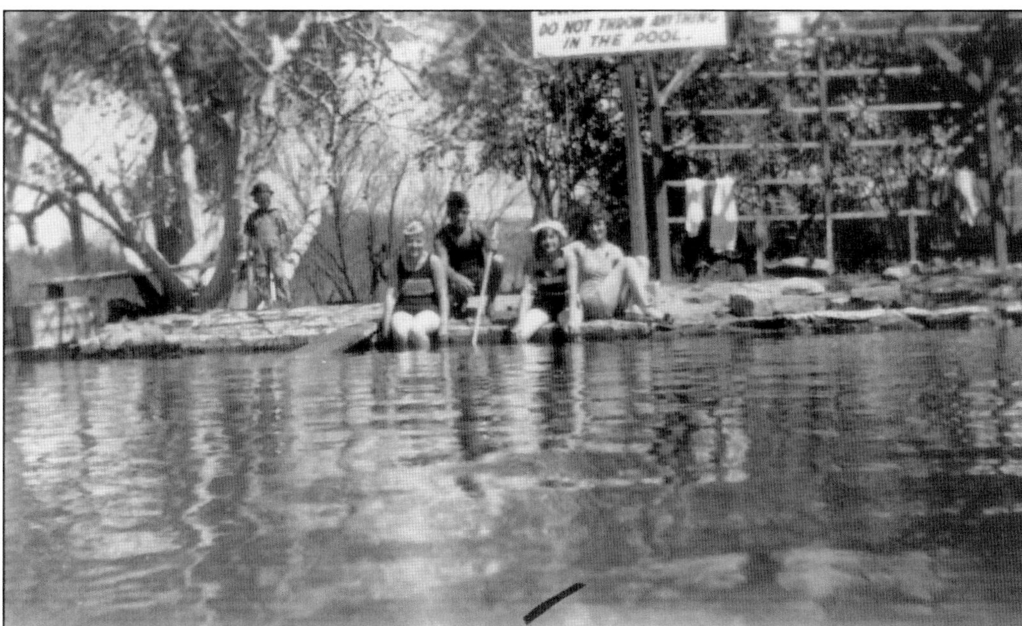

By the late 1920s, the Howard Ranch was doing well. Ed married in 1921 and had two children. He operated a general store and courted tourists, renting cabins for $1 a night. The spring-fed pool was the main attraction. In the early years of the Depression, however, Ed Howard got divorced, lost his ranch, and homesteaded elsewhere in Cave Creek before dying in 1932. His property later became the center of a new dude ranch, Rancho Mañana.

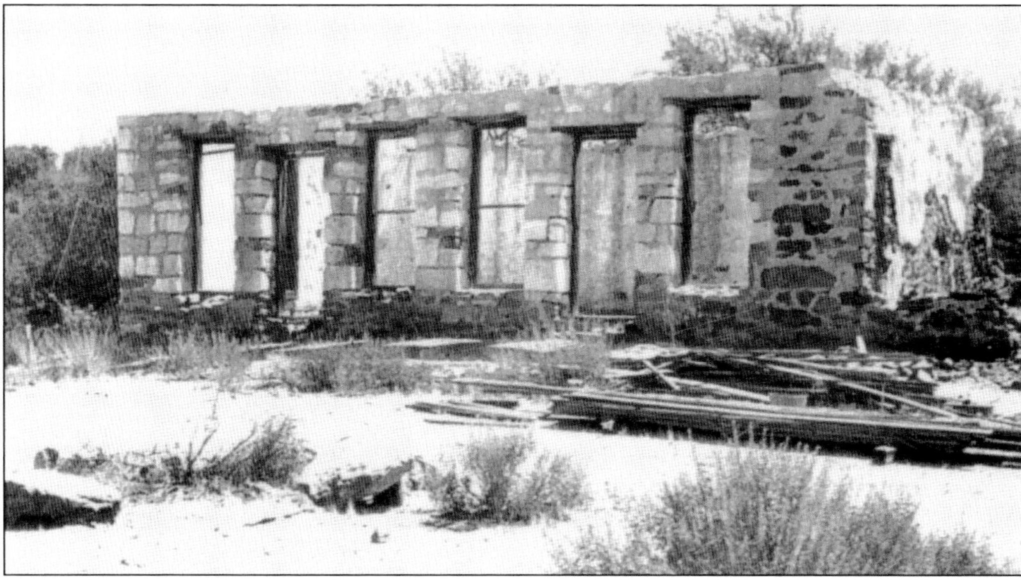

As the town center moved east, old Cave Creek Station was all but forgotten. The rock store/saloon was the last remaining structure. Later, the skeleton of the building (above) was integrated into a new residence (below). Cave Creek Station, a landmark for miners, ranchers, and travelers, was lost to the advancing progress that came to Cave Creek after World War II.

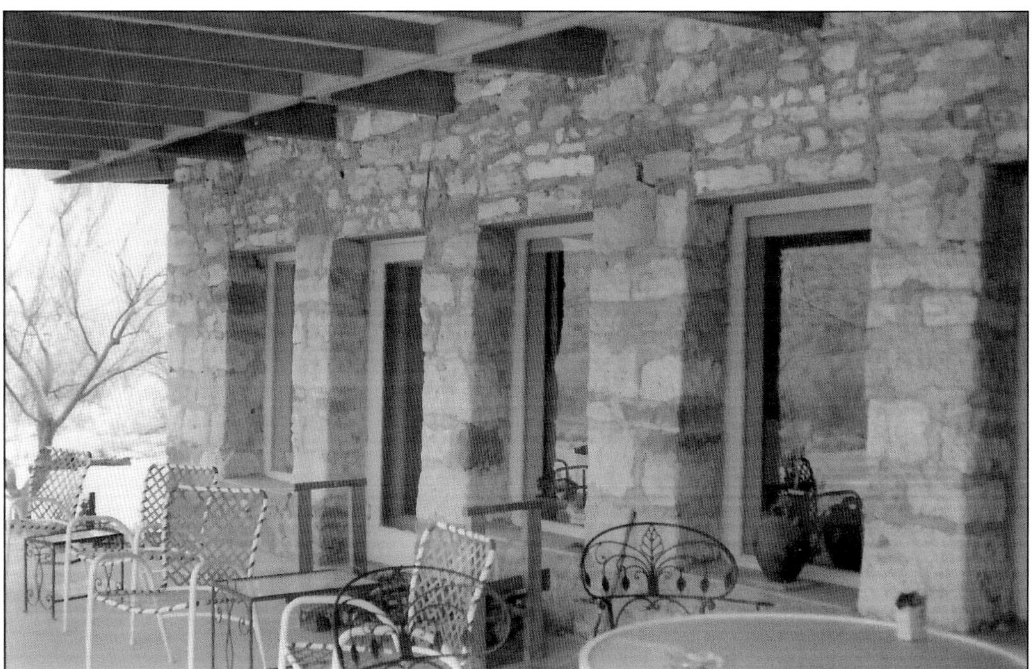

Five

Ranching

Cattle ranching in the Cave Creek area began in the late 1870s. With grasslands to the south, along the creek, on the surrounding mesas, and east to the Verde River, cattle grazed for miles on summer and winter grasses.

Jeriah Wood and Jedder Hoskin were early cattle ranchers at Cave Creek Station. They were followed by the Cartwrights, who came up to the Seven Springs area in the mid-1880s. John Rountree was north of them at the 51 Ranch. The Sears Ranch was to the south, at the confluence of Camp Creek and the Verde River. Logan Morris ranched near the Hoskinses, and Billy Cook was west of Cave Creek, closer to New River. The Linvilles and others, including Charles Hardy, ranched along Cave Creek.

Around 1900, James Houck came from the Mogollon Rim to a sheep ranch at the former Cave Creek Station. Logan Morris then moved east a mile to Grapevine Springs to create the Quarter Circle One Ranch. His son Elmer started his own spread along the creek, next to what is now the Jewel of the Creek Preserve. In the early 1900s, John and William Lewis, brothers from Missouri, started the 6L Ranch five miles up the creek, which they sold to the Cartwrights in the late 1930s because of ill health.

By 1910, the Linville and Houck ranch operations had ceased and the former extended families had moved back to Phoenix. Others would come to the area in the 1930s to try their hand at cattle ranching. Homer Smith ranched in the area near Spur Cross before moving to the old Linville homestead. Bud Miller ranched west of the mountains at Rogers Springs. The Brice family homesteaded and ranched nearby. By 1950, however, nearly all of these pioneer ranches were gone.

Only the Quarter Circle One Ranch, under the management of the Hudson family since 1944, and the Cartwright Ranch at Seven Springs remained. The Hudsons had historical grazing leases covering 120 sections over to Brown's Ranch and down to Pinnacle Peak Road to the south. The Cartwright Ranch operation covered 65,000 acres. At its peak, the ranch may have run 2,500 head of cattle. In 1980, after nearly a century of family ranching history, the Cartwright Ranch was sold.

Ranching and cooperative roundups are gone now, and houses and subdivisions occupy several of the former ranches. These pioneer cattlemen and their families left an indelible mark on Arizona and Cave Creek history.

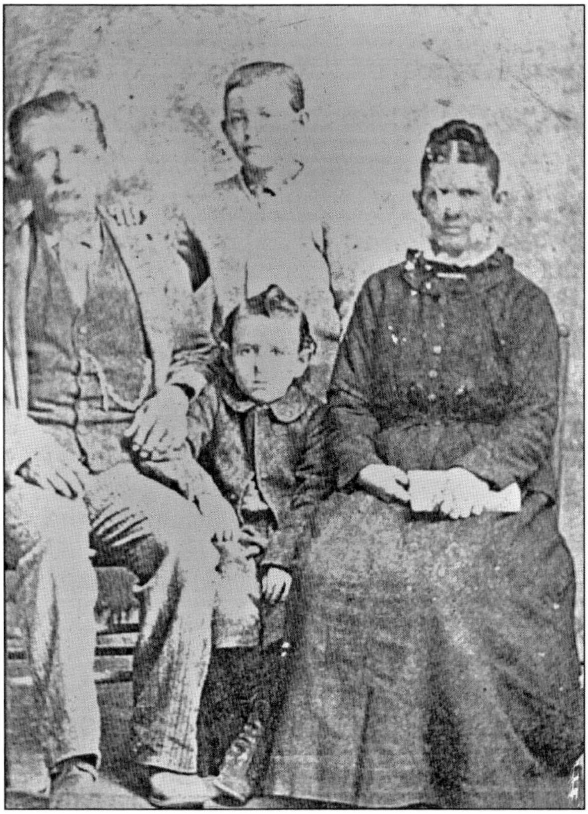

Charles and Sarah Young Hardy came from Phoenix to cattle ranch in the early 1880s. Their ranch was three miles north of Cave Creek Station. Charles's real name was Nathaniel Hickman, and he had fled Colorado in the early 1870s and resettled in Arizona under a new name. He was elected justice of the peace for Cave Creek in 1890. The family left a short time later due to continuing droughts. (Courtesy of David Hardy.)

Logan Morris (below) arrived in Cave Creek in the early 1880s. His first cattle ranch was just north of Cave Creek Station. He moved east to the Grape Vine Cattle Ranch (later renamed Quarter Circle One) in 1912 to avoid sheep grazing nearby. The ranch grew until the Depression (and perhaps Morris's drinking issues) caused problems. After Morris's death in 1943, the property was sold to Dwight and Mary Hudson in early 1944.

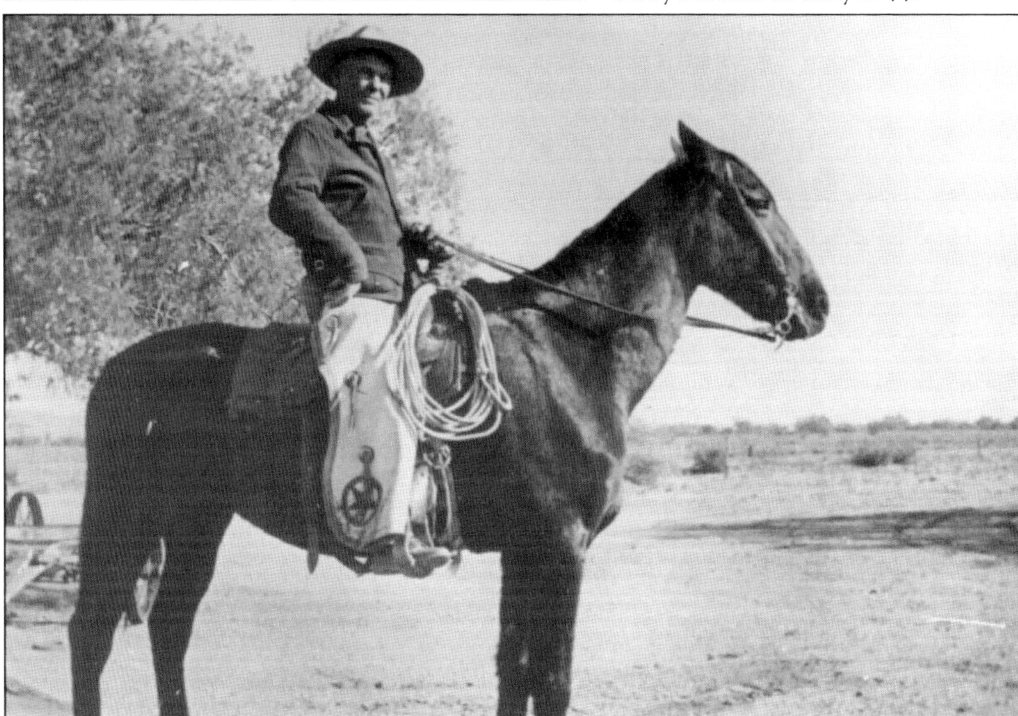

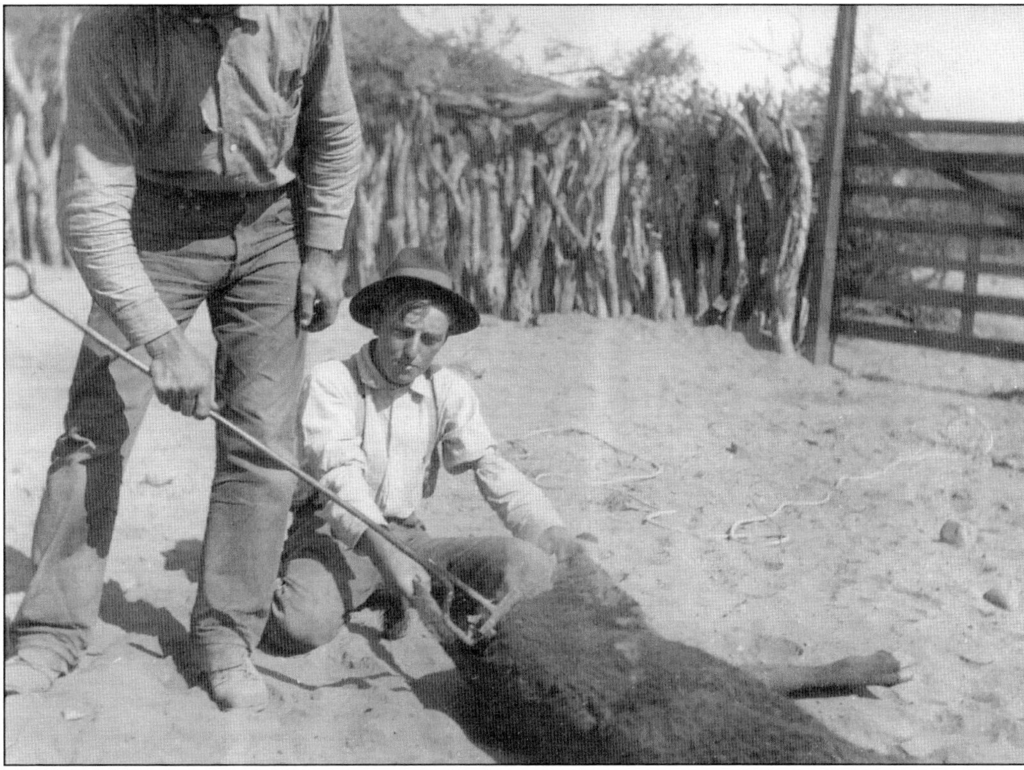

Branding was important to area ranchers, as their cattle roamed throughout the desert foothills. The young man in the photograph above was Joe Hand, a "tubercular" who came to Cave Creek from Seattle and ended up becoming a longtime forest ranger. This is a rare photograph of branding at the first Morris ranch, near the creek. The photograph below shows branding at the Quarter Circle One Ranch in the 1940s.

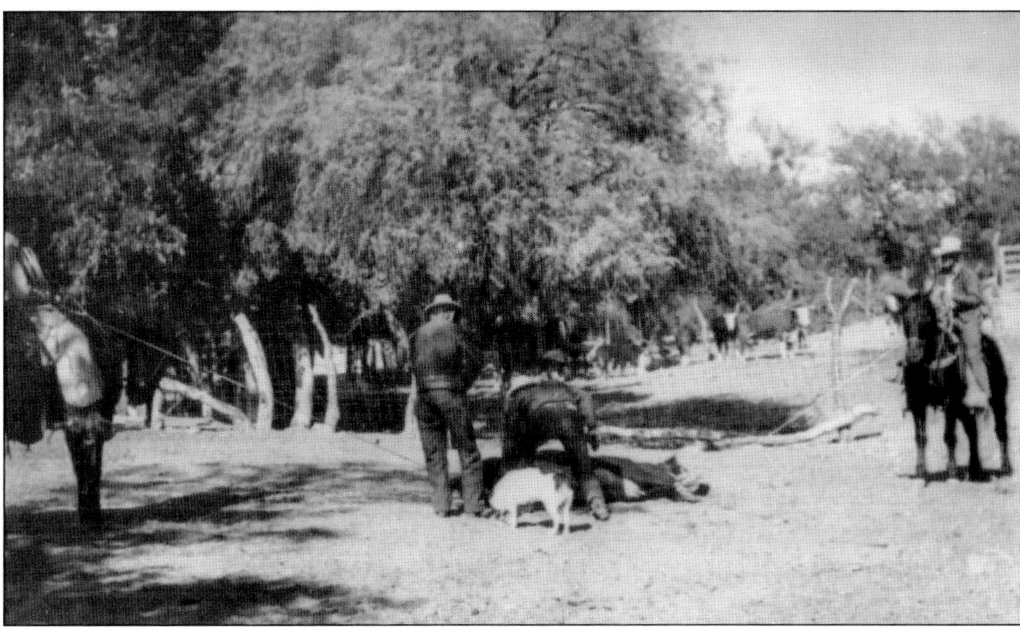

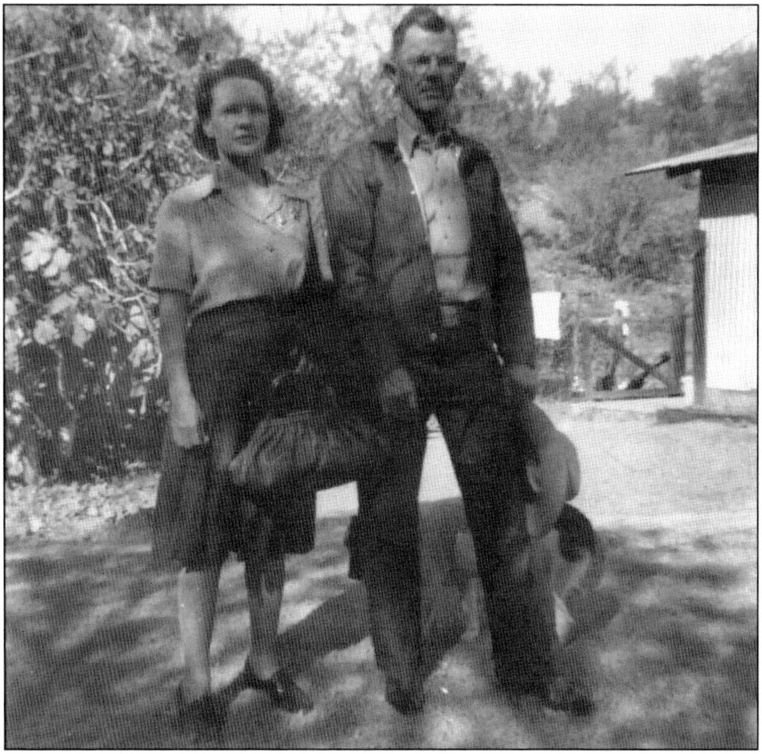

Tim Adams had run cattle all his life when he and his wife, Margaret, moved to the Quarter Circle One Ranch in 1941 to assist his uncle Logan Morris with ranch operations. They held their first deer barbecue there. The couple stayed on with the new owners for a time, later doing wrangling for both Rancho Mañana and Sierra Vista. Margaret also worked at the post office and volunteered at the Gold Mine Thrift Shop.

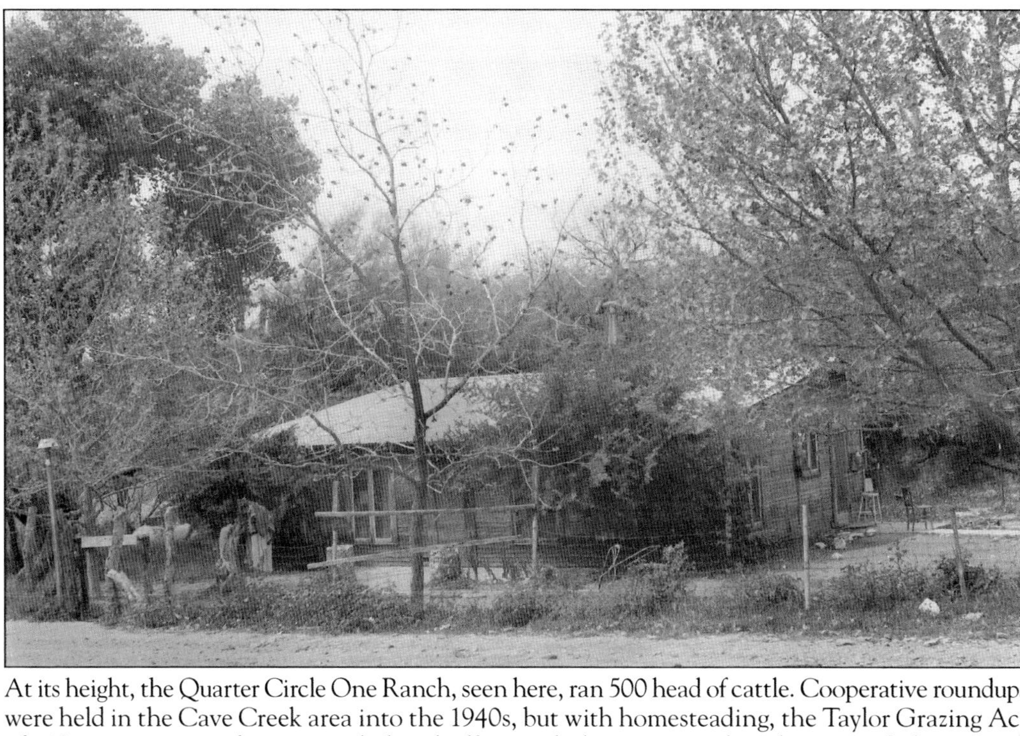

At its height, the Quarter Circle One Ranch, seen here, ran 500 head of cattle. Cooperative roundups were held in the Cave Creek area into the 1940s, but with homesteading, the Taylor Grazing Act of 1934, overgrazing, fencing, and closed-off water holes, area ranchers began to feel squeezed. When the ranch was finally sold, it had over 50 grazing leases covering 120 land sections.

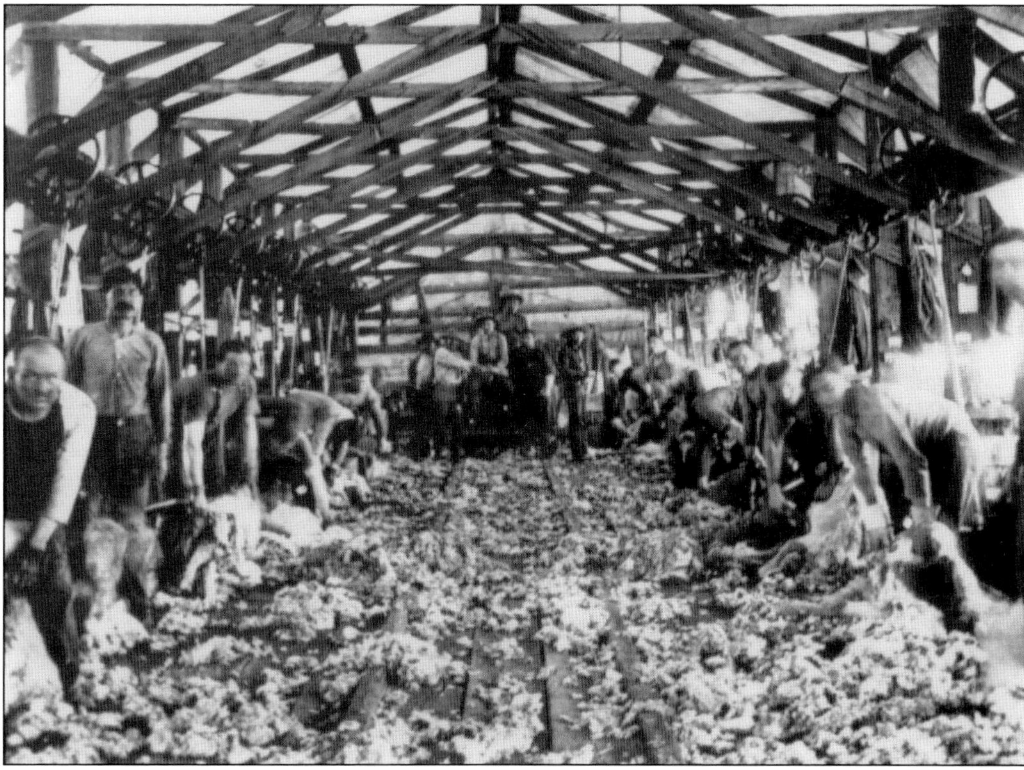

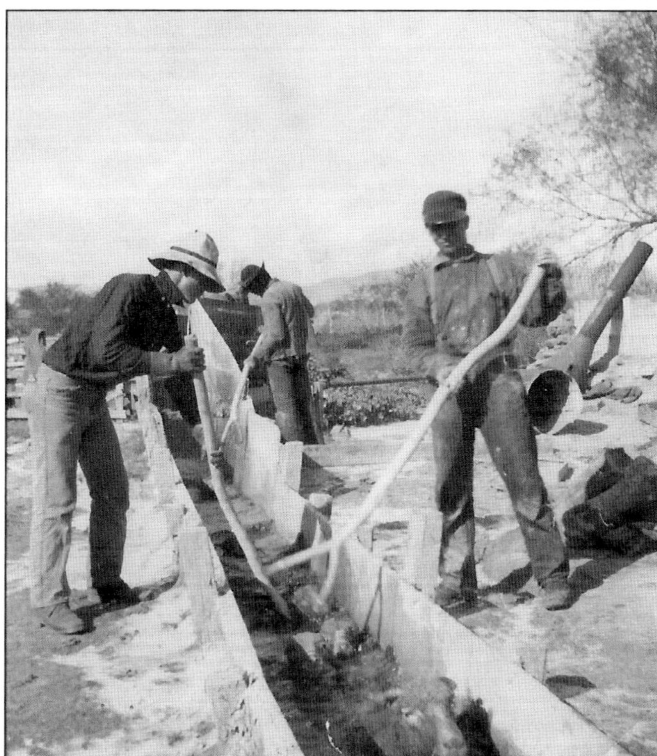

In the late fall, sheep began to arrive at Houck's ranch from northern Arizona. The shearers, 30 to 40 of them, arrived in January. In total, more than 100 men were housed and fed at the ranch. Given their long stay, packages came to the post office from sheepherder families in Italy, Greece, and Spain. The shearing shed (above) was quite a scene, with shearers clipping wool from between 60 and 200 sheep a day. Sheep were then herded to the dipping troughs (right), where they were treated for possible parasites such as mites, ticks, and lice. Men carried hooks mounted on long poles to make sure the entire body was submerged. The hooks could also be used to save sheep that were pulled or pushed under by other animals.

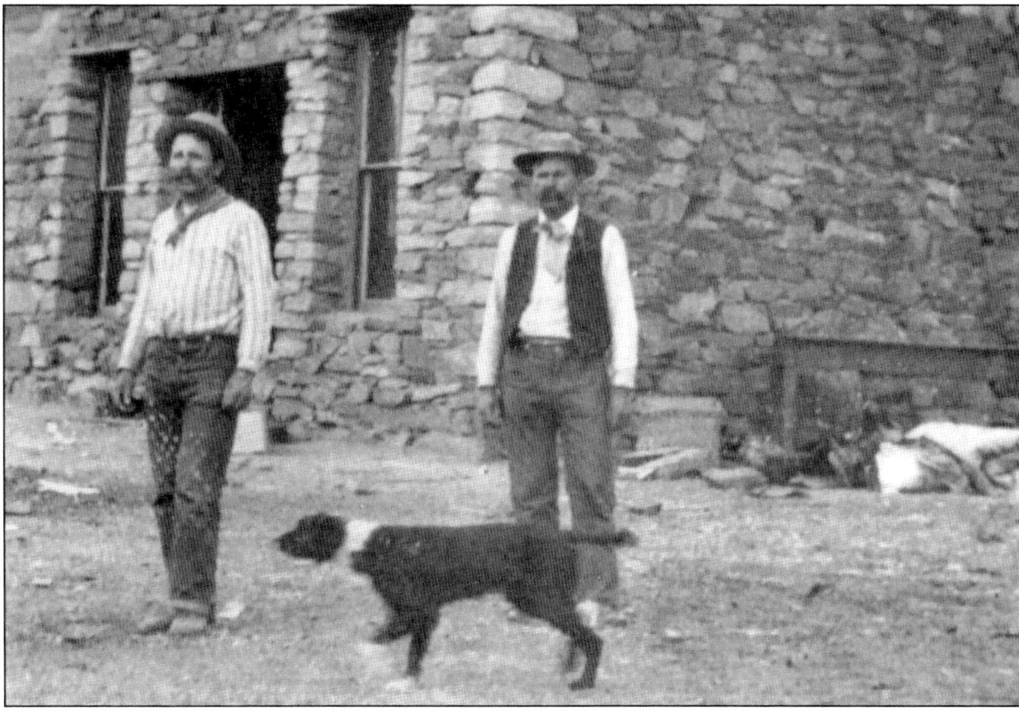

John and William Lewis came from Missouri and ran cattle in the Superstition Mountains area in the 1880s. By 1900, they had joined their uncle Boon Lewis in Cave Creek to prospect. In 1914, John Lewis filed a homestead application on 152 acres along Cave Creek, eight miles north of the town, and established the 6L Ranch. In the 1920s, the two brothers ran nearly 300 head of cattle.

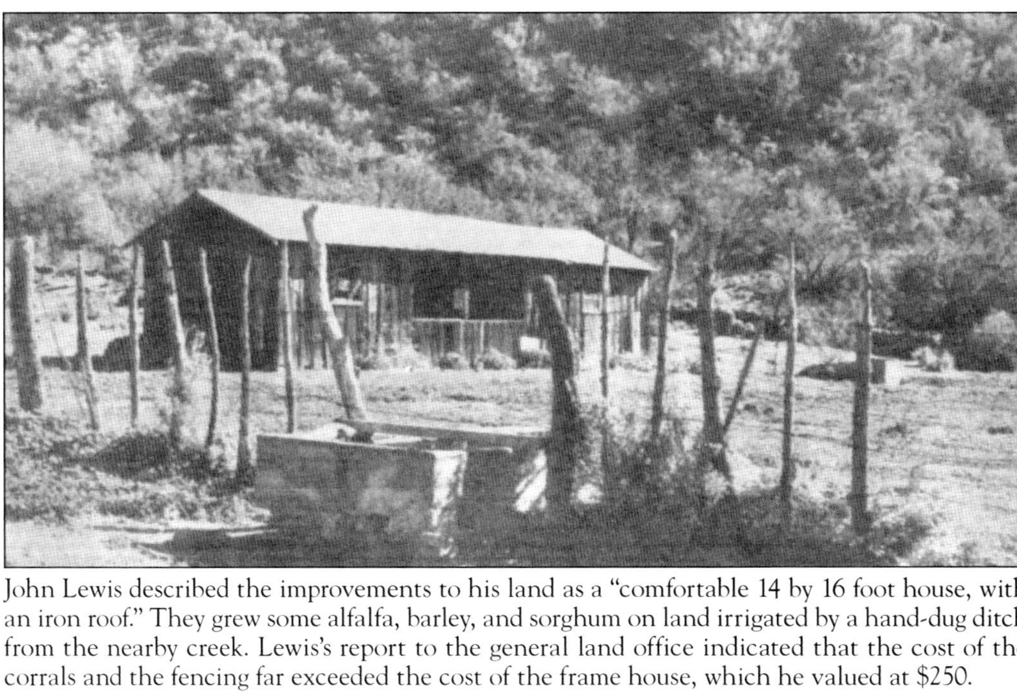

John Lewis described the improvements to his land as a "comfortable 14 by 16 foot house, with an iron roof." They grew some alfalfa, barley, and sorghum on land irrigated by a hand-dug ditch from the nearby creek. Lewis's report to the general land office indicated that the cost of the corrals and the fencing far exceeded the cost of the frame house, which he valued at $250.

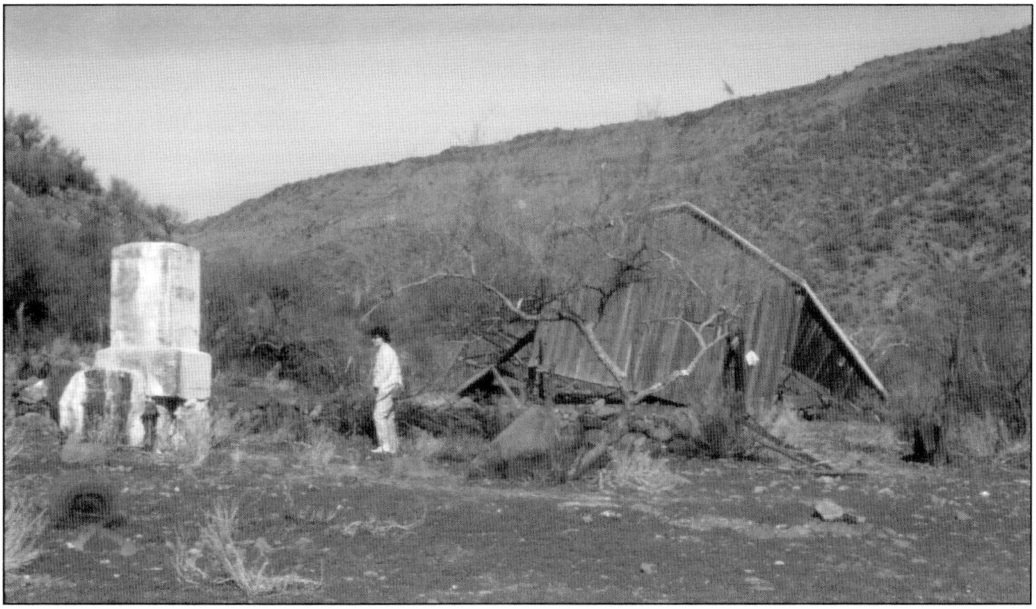

Following the deaths of the Lewis brothers in 1937 and 1938, the Cartwrights acquired the property for use as a line camp. Years later, when this photograph was taken, it had fallen into ruins.

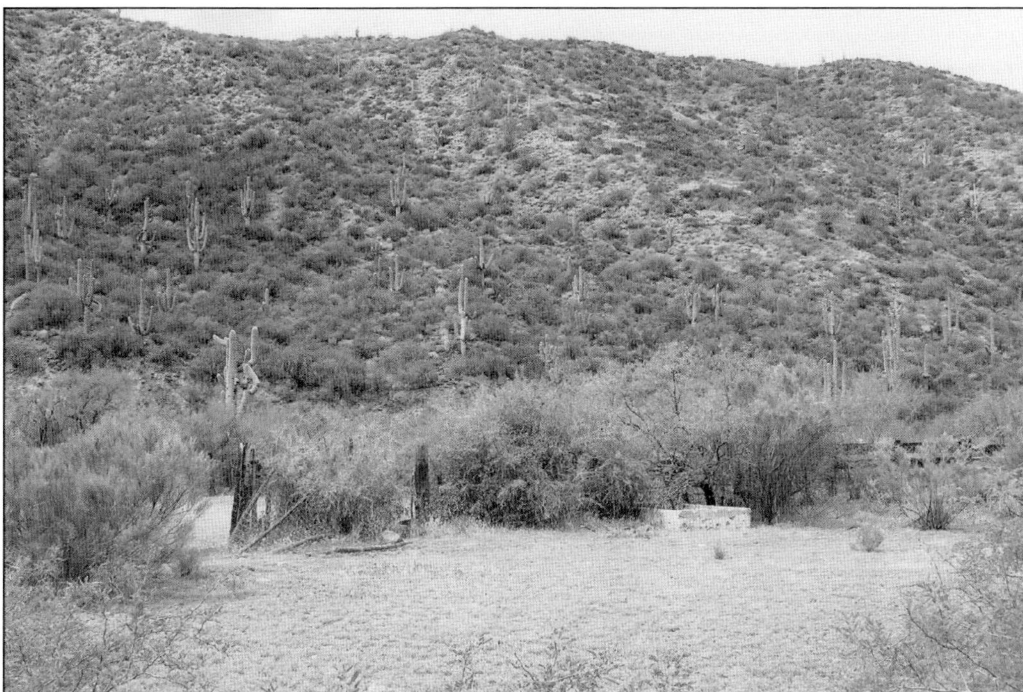

Evidence of fencing, corrals, water tanks, and even the house still remain as a faint reminder of the cowboy ranching spirit of the Lewis brothers at the remote wilderness ranch known as the 6L. The New River Mesa was immediately off to the west. Cave Creek runs along the western border, turns easterly just beyond the 6L, and then winds its way past Matty's Fork to the Cartwright Ranch and its source at Seven Springs.

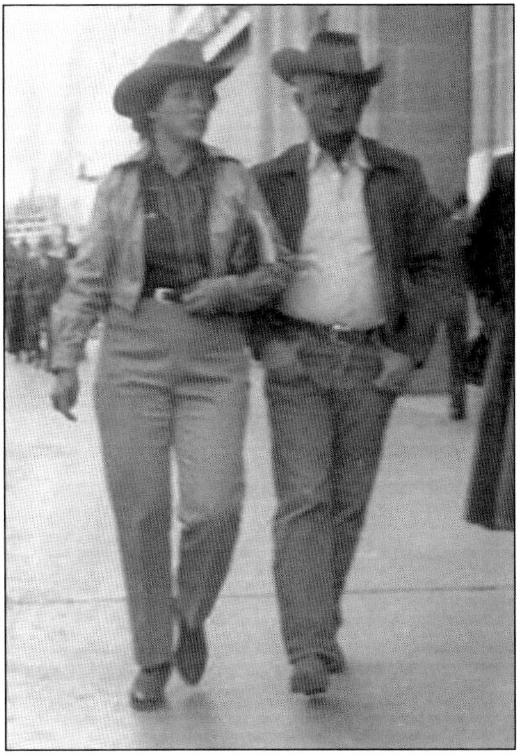

Homer and Florence Smith homesteaded in Cave Creek in 1929 after being inspired by a visit to the Quarter Circle One Ranch. Two years later, with no experience, Homer started cattle ranching. The Smiths had a small ranch north of Spur Cross Ranch on Cottonwood Wash. By the end of World War II, they owned the old Linville ranch and ran 1,200 head of cattle. The family moved to northern Arizona in 1948. (Courtesy of Glodyne Smith Cowley.)

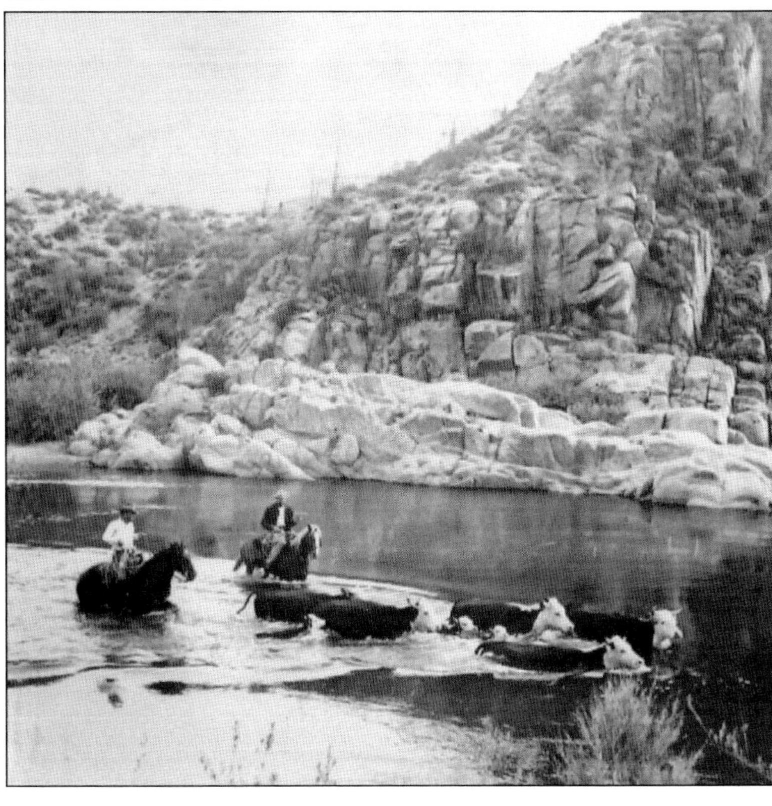

The creek was vital to cattle ranches. While portions of the creek did not always run year-round down to Cave Creek Station, it generally carried water from fall to spring, upstream, nearer its natural spring headwaters. The areas around the town and south of it were good sources of winter grass. This 1951 photograph of cowboys herding cattle across the creek appeared in *Arizona Highways*.

Jasper and Sarah Cartwright brought their family to Phoenix in early 1877. There, in the vicinity of today's Thomas Road and Fifty-first Avenue, family members homesteaded 640 acres. Jasper gave his young son Mantford some early heifers to manage. Some conflicts with neighboring farmers compelled them to move their cattle to the Cave Creek area. (Courtesy of the Cartwright family.)

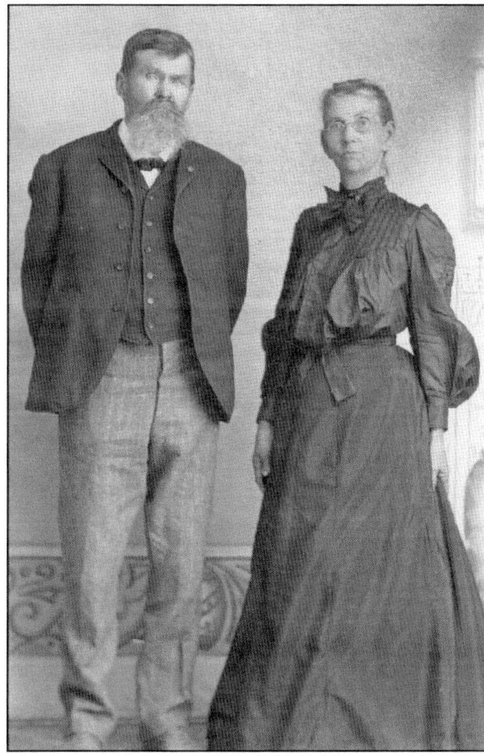

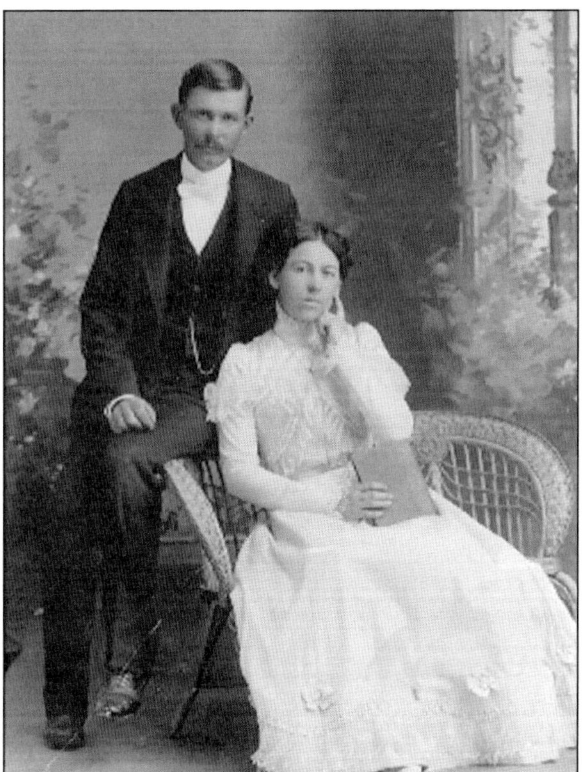

Mantford Cartwright married Beulah Greene in 1899. Mantford had been cattle ranching in the area northeast of Cave Creek known as Seven Springs. He likely had a small cabin near there in the 1890s. The Cartwrights continued to maintain their primary residence in Phoenix, in what became known as the Cartwright District. Several other family members established ranches north of Seven Springs. (Courtesy of the Cartwright family.)

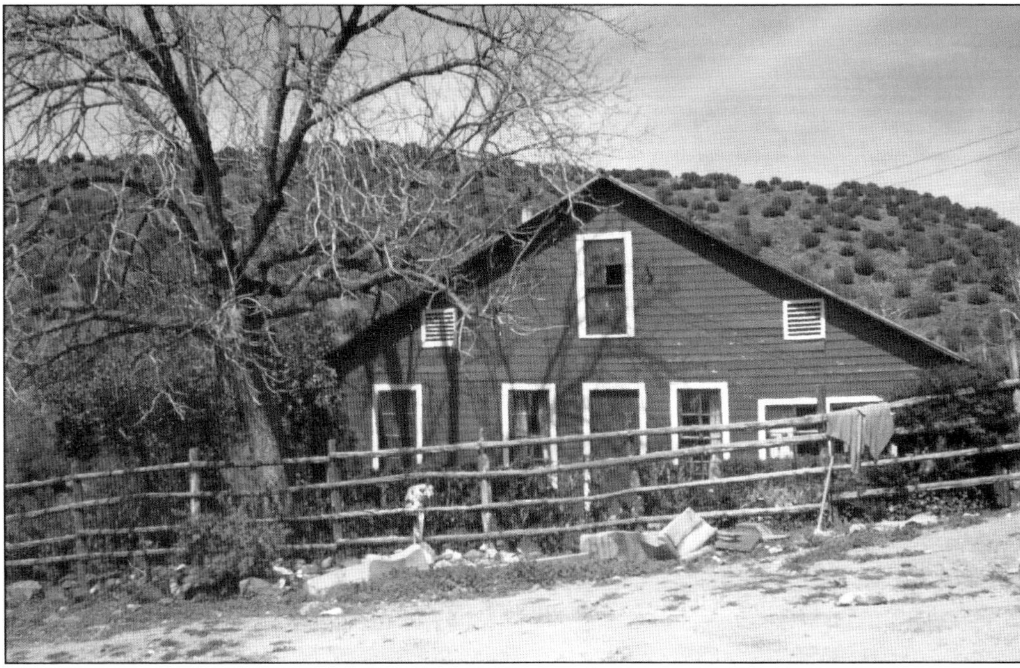

By 1906, Mantford Cartwright built this ranch on 56 acres of homesteaded land near the springs. The original 24-foot-by-24-foot home had five rooms on two stories. There was also a barn, a shed, a garage, a storeroom, and a blacksmith shop. Water was pumped a mile and a half from the springs to the house and the fields.

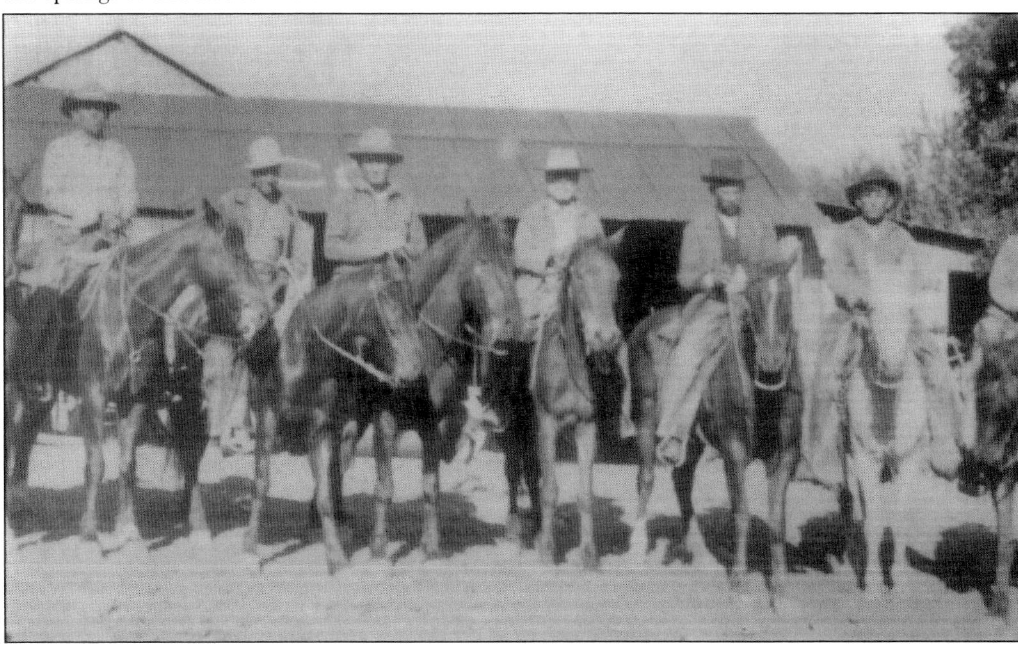

Dependable cowboys were vital to ranching, as the work was not easy. Roundups occurred twice a year, lasting more than a month each time. Trail rides herding cattle to Phoenix or Glendale could take several days, with cowboys responsible for four or five horses each. The Cartwrights had a long history of employing Hispanic cowboys. At one point, the ranch ran 2,500 head of cattle.

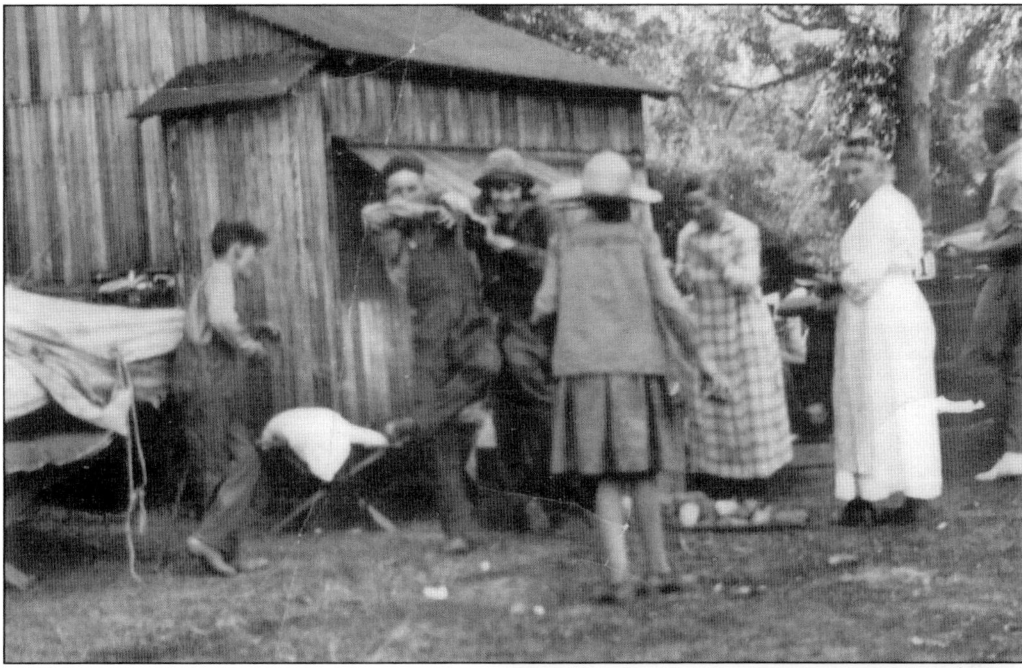

The Cartwright family often came up from Phoenix for the summer. Children took hikes, hunted for arrowheads, and fished in the creek. They even accompanied the cattle drives at times, meeting the cowboys for picnics, as seen above.

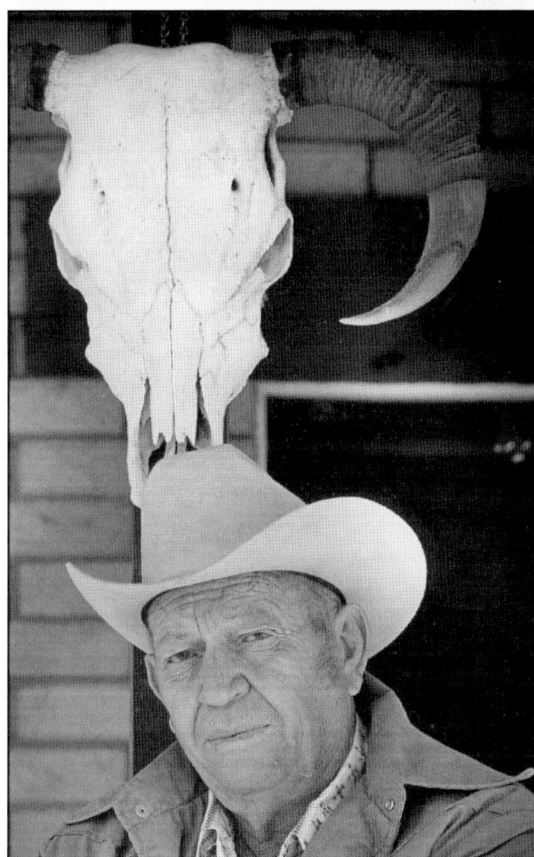

Mantford Cartwright's son Jack took over ranch operations in the late 1930s. In 1980, he reluctantly sold the ranch, ending a ranching heritage that lasted nearly a century. In 1982, he told a writer, "Every day I think about the ranch." A year later, Jack Cartwright died in his home in Cave Creek. He was the last of the old-time ranchers who lived the cowboy life along the life-giving waters of Cave Creek. (Courtesy of Cartwright family.)

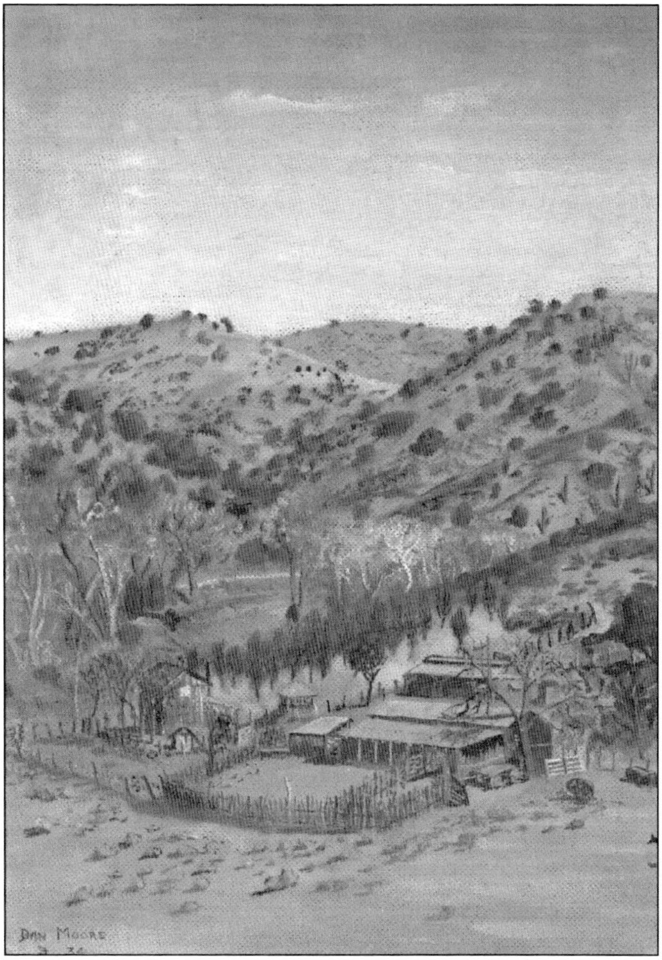

Dan Moore painted this rare picture of the Cartwright Ranch in the 1930s. Moore was a local cowboy who worked with several ranches in the 1920s and 1930s, primarily at roundup time. He recalled some of his cowboy life in the Cave Creek area and elsewhere in his book *Log of a Twentieth Century Cowboy*. (Courtesy of the Cartwright family.)

The photograph below shows the last Cartwright cattle drive, which occurred in 1979. The Cave Creek ranching era, dating from the 1880s, had finally drawn to a close on a dusty cattle trail. (Courtesy of the Cartwright family.)

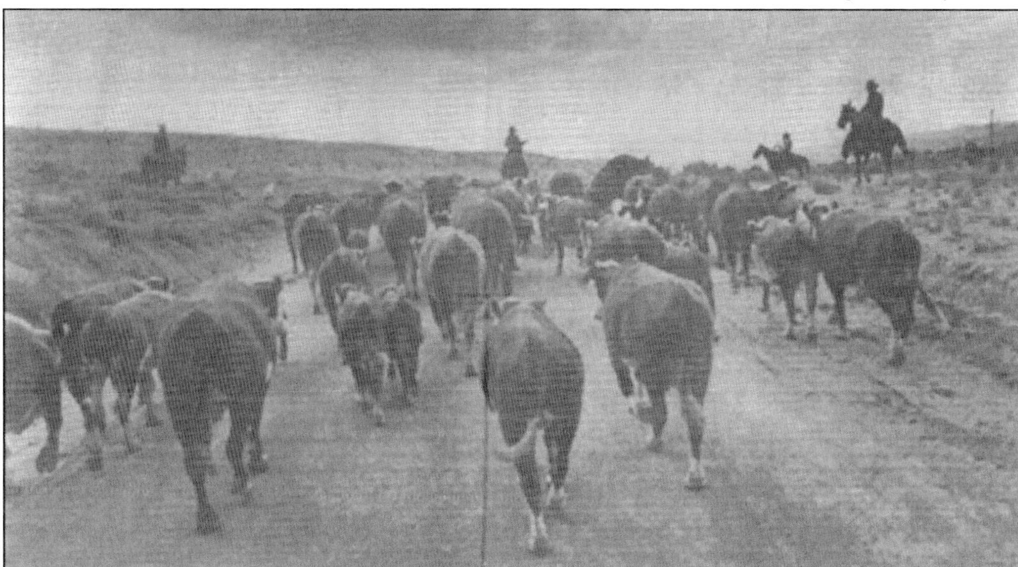

Six

Dude Ranches of Cave Creek

The Southwest has a long history of attracting those wishing to experience the life of a cowboy, if only for a week. The dude ranches of Cave Creek fulfilled those dreams, with horseback rides, barbecues, cowboy songs, storytelling, and dancing.

Spur Cross, the first dude ranch, lasted only three years. Phil Lewis and Cap Joyce started the venture in 1928 along Cave Creek, about four miles north of the town. In 1946, Warren and Billie Beaubien purchased the 2,000-acre ranch and transformed it into a successful dude ranch. Their annual Christmas party was a major community event. In 1953, tragedy struck when Warren crashed his private airplane on the ranch's landing strip, dying several days later. The ranch was closed forever shortly thereafter. Today, it is the Spur Cross Ranch Conservation Area.

Rancho Mañana was another successful dude ranch, situated near the town and the creek. Started in 1943, it owed its success to Ted and China Loring and the irrepressible Romy Lowdermilk, often called the father of Arizona dude ranching. Lowdermilk had a long history with dude ranch operations and was both a storyteller and a well-known cowboy singer. Dancing took place two to three times a week during high season. This Spanish hacienda–style ranch property also had the luxury of a swimming pool. The ranch closed in 1955, shortly after Lowdermilk's retirement.

Sierra Vista, the third dude ranch in Cave Creek, was started in 1952 by the Bloomquist family. They sold the ranch in 1955 to Dr. John "Doc" and Jean Owen, under whose leadership the ranch flourished for seven years. While they took on general property improvements, they hired Hube Yates to handle the wrangling duties. A retired Phoenix fireman with his own string of horses and a ranch in Heber, Arizona, Hube became a legend. Rugged yet kind and sociable, Hube was a masterful storyteller and an incomparable wrangler. Hube's semiannual horseback trek to Heber with his herd of horses, a 10-day, 200-mile trip, was a favorite for many. Upon Doc Owen's retirement in 1962, the Owens closed the dude ranch and transformed it into a private residence.

With that, the dude ranch era came to an end. The ranches created Cave Creek's reputation as a tourist destination. Moreover, the dude ranches played an important role in the town's social life. The equestrian culture is still alive and well in contemporary Cave Creek.

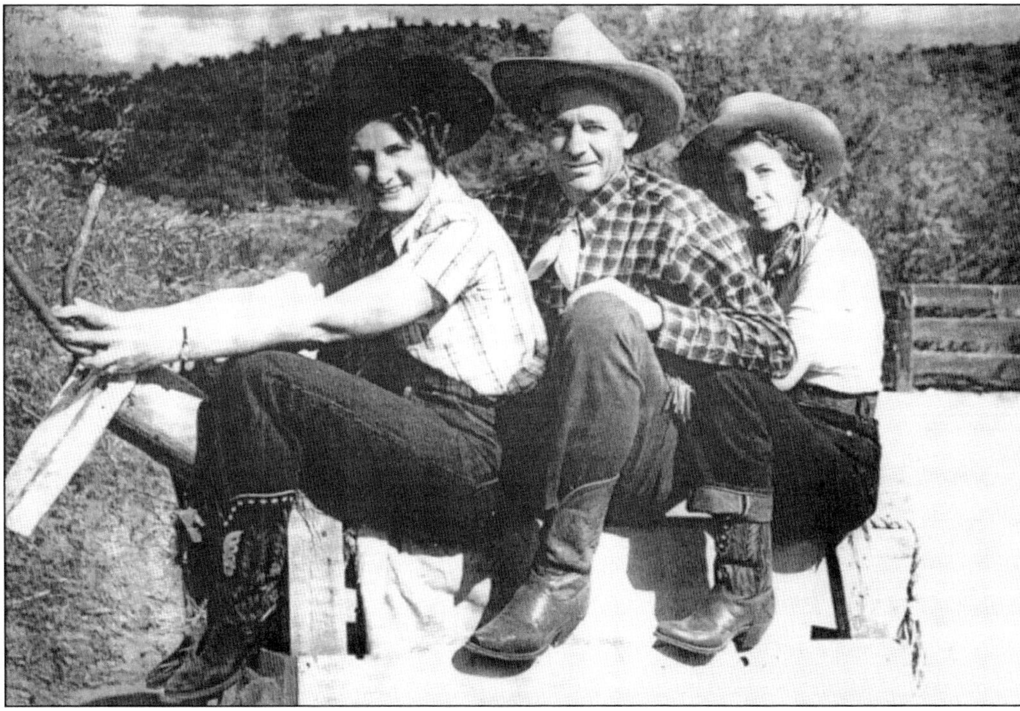

Fresh out of prison in 1928, Phil Lewis and Cap Joyce started Cave Creek's first dude ranch, Spur Cross. Their partnership dissolved within three years. Phil Lewis (center) then successfully homesteaded the land and purchased additional acreage, but as early as 1930, he and his wife, Marie (left), envisioned another dude ranch at the newly constructed Saguaro Lake. They sold Spur Cross Ranch in 1942 to Fred Knowles, who failed to revive the dude ranch. (Courtesy of Stephen Durand.)

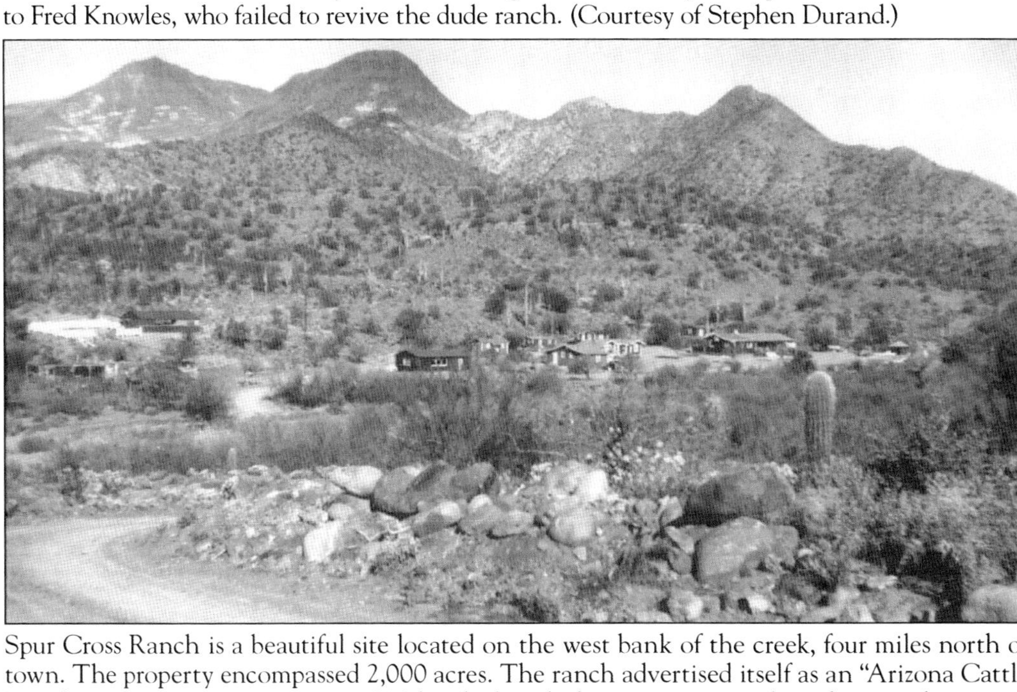

Spur Cross Ranch is a beautiful site located on the west bank of the creek, four miles north of town. The property encompassed 2,000 acres. The ranch advertised itself as an "Arizona Cattle Ranch," sometimes running up to 200 head of cattle foraging on a number of grazing leases.

Warren and Billie Beaubien purchased the Spur Cross Ranch in 1946. Warren, who had a passion for the West, was a successful general contractor, a business he continued to operate after purchasing the ranch. Billie, a five-foot-tall, spunky woman, was the hostess, cook, and social organizer.

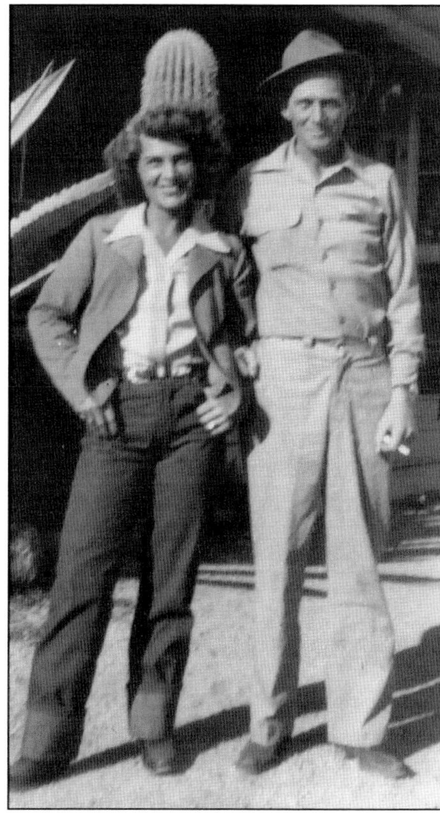

The Beaubiens raised four daughters at the ranch, (below, from left to right) Eileen, Doretta, Audrey, and Theresa. Theresa went on to marry one of the wranglers, Al Eldridge. Audrey later team-roped with her husband, Dymond Woodward, all across Arizona.

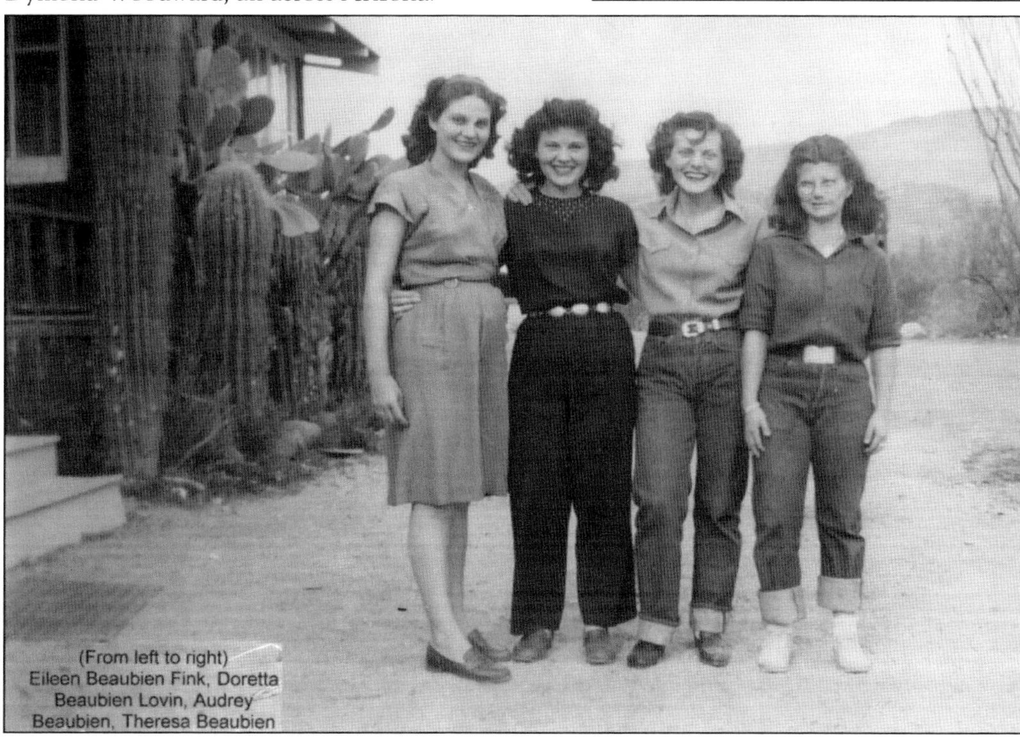

(From left to right) Eileen Beaubien Fink, Doretta Beaubien Lovin, Audrey Beaubien, Theresa Beaubien

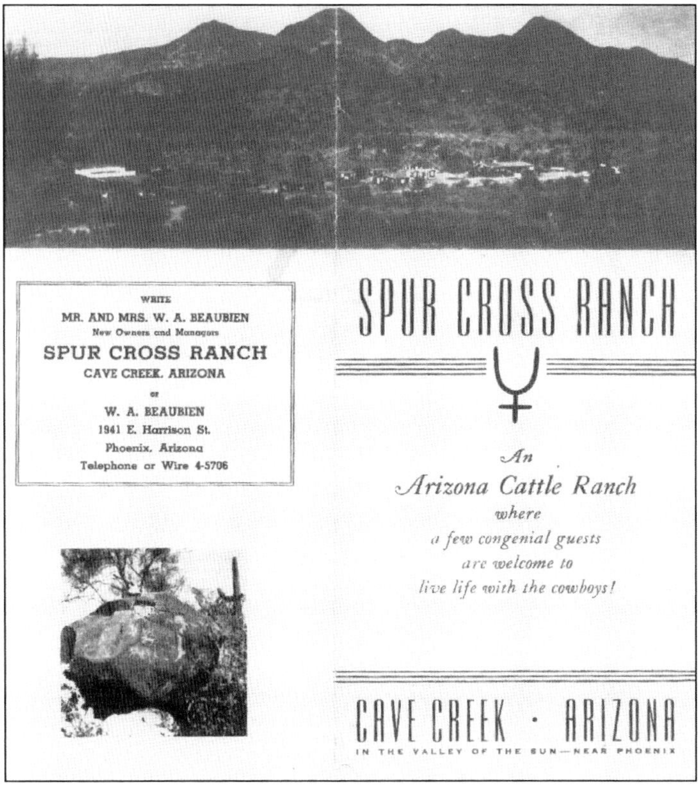

The Spur Cross Ranch could accommodate up to 24 guests. The season generally ran from October 1 to mid-May.

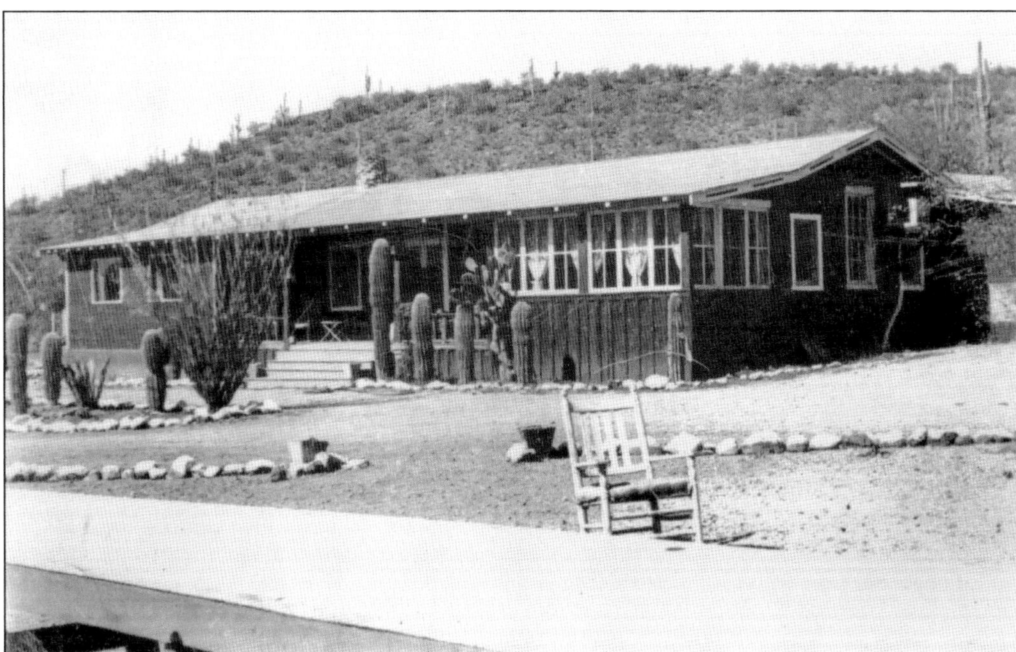

The main ranch house was the social gathering center, with the living room in the center of the lodge and the dining room, sunroom, and kitchen to the right. At the southern (left) end were the Beaubien living quarters, which also included a social room in the front.

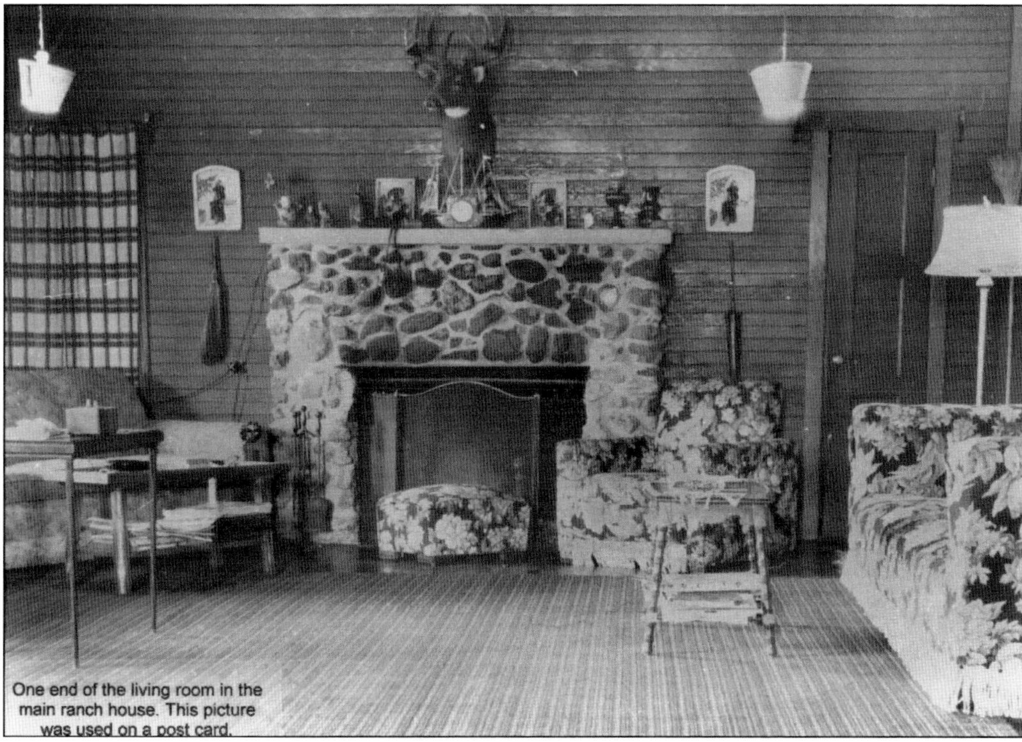

One end of the living room in the main ranch house. This picture was used on a post card.

Guests gathered in the living room for social activities. In the adjacent dining room, they were served three home-cooked meals, including a dinner of meat, potatoes, two vegetables, salad, and dessert. They ate in the dining room and the sunroom on red-checkered tablecloths. Wranglers ate in the kitchen.

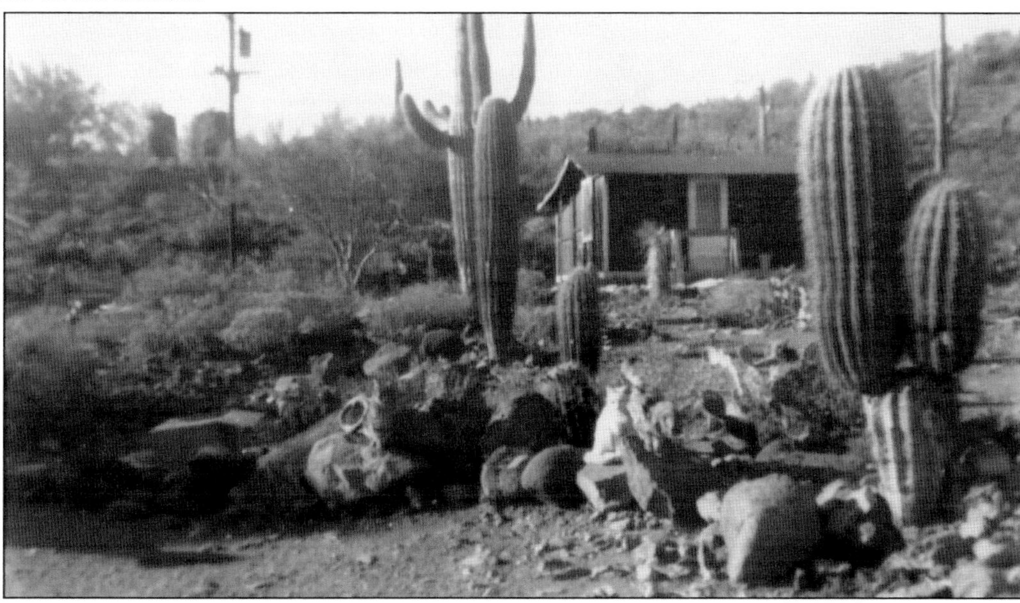

The cabins were described as "clean, modern and ranchy." All had indoor plumbing, and several had private bathrooms. There were also duplex and triplex cabins. Rates were $50 per week, and horses could be rented for an additional $15 per week.

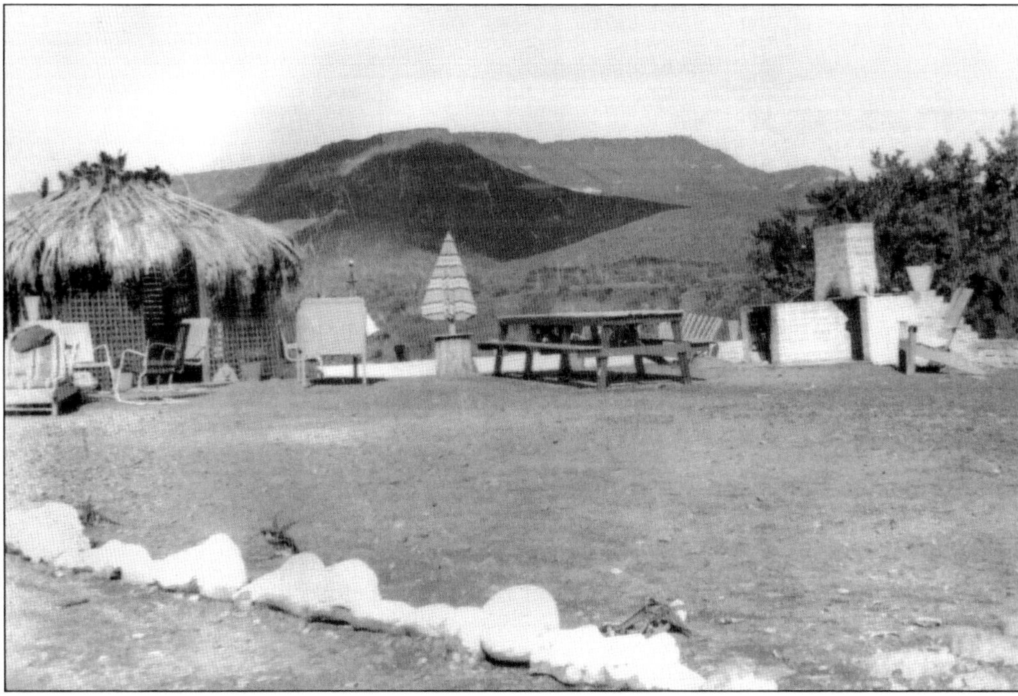

Guests at the Spur Cross Ranch enjoyed outdoor barbecues and evening cowboy stories. The Beaubiens also hosted dances in the barn for guests and Cave Creek residents. The walls were lined with bales of hay for sitting, and food and refreshments were served at midnight.

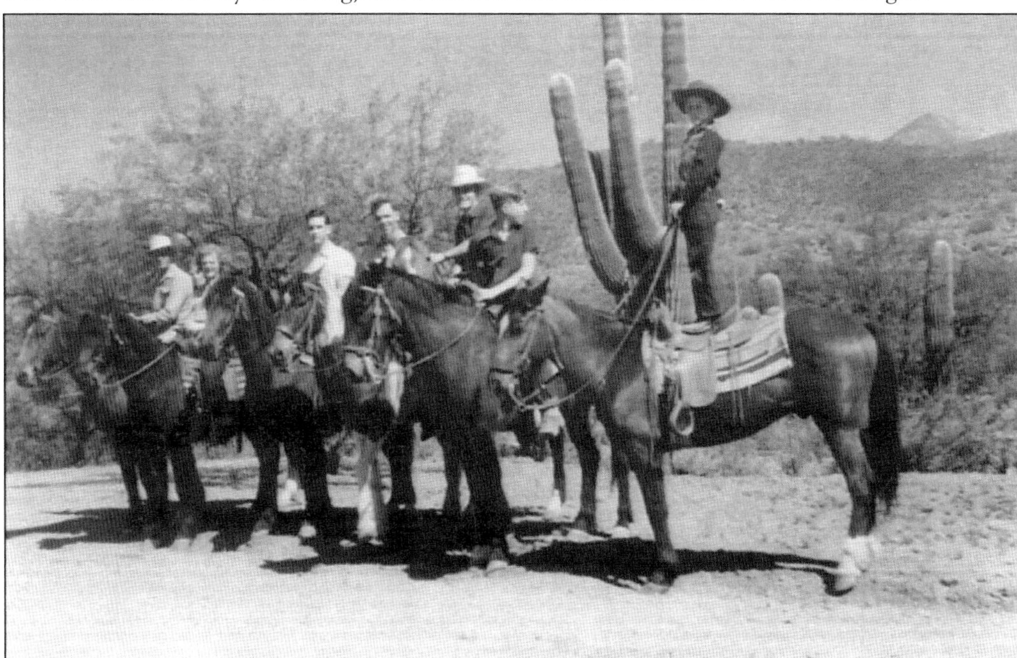

Of course, horseback riding was the favorite guest activity. Over the years, the ranch employed a number of local cowboys to lead treks into the surrounding countryside. An overnight trip to the former 6L Ranch up the creek was always a favorite.

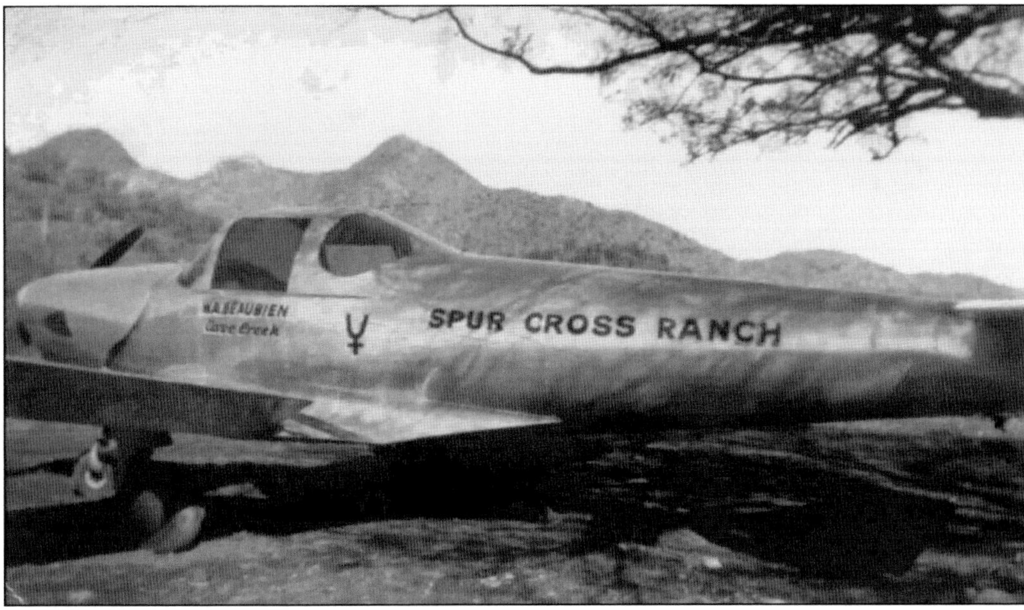

Spur Cross Ranch even had its own airstrip, for the convenience of Warren Beaubien and his business. Tragically, over Labor Day weekend in 1953, he crashed his plane on the landing strip, dying several days later from severe burns. Devastated, the Beaubien family closed the ranch shortly thereafter.

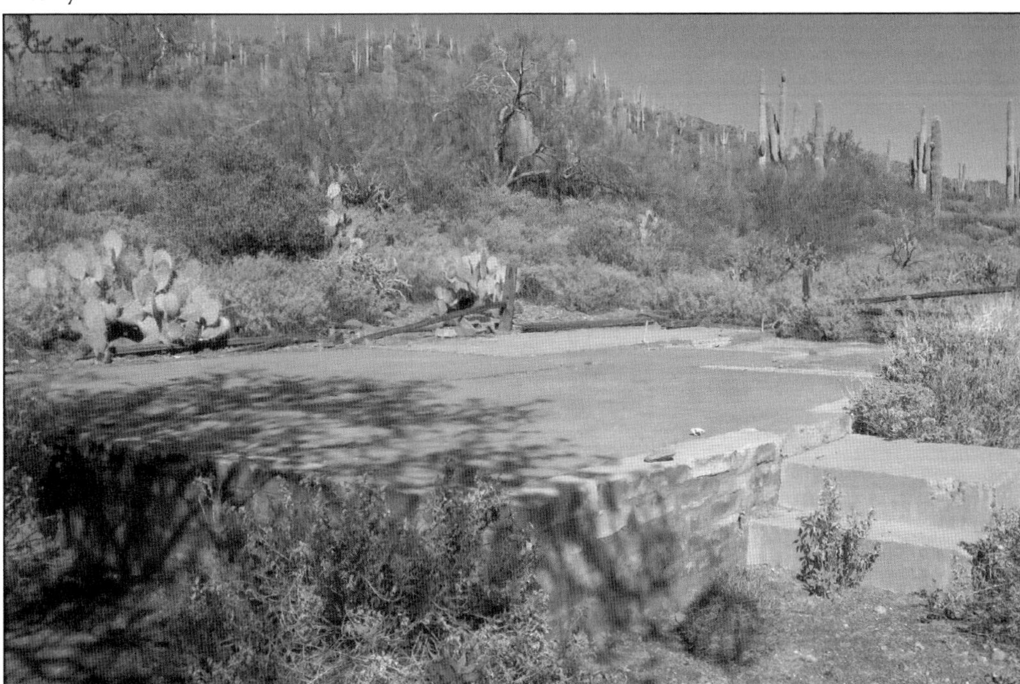

Spur Cross Ranch found new life in 2001 when a partnership of town, county, and state government purchased the property. It is quite a story of local resident initiative catalyzing the preservation of this beautiful desert oasis. The ranch and its legacy live on with the Spur Cross Ranch Conservation Area. The ruins are a reminder to hikers of the storied history of ranch life along Cave Creek.

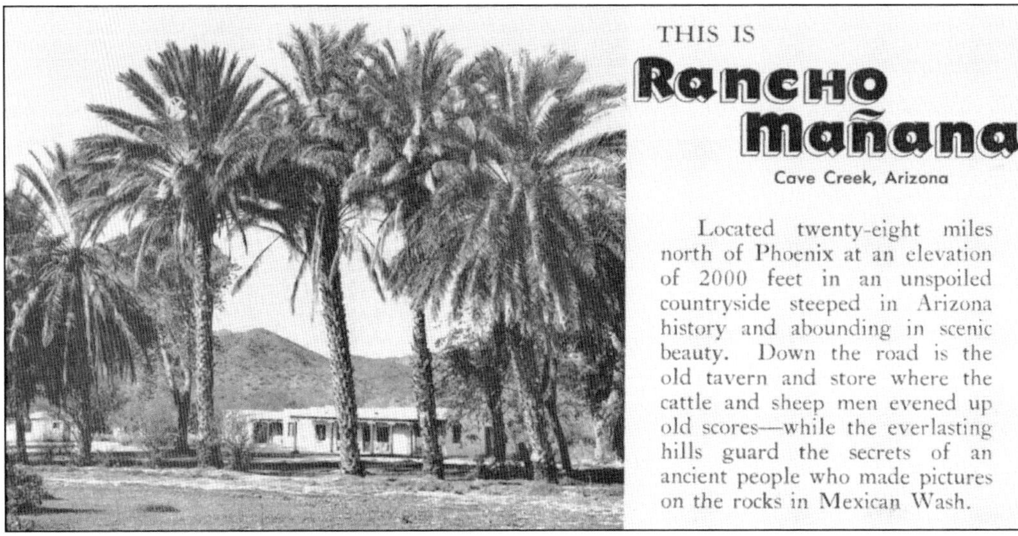

Rancho Mañana's long history includes ranching, cotton farming in the 1930s, and its transformation into a dude ranch. The beautiful resort resembling a Spanish hacienda had landscaped grounds and towering palm trees. The 750-acre property accommodated 25–40 guests. Their brochure promised "a happy combination of mountain and desert." The partnership between Romy and Jean Lowdermilk and Ted and China Loring brought new life to the property and to Cave Creek.

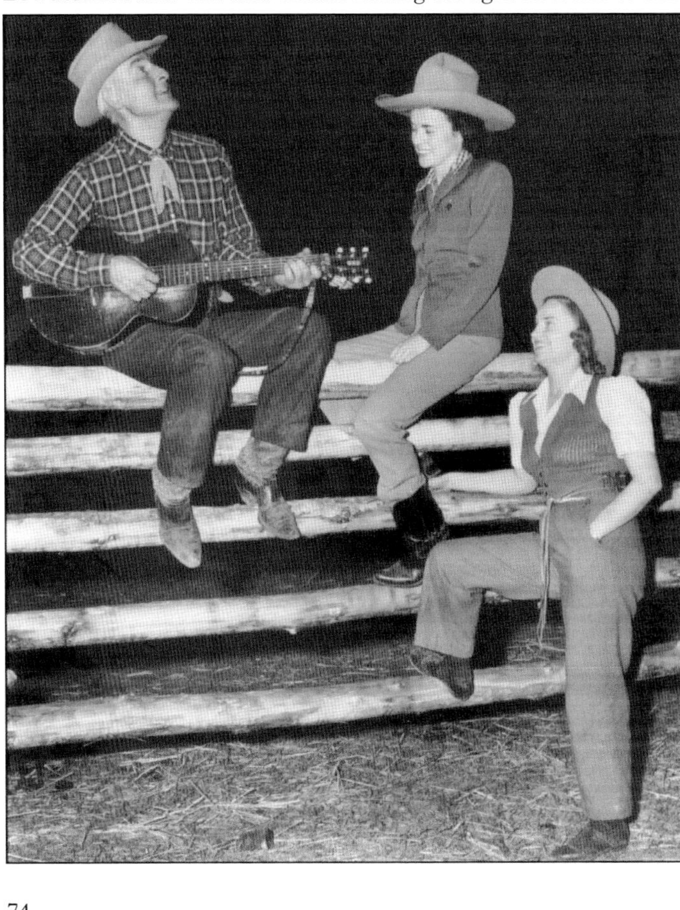

Romaine "Romy" Lowdermilk started dude ranching in 1918 on property that he homesteaded in Wickenburg. Perhaps the original singing cowboy, he was multitalented, composing both songs and short stories. Lowdermilk was the face of Rancho Mañana and his wife, Jean, managed daily guest operations. Their partnership with the Lorings was built upon time they spent together at one of his earlier dude ranches in Soda Springs, Arizona.

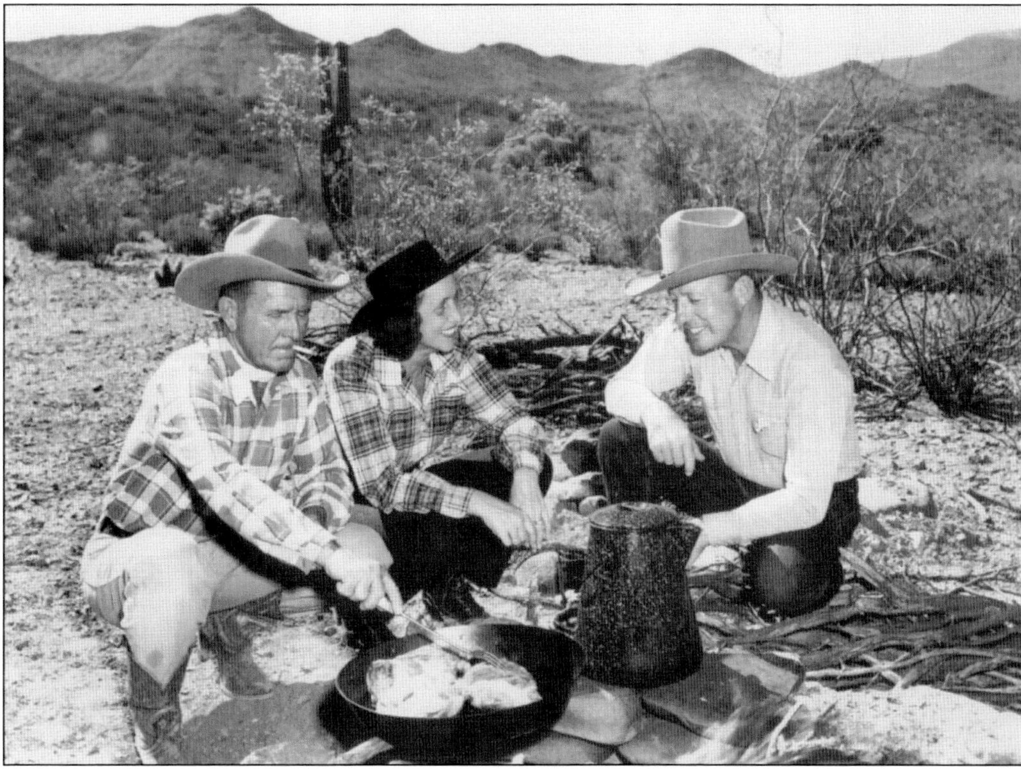

Edward "Ted" and China Loring were the unsung heroes of the ranch's revival. Hailing from Chicago, the Lorings provided the capital and the financial management behind the scenes. Each party owned a half-interest in Rancho Mañana when the property was purchased in 1945. Two years later, the Lowdermilks sold their half-interest to the Lorings. The Lorings are seen above visiting with artist Lon Megargee (right).

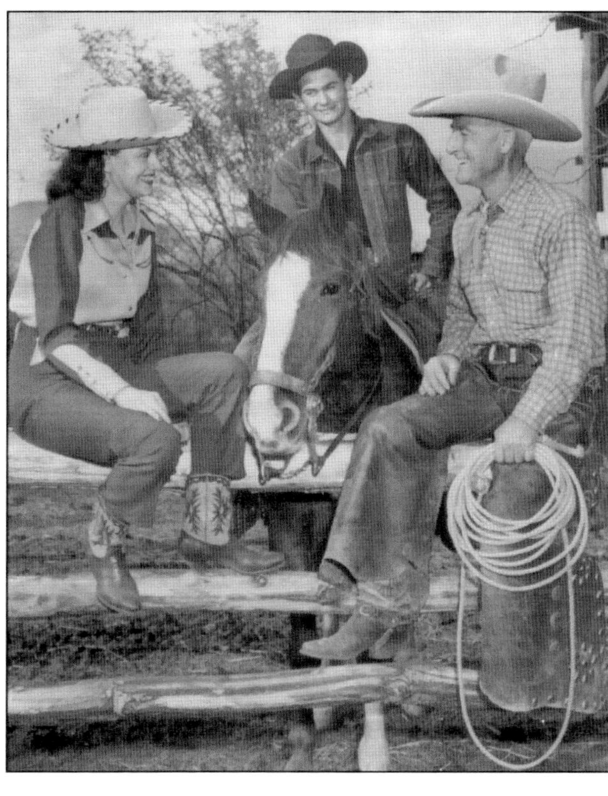

Drexel Clark (center, with Romy Lowdermilk) was a ranch wrangler at both Rancho Mañana and Spur Cross Ranch. Wranglers stayed in a bunkhouse but were sometimes forced to sleep in the barn to make room for extra guests. Clark recalled that Lowdermilk told wranglers, "Guests came out here to see what a cowboy's like, so we should be up and around."

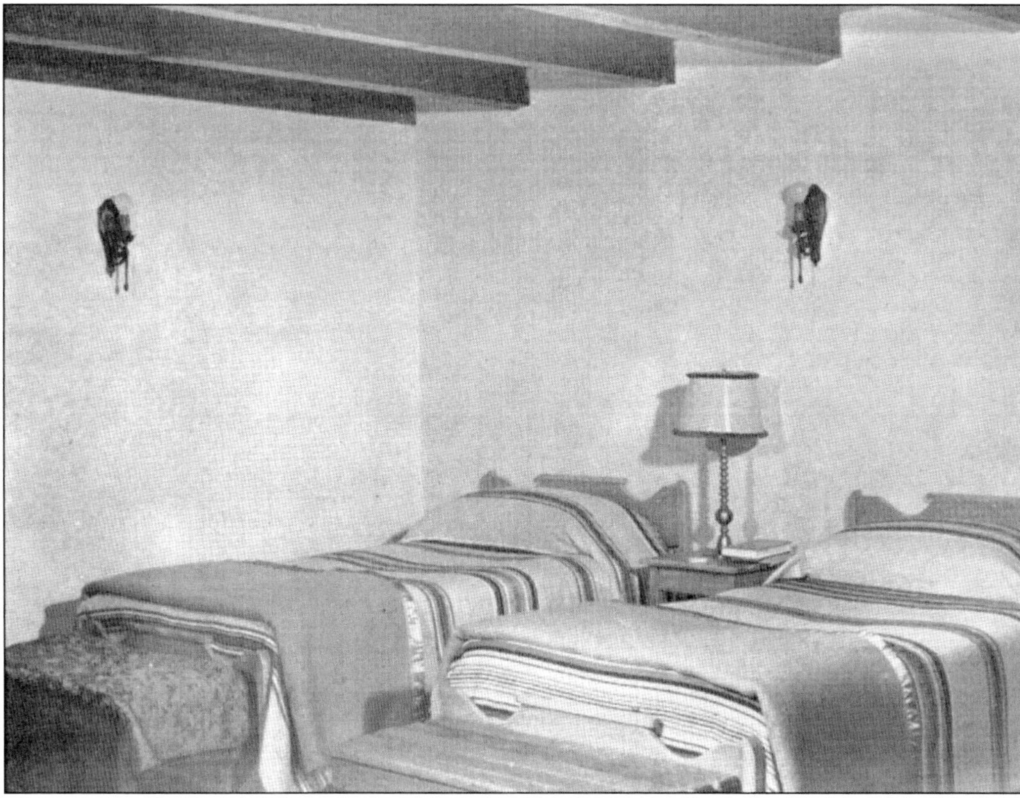

Rancho Mañana had a number of guest cottages that rented for $180 a week. Horses were rented for an additional $18 per week. Guest cottages had both electricity and water from the ranch well. The resort offered daily mail and the use of a telephone.

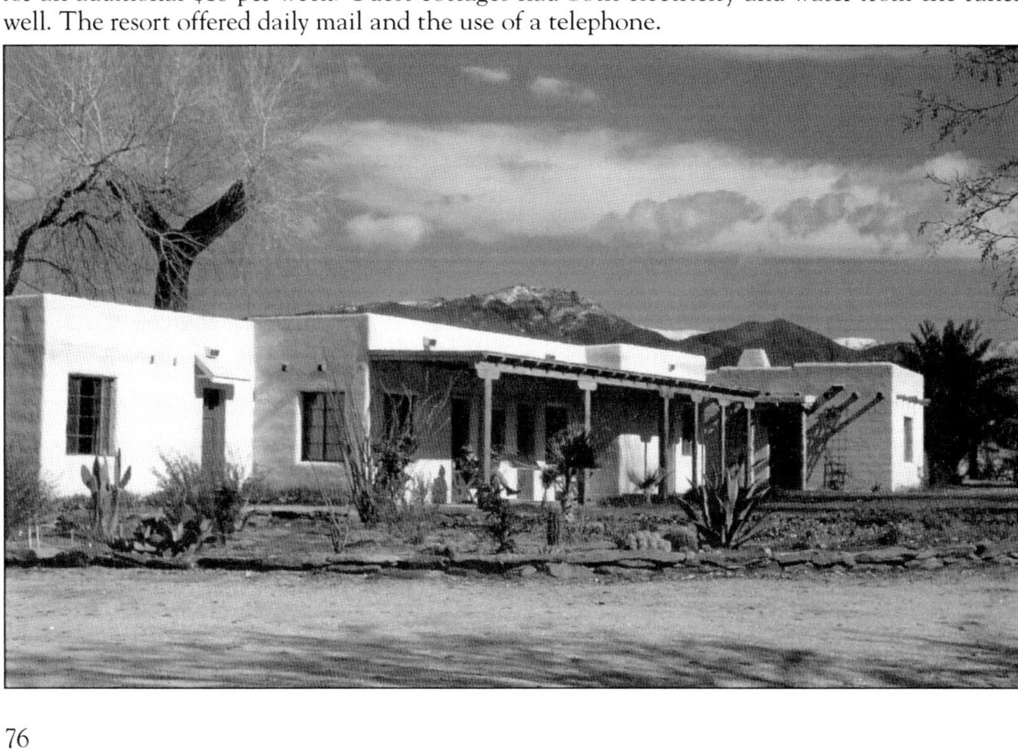

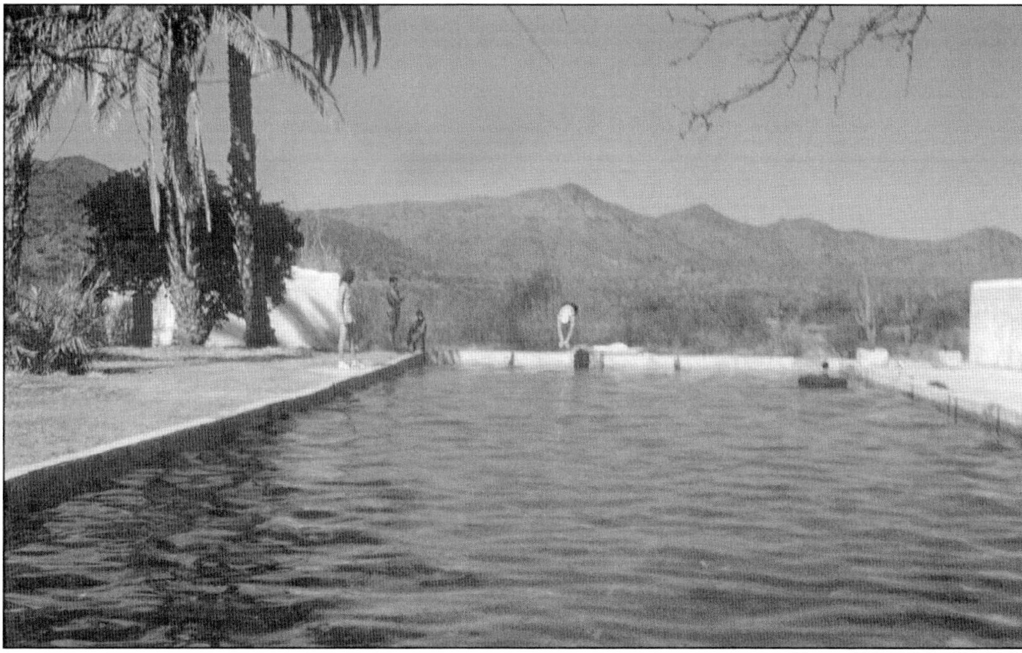

Daily events at the ranch centered around horseback riding. Guests rode east to the Boulders area for breakfast picnics of "Dutch-oven biscuits, steak, eggs, bacon, and blue cornmeal bread." Lazy afternoons were spent poolside (above). In the evening, the cantina (below) beckoned. The annual deer barbecue was a huge community-wide event. Wrangler Tim Adams and others cooked deer, covering them with 25 to 30 gallons of homemade barbecue sauce, complemented by tubs of coleslaw.

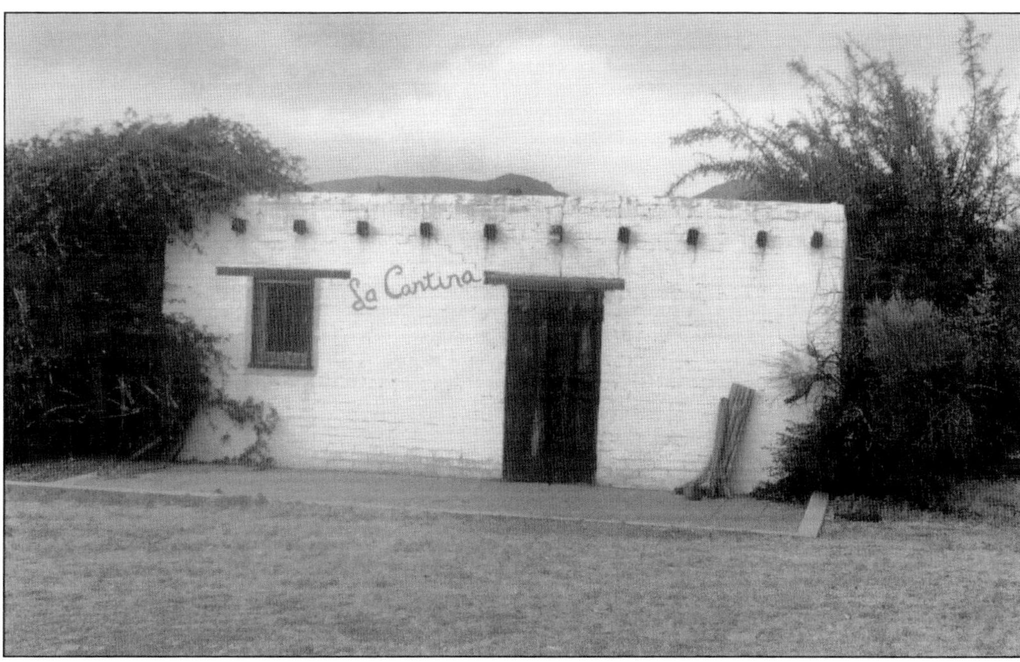

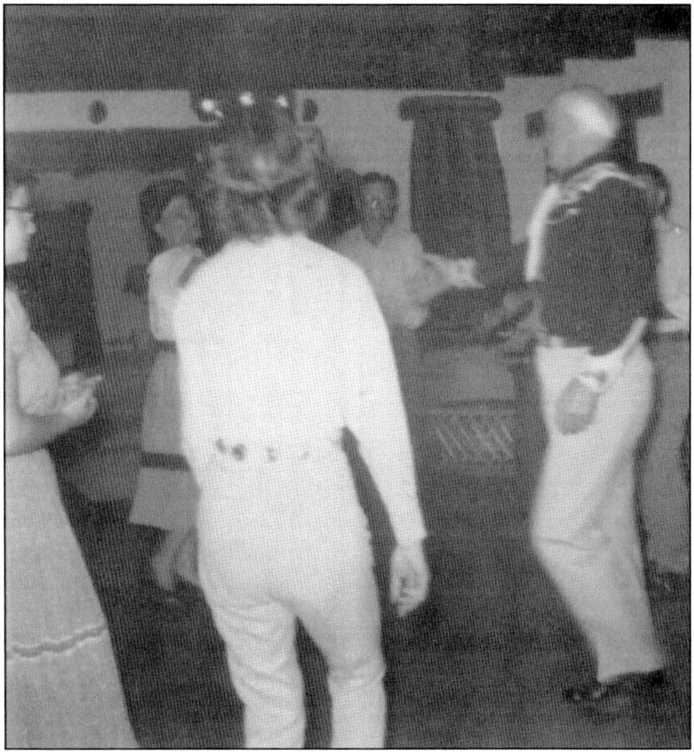

Dancing was a highlight of visits to Rancho Mañana. Trilby Gillespie, a longtime friend of Lowdermilk's, played the fiddle and called out the dances. Trilby's wife, Martina, was the ranch cook and the group's singer in the evenings. Lowdermilk was of course part of the festivities as well, as were Frank Donars, the deputy sheriff, and Herschel Simmons. The Saturday night dances would rotate weekly between the ranch, Harold's Corral, and the American Legion hall. They were community-wide events. Martina and Romy Lowdermilk are seen at left dancing. Below, Martina is singing, while Romy (left) and Trilby (right, with fiddle) accompany her.

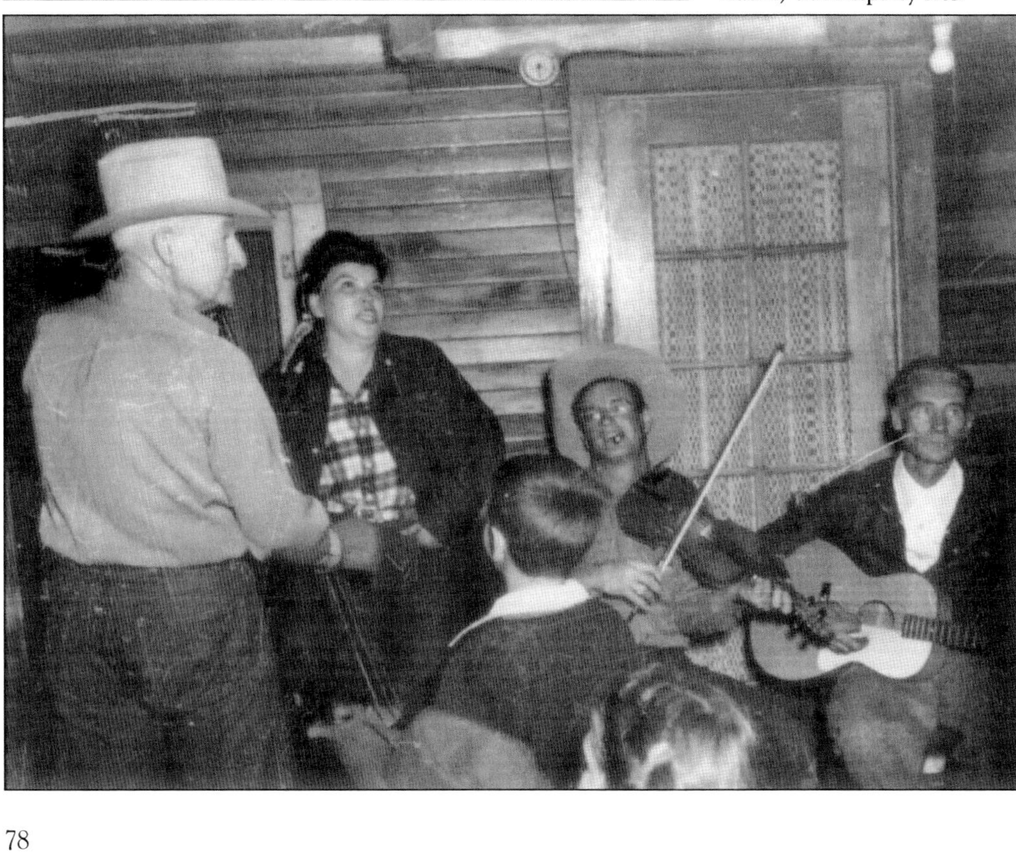

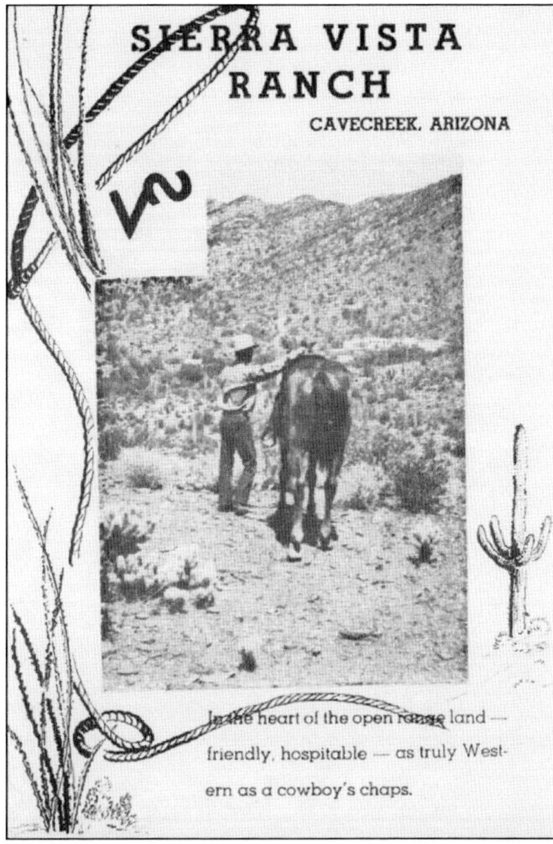

Sierra Vista enjoyed a brief time as a guest ranch in the early 1950s under the Bloomquist family. The ranch land was on the south face of the Continental Mountains, surrounding the famous mining camp of Charles Philes. Its main house was built in the 1940s by Ruth Walgreen, the daughter of Charles Rudolph Walgreen, who founded the Walgreen's drugstore chain. The Bloomquists were forced to sell in 1955.

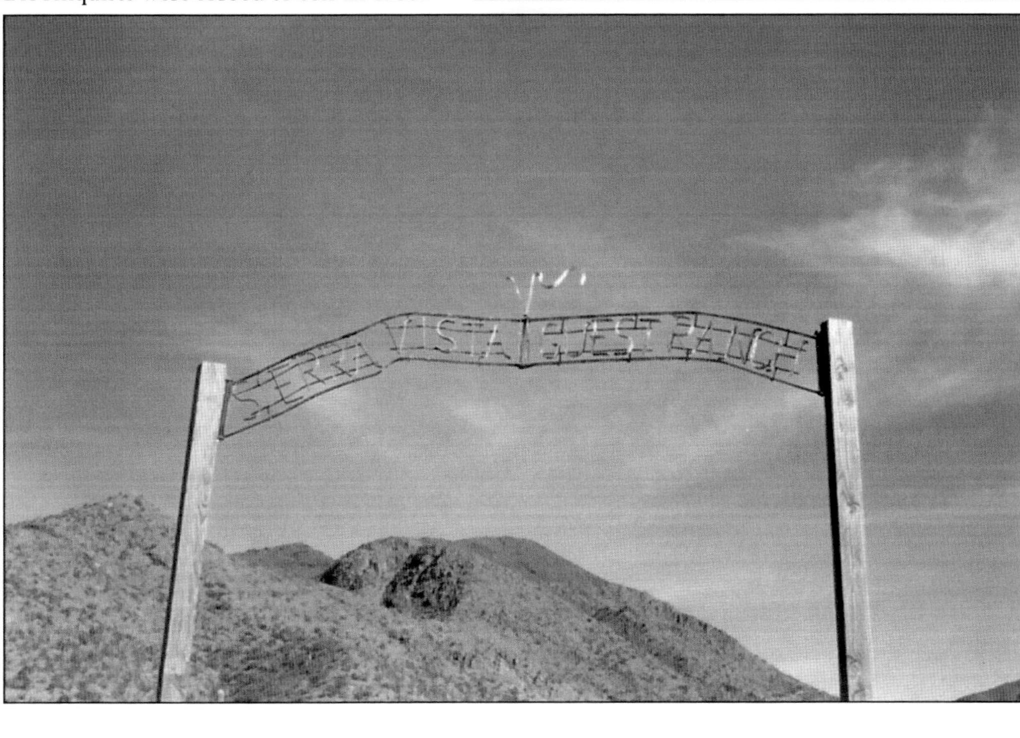

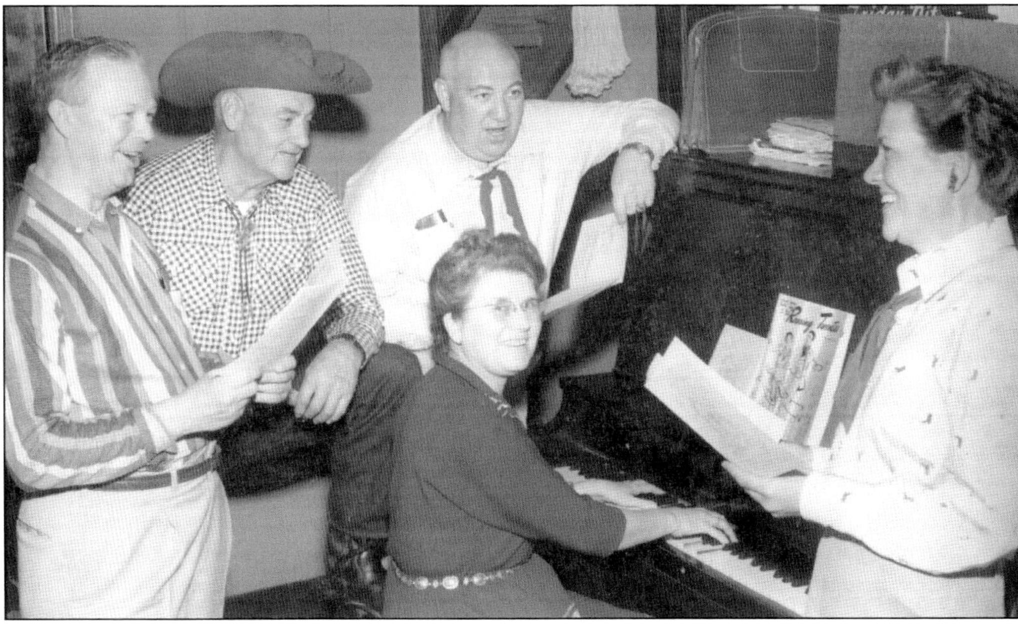

The new owners of Sierra Vista were Dr. John "Doc" Owen (center, arm on piano) and his wife, Jean (far right), of Milwaukee. Their commitment and resources gave the ranch new life. Doc Owen continued his medical practice in Milwaukee, while Jean generally arrived in November. The Owens' most important step was hiring Hube Yates (in cowboy hat) and his wife, Patsy (at piano). Hube's initial six-week contract turned into six years, while Patsy ran the kitchen and played piano for evening social gatherings.

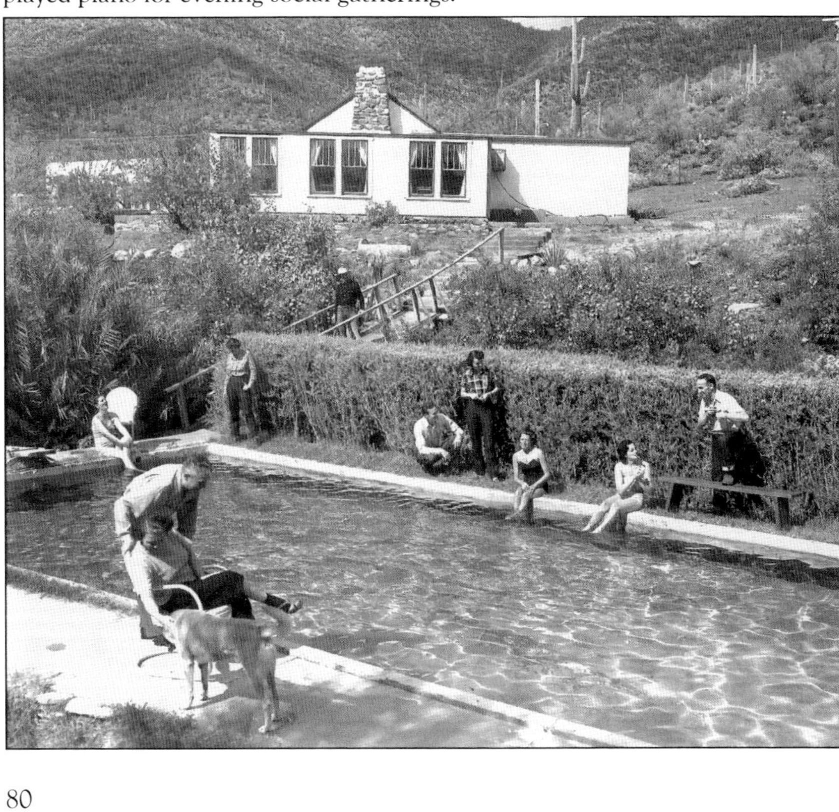

This spring-fed pool was nestled into the side of the mountain, shielded by trees and shrubs, near the main ranch house. The winter rates were $215 a week for a double room, which included all meals and horseback riding. Rates went down to $90 a week in the summer.

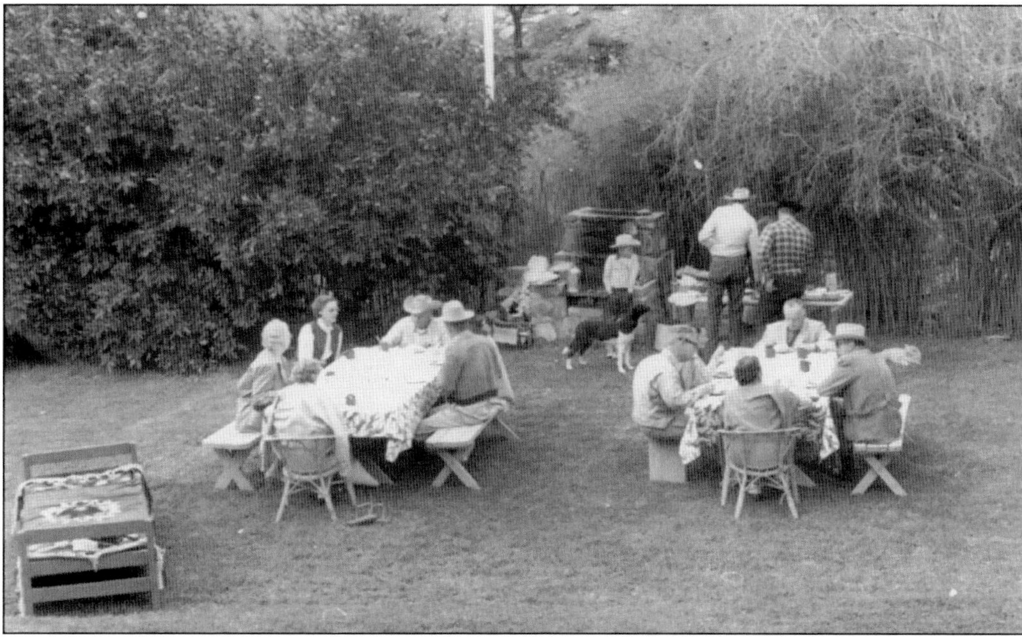

Dude ranches emphasized the casualness of the Western way of life. "Most of the time we wear Western jeans and boots, nothin' fancy," read one brochure. Barbecues were put on in that same spirit. "You're going to have to be here and sample a REAL steak, cooked over mesquite coals, to know what it's like!" boasted another brochure.

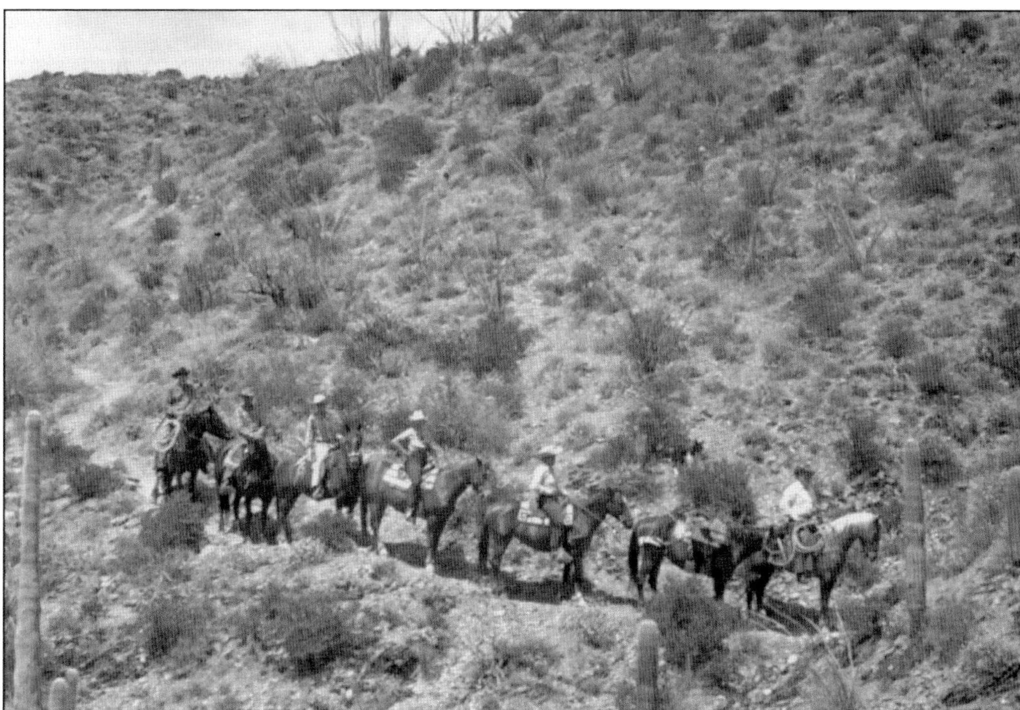

It was the trail rides that created the memories of the Western dude ranch experience. Trail rides up to the top of Skull Mesa or to Hohokam petroglyphs were both panoramic and educational.

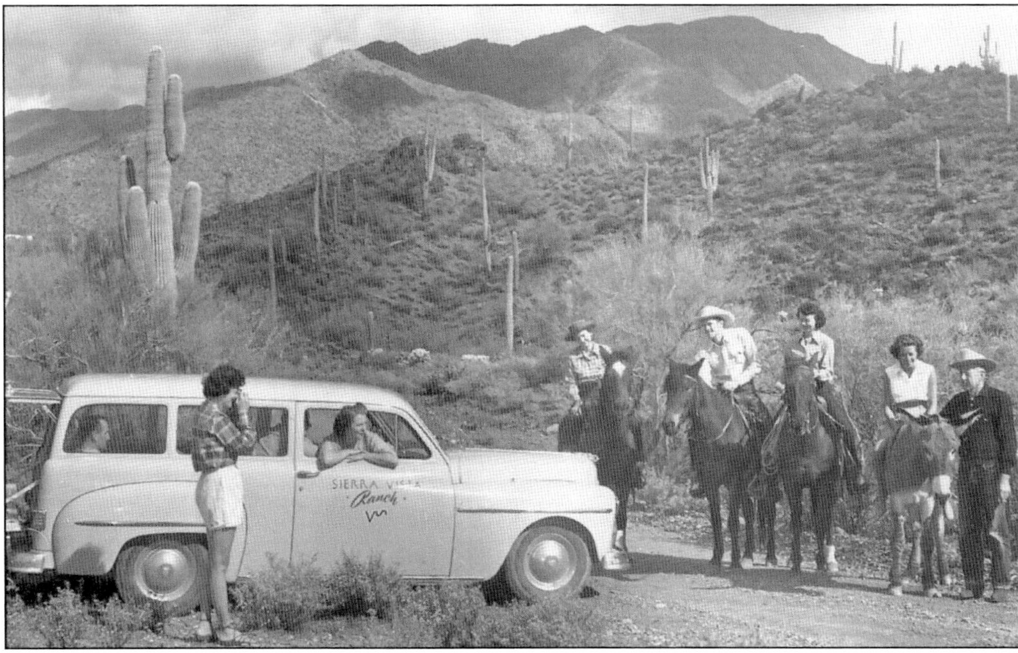

No one could create trail ride memories better than Hube Yates, seen above on the far right and below in the foreground. He arrived in Arizona from Oklahoma in two covered wagons with his family in 1914 and served as a decorated firefighter with the Phoenix Fire Department. His inimitable style and wonderful homespun stories are captured in his book *From Thunder to Breakfast*, written with Gene Garrison.

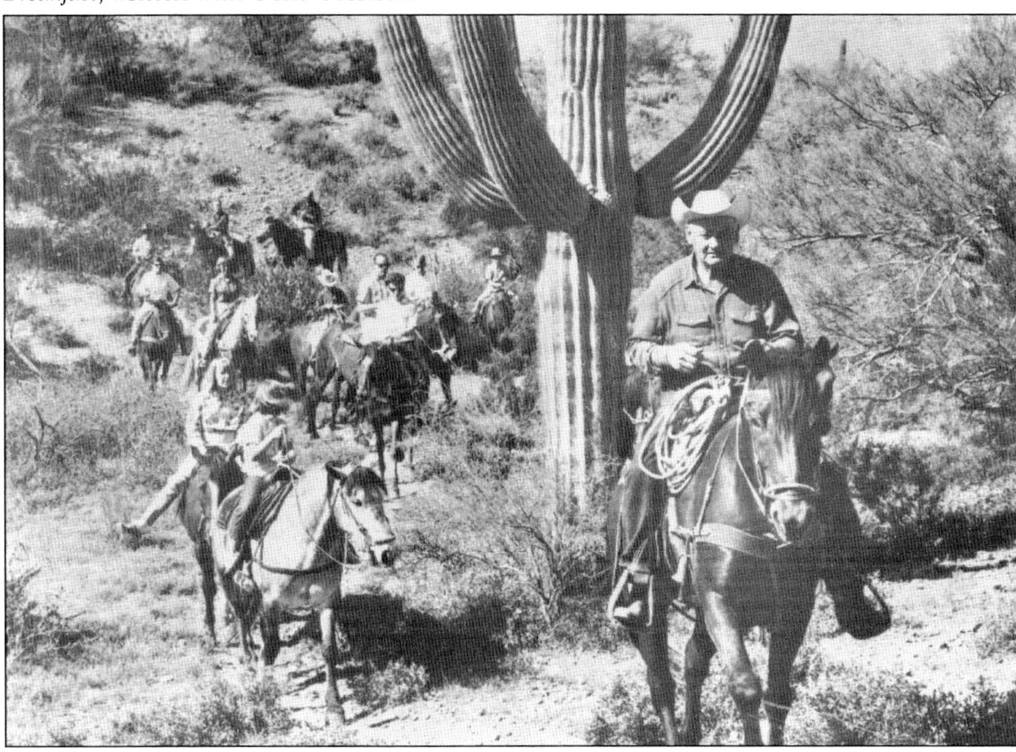

Seven

Cave Creek Village

In 1924, a change in road alignment shifted the town center from Cave Creek Station and the Howard Ranch (later Rancho Mañana) to the east and into the desert. Cave Creek Road connected to Camp Creek, the Cartwright Ranch at Seven Springs, and the Red Rover and onyx mines. Later, workers traveled it to build the Bartlett (1936–1938) and Horseshoe (1944–1946) Dams on the Verde River.

The village core developed between the 1930s and the 1950s, with the Black Mountain Store (later called the Cave Creek Inn) serving as the landmark entrance. Grocery stores, gas stations, a barbershop, restaurants, bars, guesthouses, real estate offices, and tuberculosis sanitariums dotted the landscape. The school moved from the old New River Road to Schoolhouse Road. The post office, which had various locations, became the center of town activity. With a sparse population living in far-reaching locations, the post office was the one place everyone visited not only for mail, but to gather, play cards, gossip, and post messages about sales, births, deaths, and dances.

Nighttime in Cave Creek, particularly on weekends, contributed to the town's early and ongoing reputation. The Cave Creek Corral, originally built in 1936 and later purchased by Harold Gavagan and renamed Harold's Corral, was the nightspot known around the valley for drinking and dancing. With Gavagan serving and drinking, cowboys, construction workers, ranchers, and even college students from Tempe gathered around the bar. Residents spent many a Saturday night dancing there or at the American Legion Hall, built in 1946.

Village growth and the booming tourist trade, catalyzed by three successful dude ranches, brought the need for civic improvements. In 1946, electricity arrived. Telephone lines came later, and party lines were used until the mid-1960s. In 1949, the Cave Creek Improvement Association formed. The organization successfully lobbied to have Cave Creek Road paved from Bell Road to the village in 1952. The Cave Creek Water Company formed in the late 1950s.

In 1952, led by a 4-H group, the community came together to launch the Christmas pageant, a tradition that endures today. In 1955, a group of women established the Mothers' Club. In 1957, they published the *Vacuum Cleaner* newspaper, as well as the area's first phone book, which had barely one page of listings.

The population was about 400 in 1960. Cave Creek remained quiet and remote until Phoenix-area real estate boomed years later.

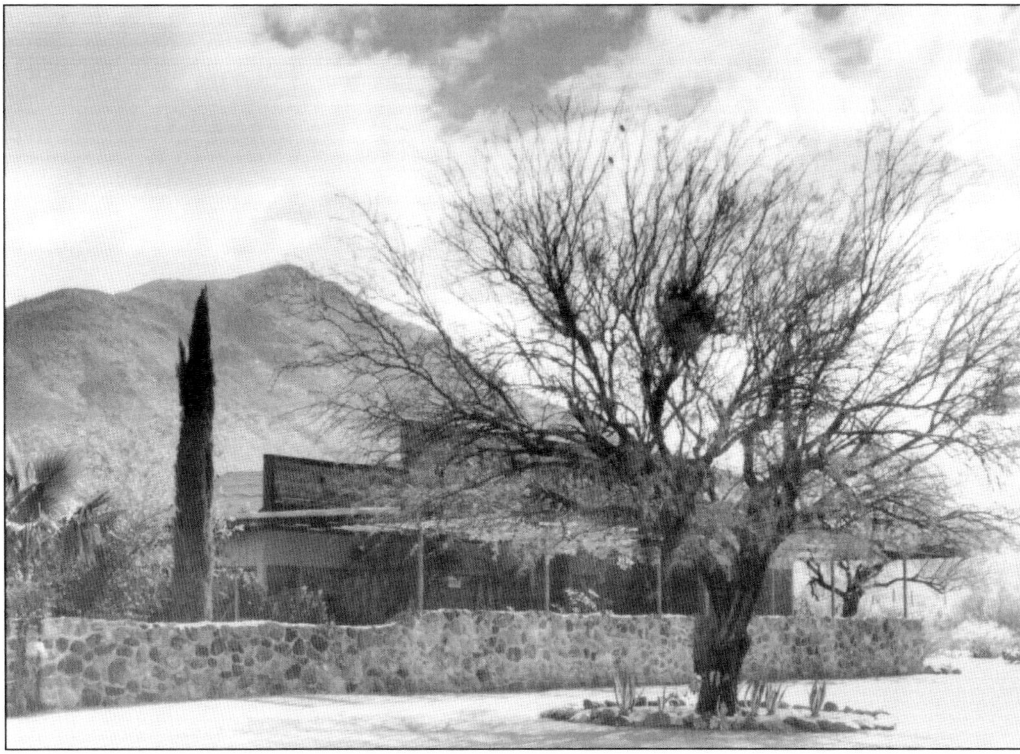

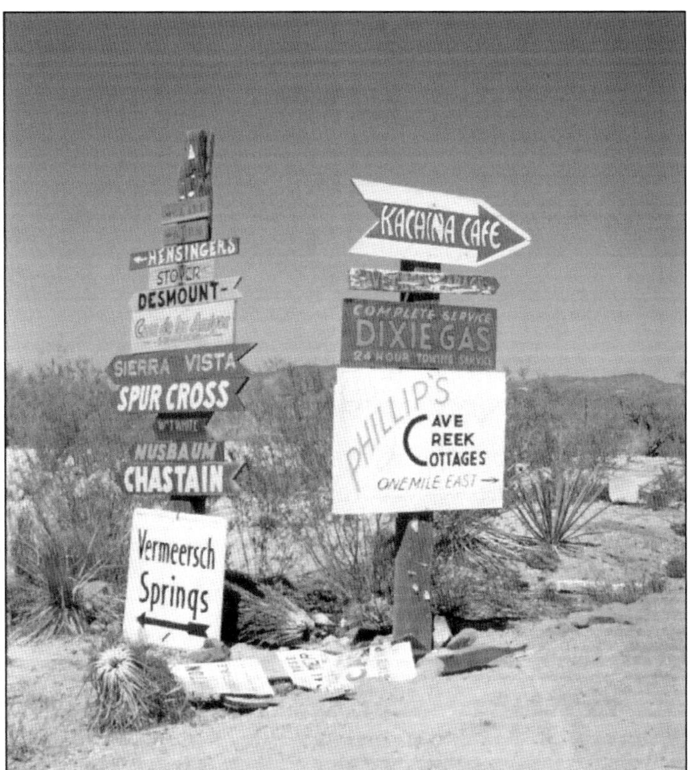

Located across from town hall, the building above, one of Cave Creek's oldest, was constructed in 1928. It was originally the Black Mountain Store, where one could buy food and, in later years, rent a cottage as well. Two other stores, Idlewild and a store at the Howard Ranch, also served the town. The Howard Ranch store closed in 1943. This 1950s photograph shows the Black Mountain Store building when it was the Cave Creek Inn.

This much-photographed sign was located at the intersection of Cave Creek and Spur Cross Roads.

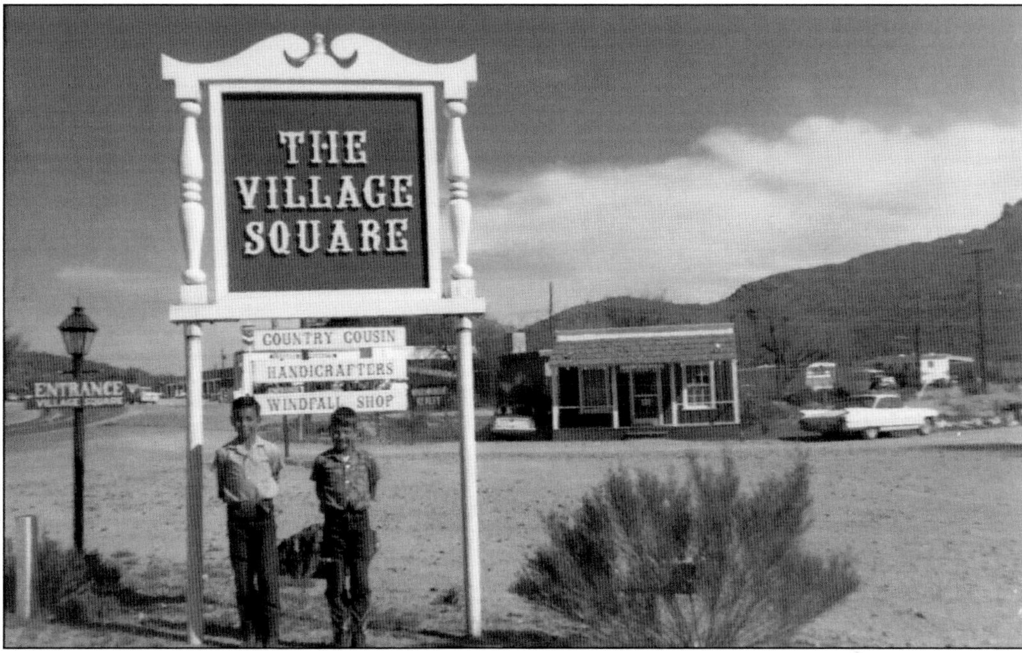

This area, next to the Salvation Army Youth Park, was developed in the late 1950s. The first building (not in view) held businesses. The building shown was a real estate office. It is southeast of Hidden Valley and Cave Creek Roads. In later years, the community gazebo would be in this photograph. The gazebo has since been relocated to the property of the Cave Creek Museum.

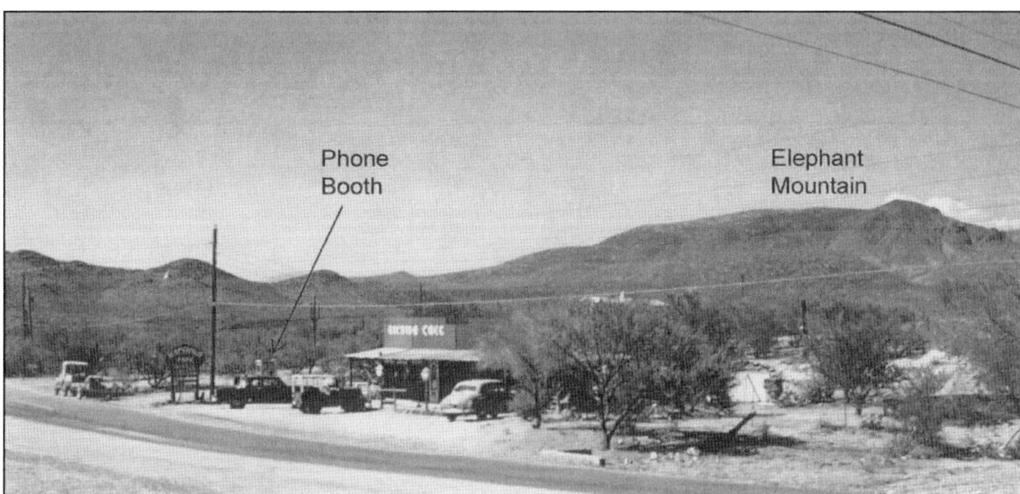

The Kachina Cafe was just north of the village square at the northeast intersection of Cave Creek and Hidden Valley Roads. The only phone booth the town ever had is barely visible behind the dark sedan. In 1962, the restaurant was purchased by Harold Gavagan, the owner of the Cave Creek Corral. Shortly thereafter, Gavagan moved the building and made it part of what became Harold's Corral.

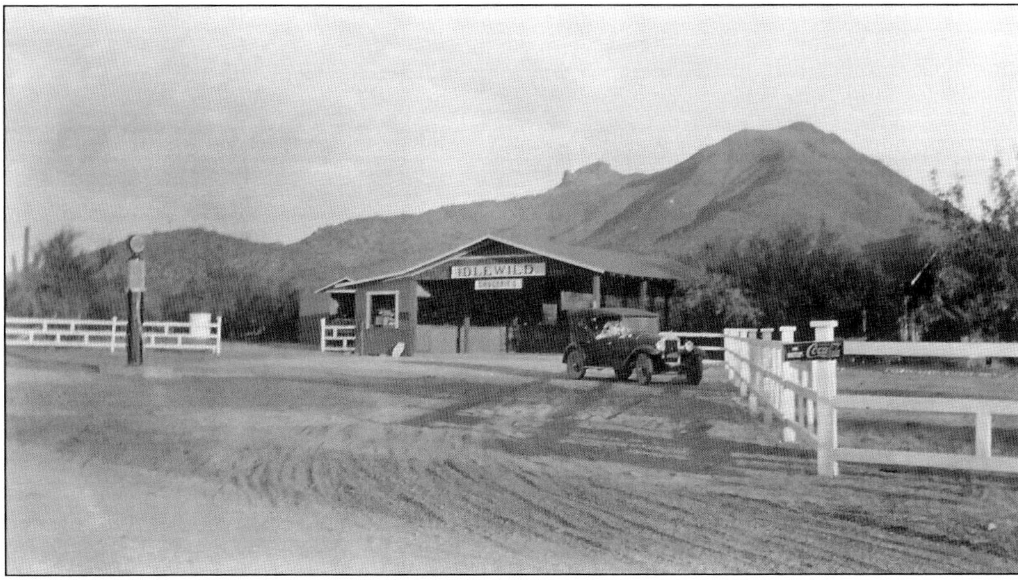

The Idlewild store, built in the late 1920s by George Smith for owners Robert and Jean Barry, was one of only a few locations for purchasing the necessities of life. Its use and appearance have changed, but it is still located at the southwest corner of Basin and Cave Creek Roads.

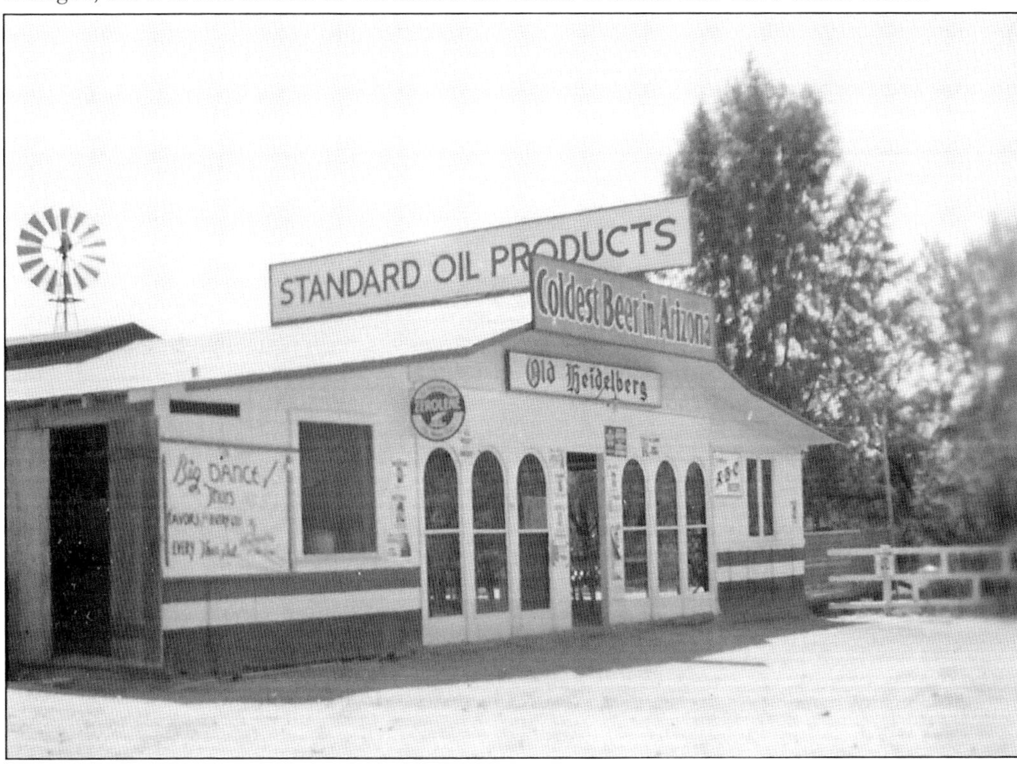

In addition to buying goods at the Idlewild store, patrons also went there to leave news to be collected by the local newspaper for submission and publication. The *Cave Creek Chronicle*, founded in 1942, was published to keep those serving in the military in touch with what was going on at home. This photograph was taken in 1938.

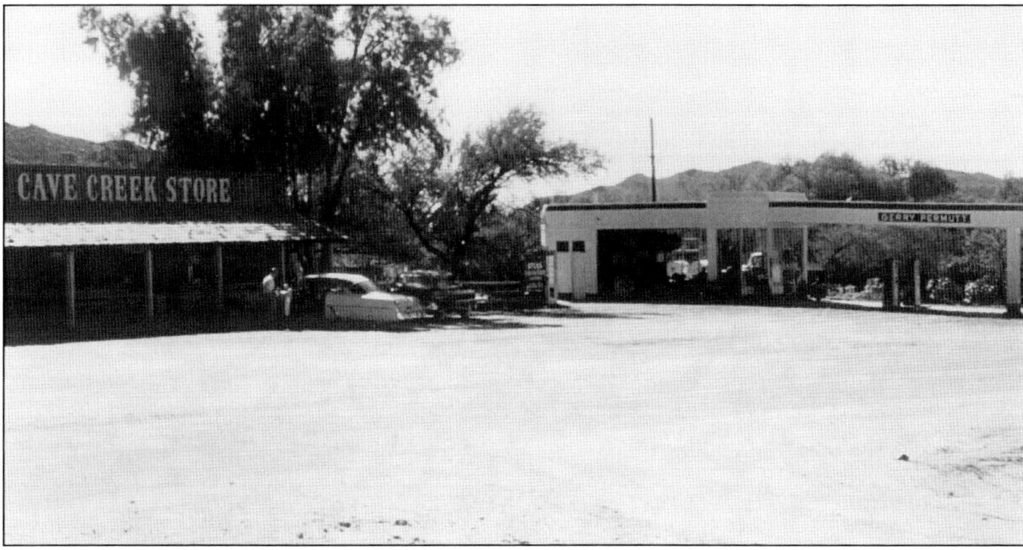

Later, the Idlewild was updated and became known as the Cave Creek Store. It remained the principal choice for shopping until a modern supermarket opened in Carefree in 1962. Still, many continued to shop there until the mid-1970s. A full-service gas station owned by Gerry Permutt was moved from Phoenix and relocated next door.

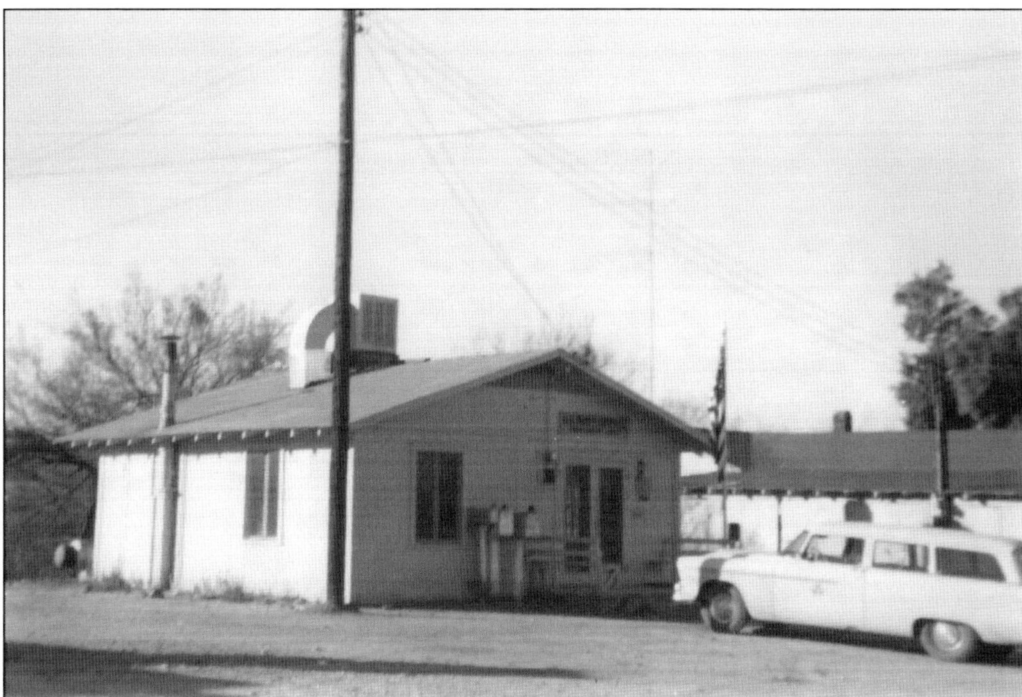
Through the mid-1950s, mailings were addressed "Cave Creek Stage Route." In May 1944, the post office moved to this building, at the southwest corner of Basin and Cave Creek Roads. Since the late 1800s, early writings spelled the town name two ways: as one word, Cavecreek, as well as Cave Creek. On February 1, 1962, the US Postal Service officially clarified the spelling, identifying the town as Cave Creek.

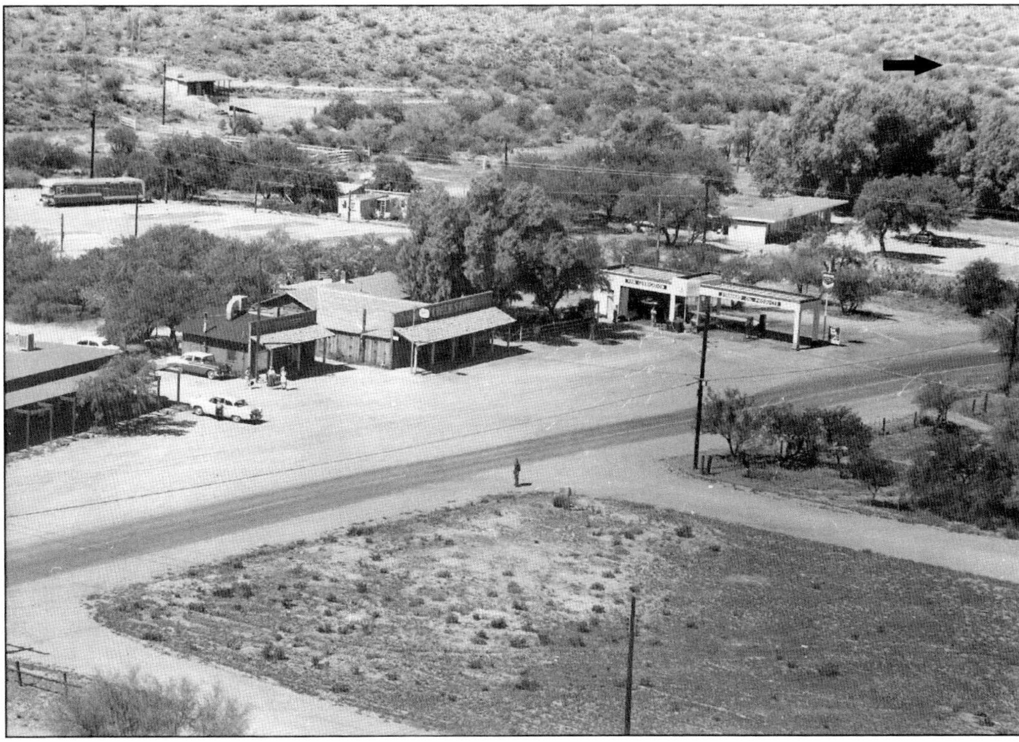

This 1956 aerial view of downtown Cave Creek shows early structures in town, including, from left to right, Wishing U Well Gift Shop, the post office (currently the Flat Tire Bike Shop), the Cave Creek Store, and Gary Permutt's gas station. The arrow points to a segment of Cave Creek Road on the west side of downtown before the road curves.

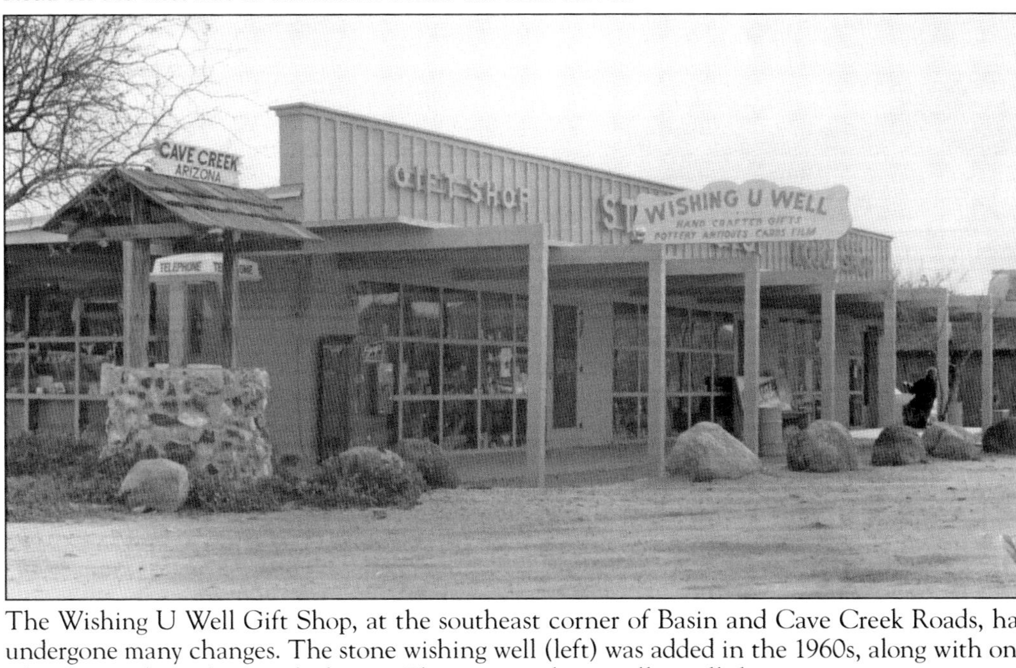

The Wishing U Well Gift Shop, at the southeast corner of Basin and Cave Creek Roads, has undergone many changes. The stone wishing well (left) was added in the 1960s, along with one of Cave Creek's only pay telephones. The stone wishing well is still there.

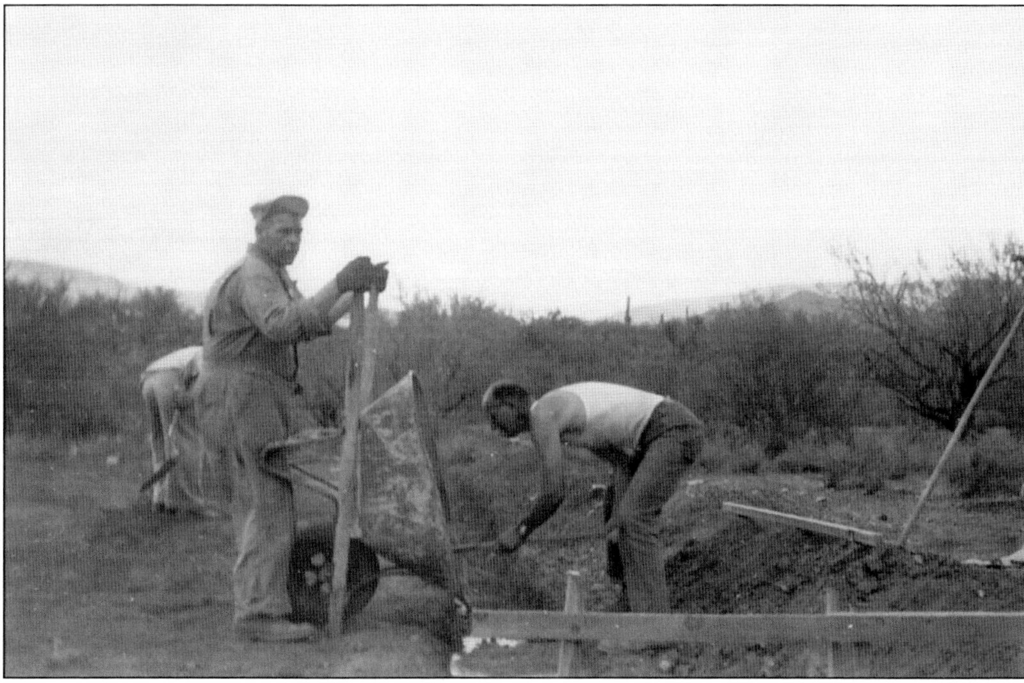

On April 6, 1946, ground was broken to build the American Legion hall. Monies were raised through various fundraisers, and most of the work and materials were donated. At this time, according to the Legion newsletter, American Legion Post 34 in Cave Creek had the second-highest membership in Arizona.

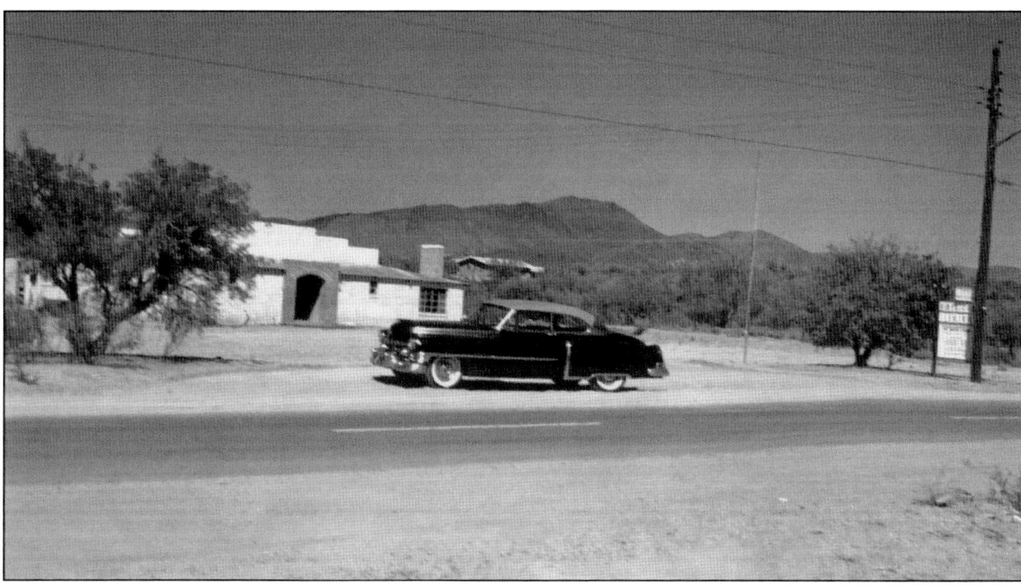

The American Legion building was completed late in 1947 and continues to serve the community and its Legionnaires. Since that time, an addition has been built. Frank and Hazel Wright, who contributed greatly to the American Legion and to the town, lived in the pitched-roof house seen in the background.

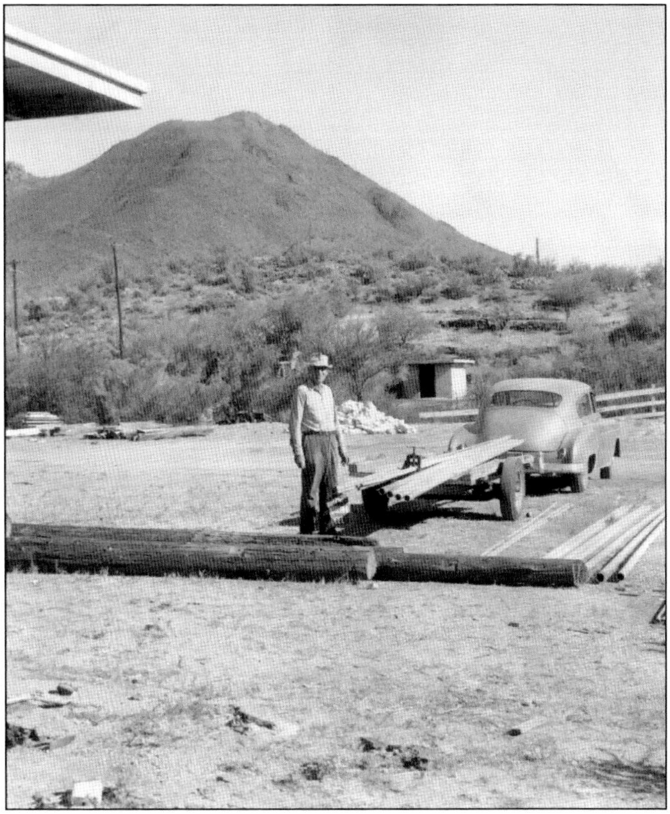

The Cave Creek Water Company was established in the late 1950s by Frank Wright, seen here, and a few partners. This photograph was taken near the original well site, behind the area once known as the village square on Hidden Valley Road. The pipe in the photograph was used to carry water to residents all the way into the 21st century.

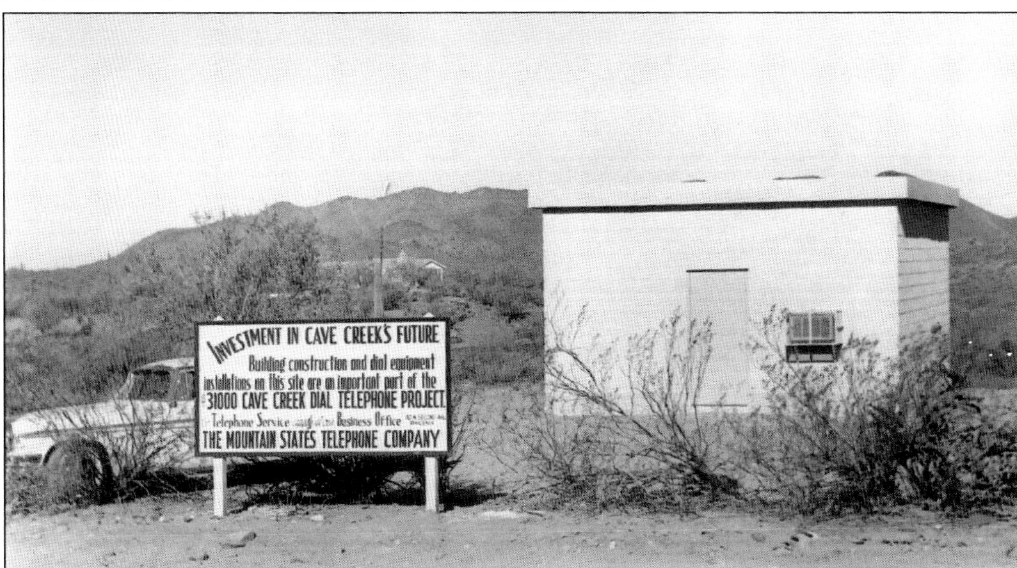

Central Arizona Light & Power brought electricity to Cave Creek on May 7, 1946. In early 1947, telephones became available. The Idlewild store collected applications for telephone installations in homes and businesses. In 1958, direct dialing was introduced. This substation was built in 1963 on the north side of Basin and Cave Creek Roads, along with a relay screen atop Wright's Hill. As a result, party line service soon ended.

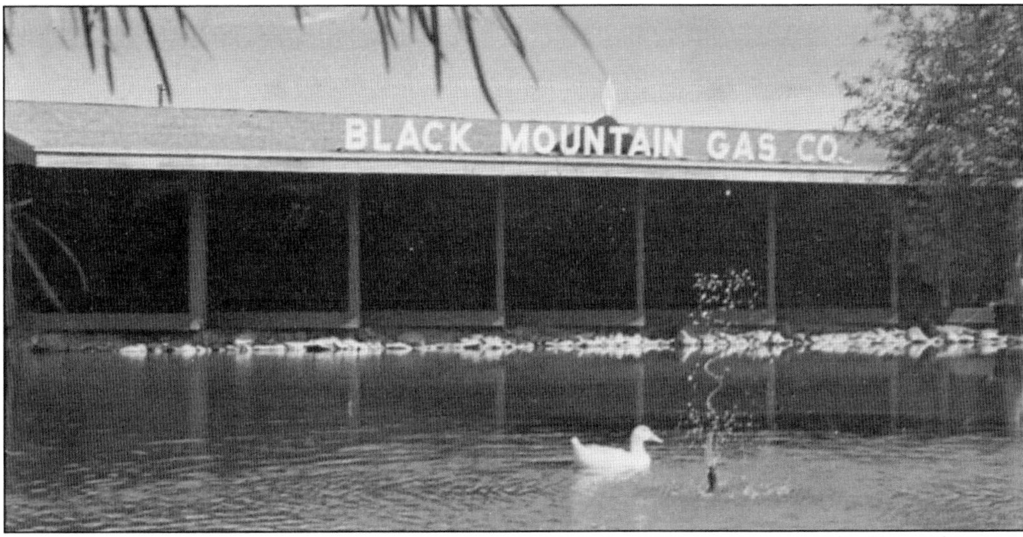

Black Mountain Gas Company served Cave Creek and Carefree. Its general offices were on a beautiful "oriental pond setting," according to an early brochure. The pond was dug and then filled with water, but the next day, all the water was gone. The pond was then sealed with gunite and successfully, permanently filled, luring children who snuck in to float toy boats. El Encanto Restaurant currently occupies the site.

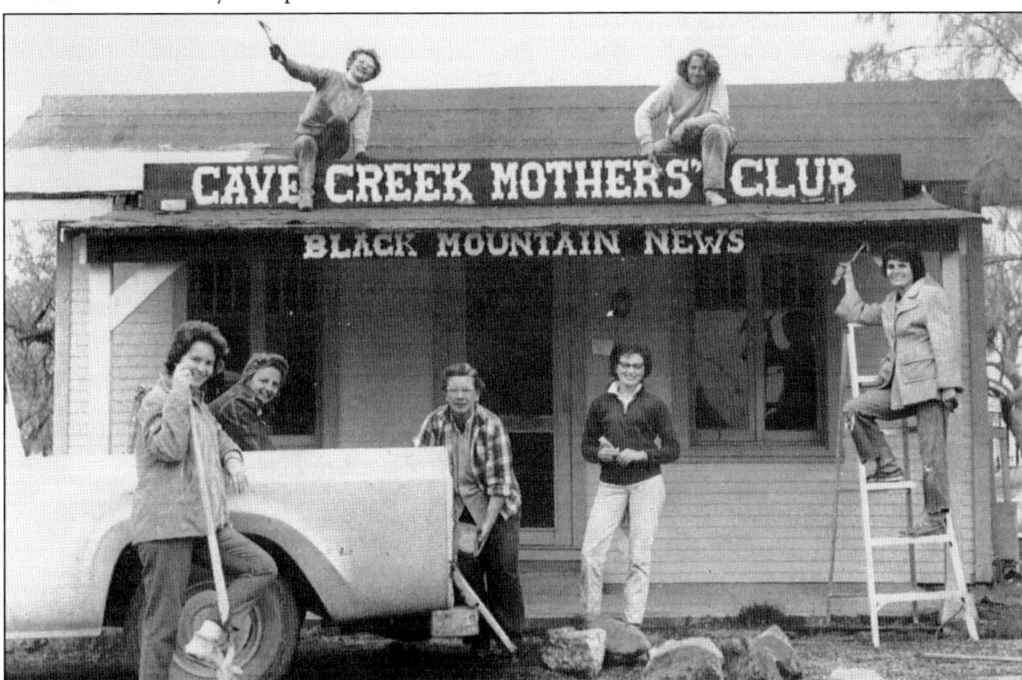

Energetic women raised funds, raised roofs, and raised a little Cain to improve the lives of their families. In 1966, the Mothers' Club moved into their office. These members are, from left to right, (standing) Jackie Snively, Margot Crooks, Alma Veres, Beverly Metcalfe Brooks, and Connie Alford; (on roof) Leonie Sutton and Doris Binkley. Among its many projects, the club published the *Black Mountain News* and area phone books. (Courtesy of Connie Alford.)

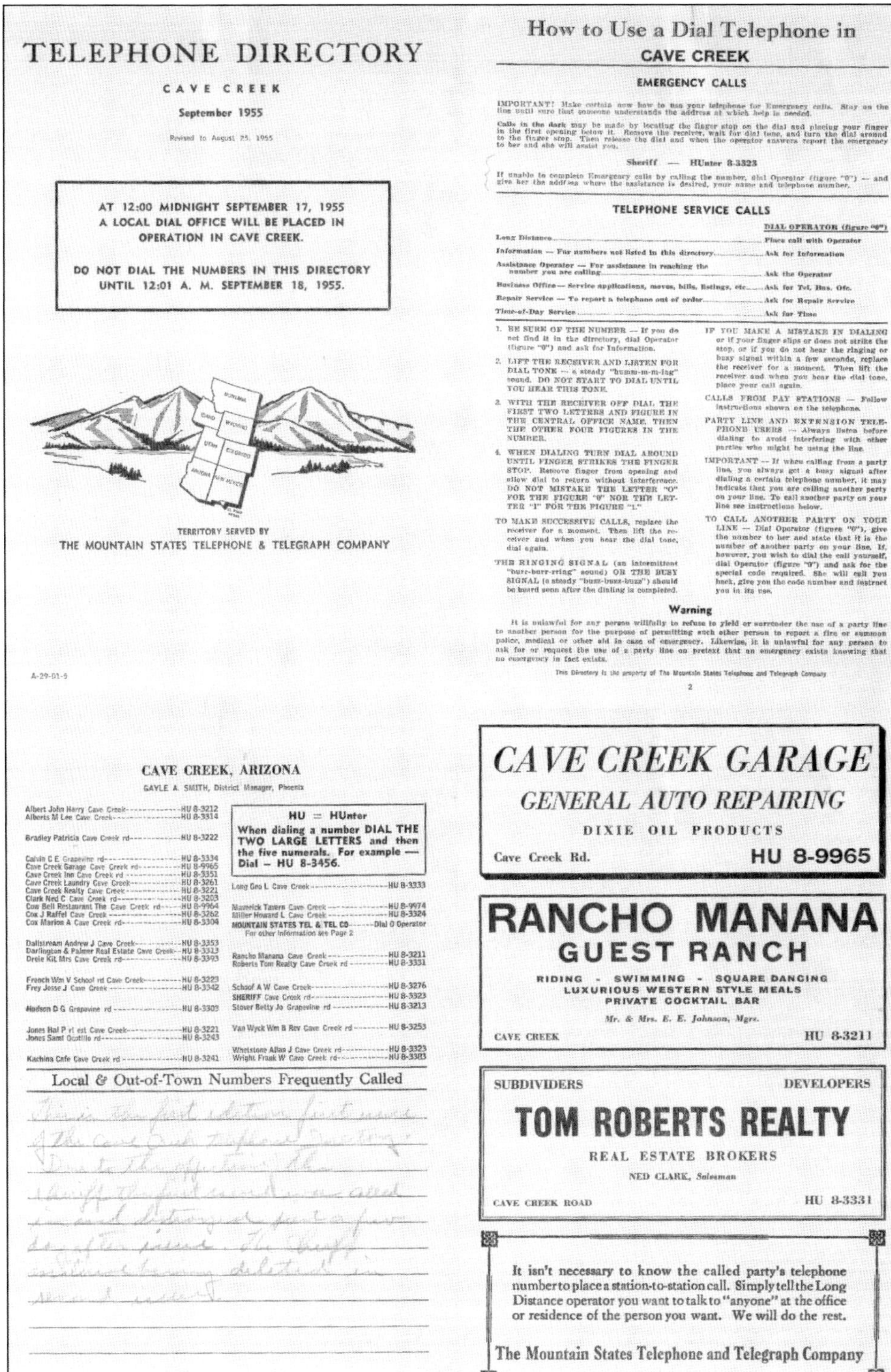

TELEPHONE DIRECTORY

CAVE CREEK

September 1955

Revised to August 25, 1955

AT 12:00 MIDNIGHT SEPTEMBER 17, 1955 A LOCAL DIAL OFFICE WILL BE PLACED IN OPERATION IN CAVE CREEK.

DO NOT DIAL THE NUMBERS IN THIS DIRECTORY UNTIL 12:01 A. M. SEPTEMBER 18, 1955.

TERRITORY SERVED BY
THE MOUNTAIN STATES TELEPHONE & TELEGRAPH COMPANY

A-29-01-5

How to Use a Dial Telephone in CAVE CREEK

EMERGENCY CALLS

IMPORTANT! Make certain now how to use your telephone for Emergency calls. Stay on the line until sure that someone understands the address at which help is needed.

Calls in the dark may be made by locating the finger stop on the dial and placing your finger in the first opening below it. Remove the receiver, wait for dial tone, and turn the dial around to the finger stop. Then release the dial and when the operator answers report the emergency to her and she will assist you.

Sheriff — HUnter 8-3323

If unable to complete Emergency calls by calling the number, dial Operator (figure "0") — and give her the address where the assistance is desired, your name and telephone number.

TELEPHONE SERVICE CALLS

	DIAL OPERATOR (figure "0")
Long Distance	Place call with Operator
Information — For numbers not listed in this directory	Ask for Information
Assistance Operator — For assistance in reaching the number you are calling	Ask the Operator
Business Office — Service applications, moves, bills, listings, etc.	Ask for Tel. Bus. Ofc.
Repair Service — To report a telephone out of order	Ask for Repair Service
Time-of-Day Service	Ask for Time

1. BE SURE OF THE NUMBER — If you do not find it in the directory, dial Operator (figure "0") and ask for Information.
2. LIFT THE RECEIVER AND LISTEN FOR DIAL TONE — a steady "humm-m-m-ing" sound. DO NOT START TO DIAL UNTIL YOU HEAR THIS TONE.
3. WITH THE RECEIVER OFF DIAL THE FIRST TWO LETTERS AND FIGURE IN THE CENTRAL OFFICE NAME. THEN THE OTHER FOUR FIGURES IN THE NUMBER.
4. WHEN DIALING TURN DIAL AROUND UNTIL FINGER STRIKES THE FINGER STOP. Remove finger from opening and allow dial to return without interference. DO NOT MISTAKE THE LETTER "O" FOR THE FIGURE "0" NOR THE LETTER "I" FOR THE FIGURE "1."

TO MAKE SUCCESSIVE CALLS, replace the receiver for a moment. Then lift the receiver and when you hear the dial tone, dial again.

THE RINGING SIGNAL (an intermittent "burr-burr-rring" sound) OR THE BUSY SIGNAL (a steady "buzz-buzz-buzz") should be heard soon after the dialing is completed.

IF YOU MAKE A MISTAKE IN DIALING or if your finger slips or does not strike the stop, or if you do not hear the ringing or busy signal within a few seconds, replace the receiver for a moment. Then lift the receiver and when you hear the dial tone, place your call again.

CALLS FROM PAY STATIONS — Follow instructions shown on the telephone.

PARTY LINE AND EXTENSION TELEPHONE USERS — Always listen before dialing to avoid interfering with other parties who might be using the line.

IMPORTANT — If when calling from a party line, you always get a busy signal after dialing a certain telephone number, it may indicate that you are calling another party on your line. To call another party on your line see instructions below.

TO CALL ANOTHER PARTY ON YOUR LINE — Dial Operator (figure "0"), give the number to her and state that it is the number of another party on your line. If, however, you wish to dial the call yourself, dial Operator (figure "0") and ask for the special code required. She will call you back, give you the code number and instruct you in its use.

Warning

It is unlawful for any person willfully to refuse to yield or surrender the use of a party line to another person for the purpose of permitting such other person to report a fire or summon police, medical or other aid in case of emergency. Likewise, it is unlawful for any person to ask for or request the use of a party line on pretext that an emergency exists knowing that no emergency in fact exists.

This Directory is the property of The Mountain States Telephone and Telegraph Company

2

CAVE CREEK, ARIZONA

GAYLE A. SMITH, District Manager, Phoenix

Albert John Harry Cave Creek — HU 8-3212
Alberts M Lee Cave Creek — HU 8-3314

Bradley Patricia Cave Creek rd — HU 8-3222

Calvin C E Grapevine rd — HU 8-3334
Cave Creek Garage Cave Creek rd — HU 8-9965
Cave Creek Inn Cave Creek rd — HU 8-3351
Cave Creek Laundry Cave Creek — HU 8-3261
Cave Creek Realty Cave Creek — HU 8-3221
Clark Ned C Cave Creek rd — HU 8-3203
Cow Bell Restaurant The Cave Creek rd — HU 8-9964
Cox J Raffel Cave Creek — HU 8-3262
Cox Marion A Cave Creek rd — HU 8-3304

Dallstream Andrew J Cave Creek — HU 8-3353
Darlington & Palmer Real Estate Cave Creek — HU 8-3313
Dreie Kit Mrs Cave Creek rd — HU 8-3393

French Wm V School rd Cave Creek — HU 8-3223
Frey Jesse J Cave Creek — HU 8-3342

Hodson D G Grapevine rd — HU 8-3303

Jones Hal P rl est Cave Creek — HU 8-3221
Jones Saml Ocotillo rd — HU 8-3243

Kachina Cafe Cave Creek rd — HU 8-3241

HU = HUnter
When dialing a number DIAL THE TWO LARGE LETTERS and then the five numerals. For example — Dial – HU 8-3456.

Long Geo L Cave Creek — HU 8-3333

Maverick Tavern Cave Creek — HU 8-9974
Miller Howard L Cave Creek — HU 8-3324
MOUNTAIN STATES TEL & TEL CO — Dial 0 Operator
For other Information see Page 2

Rancho Manana Cave Creek — HU 8-3211
Roberts Tom Realty Cave Creek rd — HU 8-3331

Schoof A W Cave Creek — HU 8-3276
SHERIFF Cave Creek rd — HU 8-3323
Stover Betty Jo Grapevine rd — HU 8-3213

Van Wyck Wm B Rev Cave Creek rd — HU 8-3253

Whetstone Allan J Cave Creek rd — HU 8-3323
Wright Frank W Cave Creek rd — HU 8-3383

Local & Out-of-Town Numbers Frequently Called

3

CAVE CREEK GARAGE
GENERAL AUTO REPAIRING
DIXIE OIL PRODUCTS
Cave Creek Rd. HU 8-9965

RANCHO MANANA
GUEST RANCH
RIDING - SWIMMING - SQUARE DANCING
LUXURIOUS WESTERN STYLE MEALS
PRIVATE COCKTAIL BAR
Mr. & Mrs. E. E. Johnson, Mgrs.
CAVE CREEK HU 8-3211

SUBDIVIDERS DEVELOPERS
TOM ROBERTS REALTY
REAL ESTATE BROKERS
NED CLARK, Salesman
CAVE CREEK ROAD HU 8-3331

It isn't necessary to know the called party's telephone number to place a station-to-station call. Simply tell the Long Distance operator you want to talk to "anyone" at the office or residence of the person you want. We will do the rest.

The Mountain States Telephone and Telegraph Company

This photograph shows the entire 1955 telephone directory for Cave Creek, which included instructions as to how to use a rotary dial.

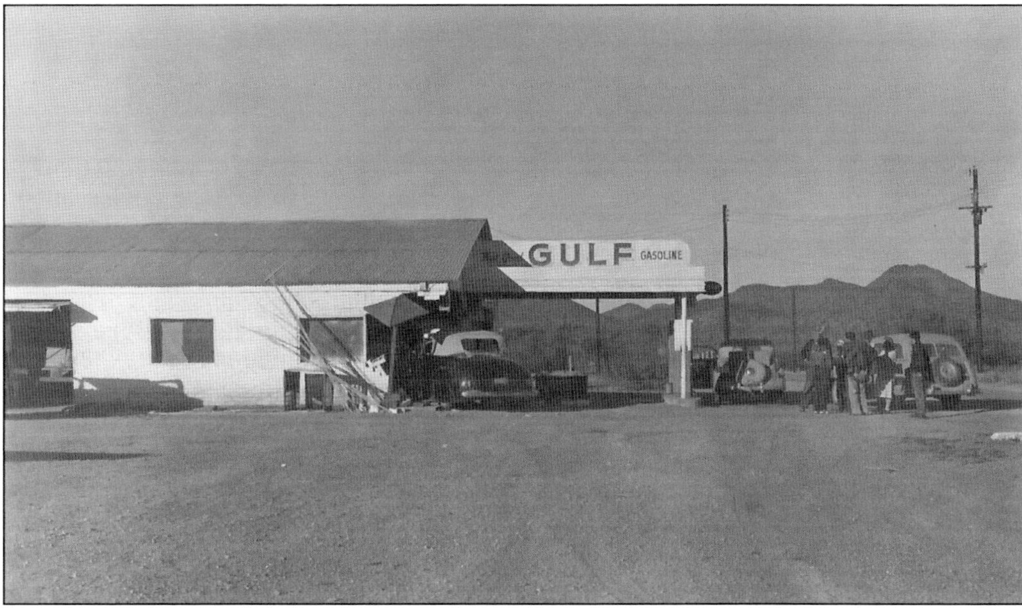

Seen here is Cave Creek's first full-service garage. Built by C.V. Smith and Red Mattingly in 1946, it opened on April 7, 1947. The garage continued operations into the 1960s. Note the automobile that crashed into the corner of the building. Much of the garage site is currently a hotel, situated between Linda Lane and Schoolhouse Road. West of the hotel, a building slab from the garage is still visible.

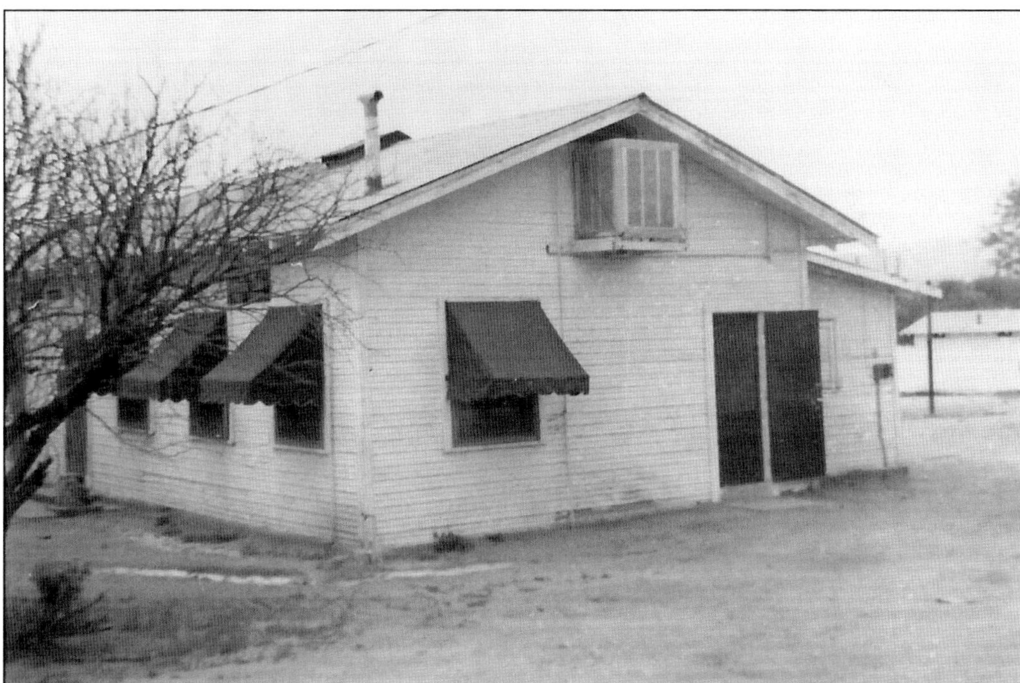

The Cave Creek School was located at the northeast corner of Schoolhouse and Cave Creek Roads. When a new school was constructed, this building became the library. It has seen many uses since that time. The current library is now just north of the old school, on Saguaro Hill.

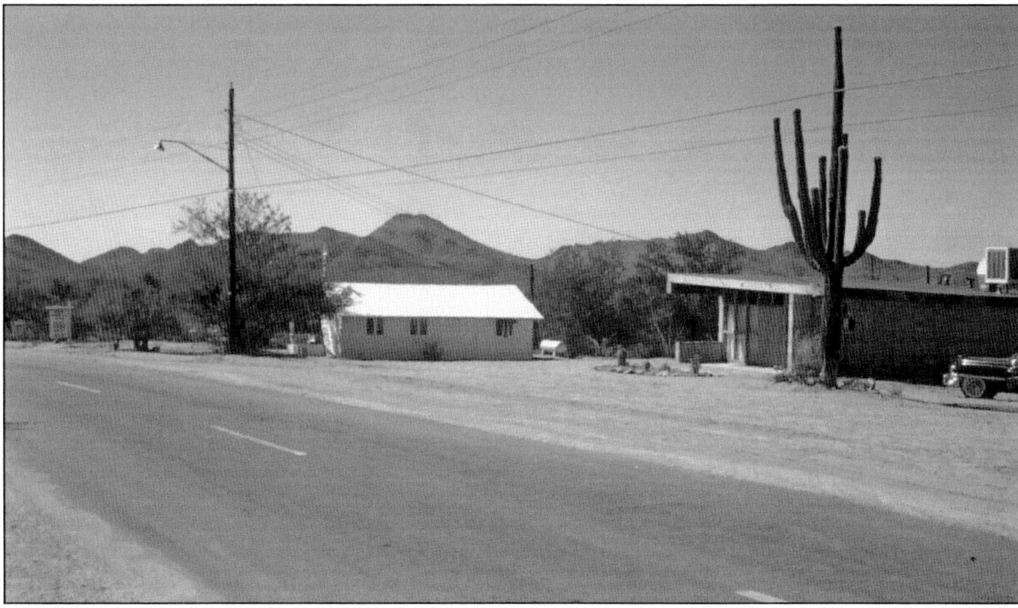

This 1957 photograph shows the original Good Shepherd of the Hills Episcopal Church (white building) and parish hall (right). The congregation later outgrew the small church, and a larger building now serves them. The tiny church was moved to become part of the Cave Creek Museum.

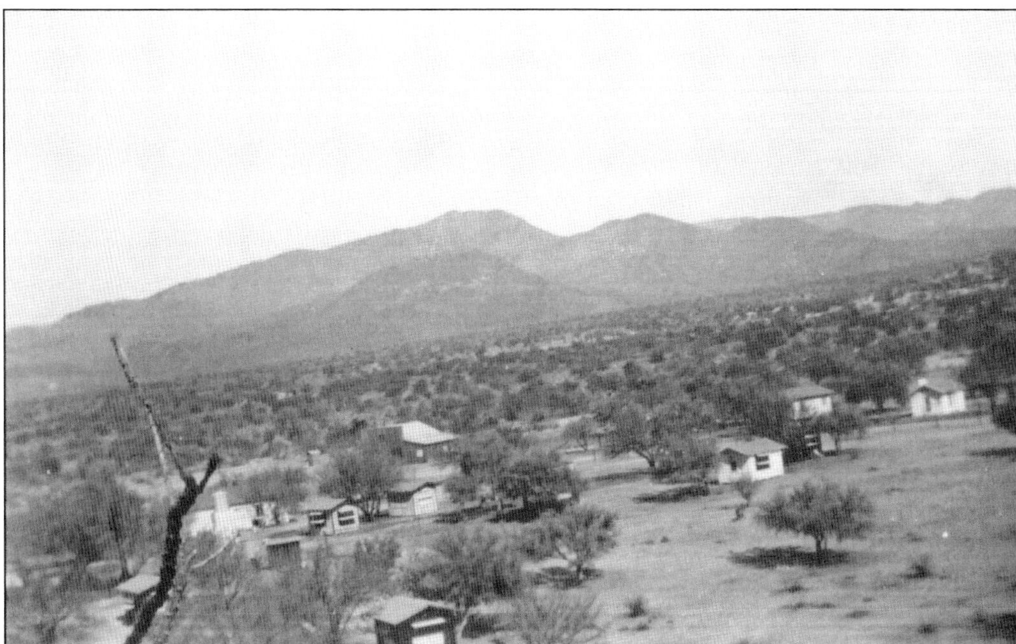

The Desmount station, a tubercular sanitarium, housed those suffering with lung ailments in rustic cabins. The station was located near where the Horny Toad Restaurant is today. Previously, the sanitarium was located farther east, near where Le Sans Souci Restaurant is now. The last remaining tubercular cabin from the Desmount station is now listed in the National Register of Historic Places and sited at the Cave Creek Museum.

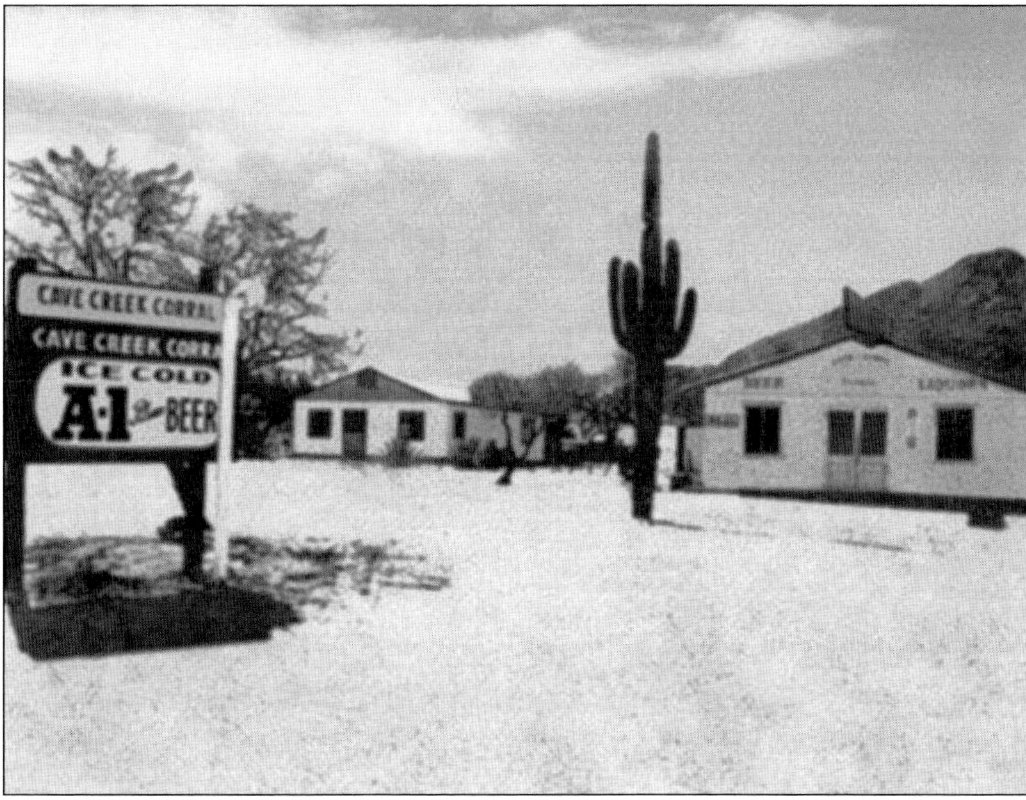

In this early photograph, the Cave Creek Corral bar is pictured to the right. This building still stands as part of an enlarged restaurant that is now Harold's Cave Creek Corral, a landmark of Cave Creek. The residence pictured to the left became Harold's business office. The Corral attracted locals for lively evenings of drinking and dancing for many years, a custom that continues to this very day.

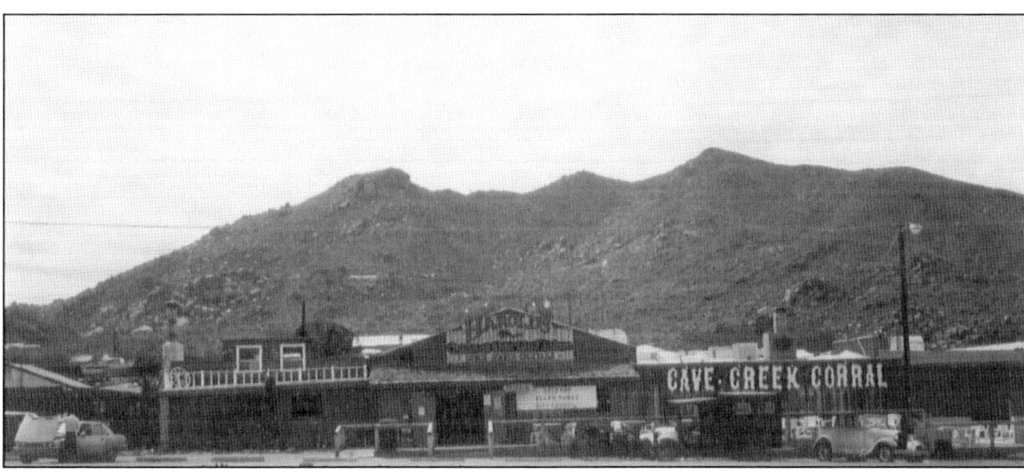

In 1958, Harold Gavagan repurchased the Cave Creek Corral, expanded it considerably, and began serving food. In 1962, he bought the Kachina Café in Cave Creek and moved it to the Corral site, and it is now part of Harold's Corral.

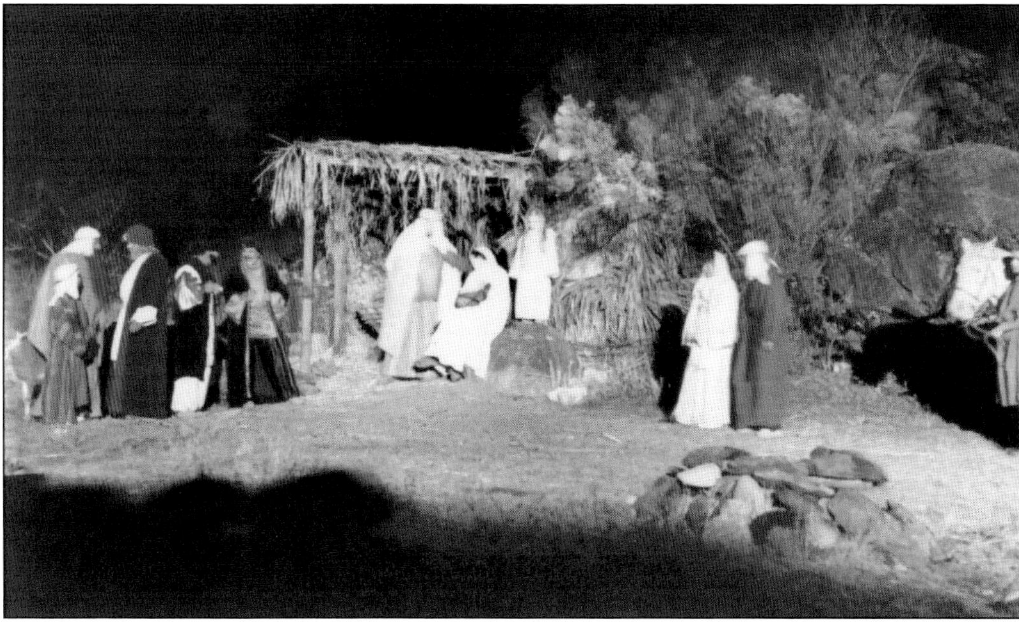

The entire population of tiny Cave Creek banded together to support a 4-H group that started the Christmas pageant, a perennial favorite. Originally presented on the north side of Black Mountain, the pageant involved young and old as both participants and enthusiastic audience members. The dramatic mountainside setting under brilliant, clear skies created a moving enactment of the Christmas story that continues today.

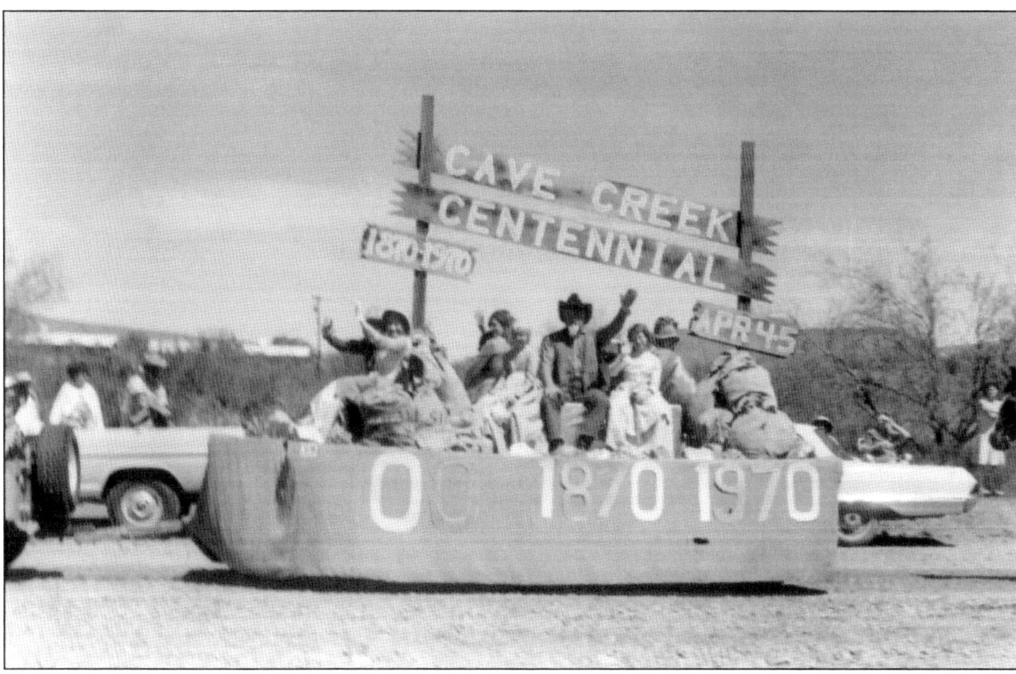

The centennial parade, on April 4, 1970, brought the community together to celebrate its origins and generated enthusiasm for the creation of the Cave Creek Museum.

Eight

People of Interest

The richness of a community is determined by the quality of its people. By such a measure, the Cave Creek-Carefree area is wealthy indeed.

Among those people were cowboys, who where essential to the ranches. George Mileham has been called "the last cowboy." He described himself as "stoved up," having been gored by bulls, shot, and thrown off horses. He spent much of his life punching cows or punching bar mates on rowdy nights at Harold's Corral.

In the 1950s, dude ranches needed cowboys like the popular Romy Lowdermilk, who entertained guests with rope tricks, cowboy songs, and tales, many of which he wrote. Perhaps the most beloved cowboy was Hube Yates, who was also a bicycle racing champion, a boxer, an ordained minister, and a fireman who was awarded the Carnegie Medal for heroism.

Less ribald members of the community included Frank and Hazel Wright. After being gassed in World War I, Frank was advised by doctors to "find a nice place to die." He found Cave Creek in 1922, where he did die—in 1982. Between those years, he and Hazel, a tuberculosis victim from Colorado, adopted Cave Creek as the child they never had. Mr. Cave Creek, as many locals called Frank, did much for the tiny community, wrangling with authorities to pave Cave Creek Road and bring in electricity.

Contrasting with the sedate Wrights were Harold and Ruth Gavagan, who ran the popular Harold's Corral. Over the years, the bar hosted construction workers, cowboys, and even lions and tigers, reportedly refugees from a circus.

Artists drawn to the dramatic beauty of the foothills often had a history in the saddle. Former cowboy Lon Megargee sketched what he saw on ranches. His art ranged from commercial posters to classical murals for the Arizona capitol. John Wade Hampton, a renowned painter and sculptor, said he was inspired to begin the exclusive Cowboy Artists of America in 1965 while strolling Cave Creek's tamarisk grove. Carefree resident Ray Swanson, a two-time president of Cowboy Artists of America, was noted for his Navajo portraits. Many of the area's contemporary artists created the Sonoran Arts League, which each year features the well-respected Hidden in the Hills art show and tour of studios.

The sister towns of Cave Creek and Carefree have developed their own personalities and lifestyles, identified with charming monikers such as "Denim and Diamonds" and "Cowboys and Caviar."

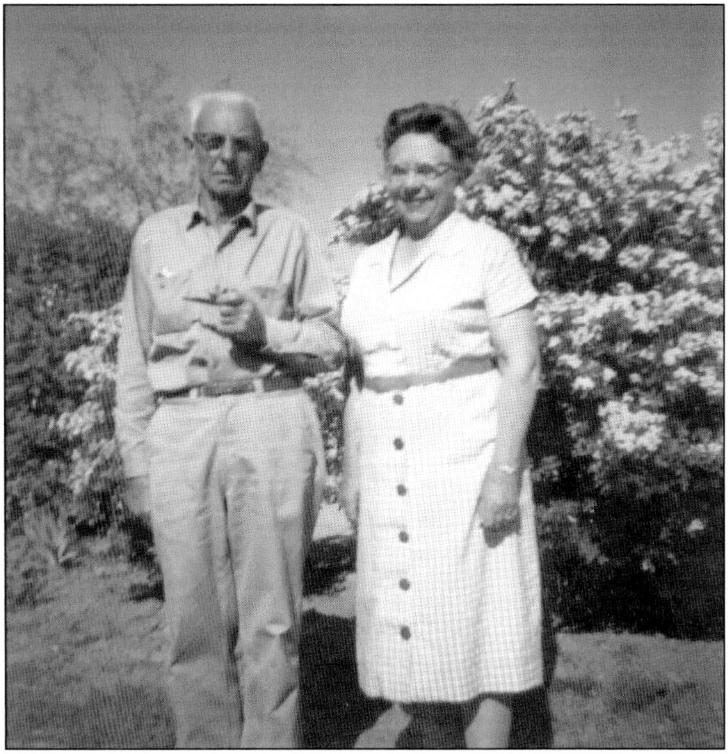

After being gassed in World War I, Frank Wright came to Cave Creek to die, which he did, but not until he was in his 80s. His wife, Hazel, came to town seeking relief from tuberculosis. The pair had no children but considered Cave Creek their baby. They brought in water and power and donated land to community organizations. Hazel said, "Cave Creekers often fussed among themselves, but they always stuck together when anyone was in trouble."

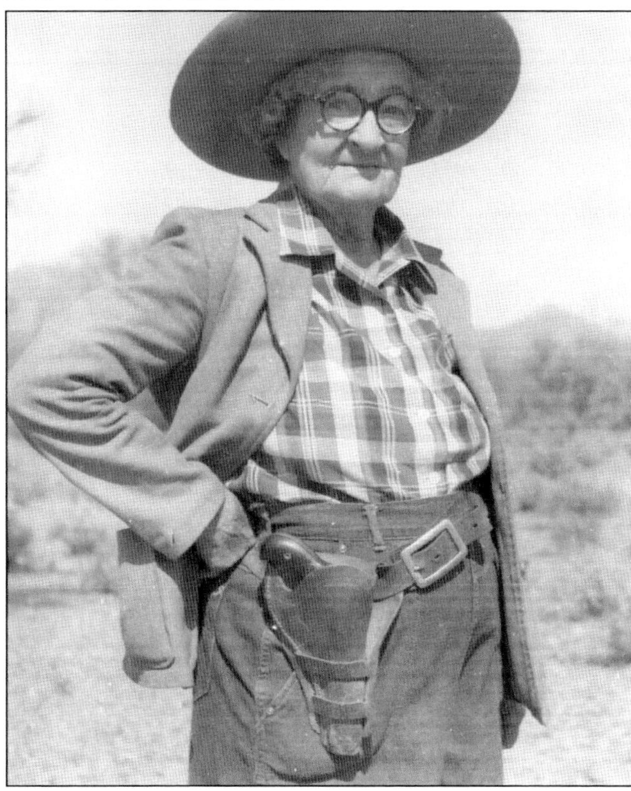

Catherine "Cattle Kate" Jones, a deputy sheriff, patrolled Cavecreek, as it was then spelled, armed with her six-shooter. Prohibition-era stills in the area disappeared when the tiny, feisty rancher shot the ear off a moonshiner who laughed at her authority. After the encounter, miscreants avoided Cavecreek. In contrast to her law enforcement duties, Jones also painted beautiful landscapes, published poetry, and skillfully ran Cahava Ranch with her husband, Theodore.

Dwight "Doc" Hudson never wanted to continue the hard life of ranching he had experienced growing up. He decided to become a dentist so that every Wednesday he could hang a "Gone Fishing" sign on his office door. Fates intervened, however, and Hudson returned to own and run the Quarter Circle One Ranch. In the late 1950s, he sold part of the ranch to the developers of Carefree.

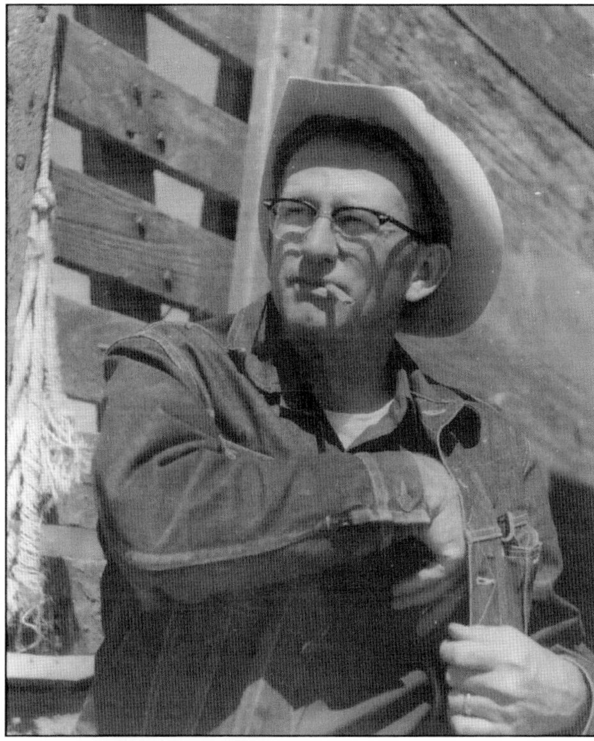

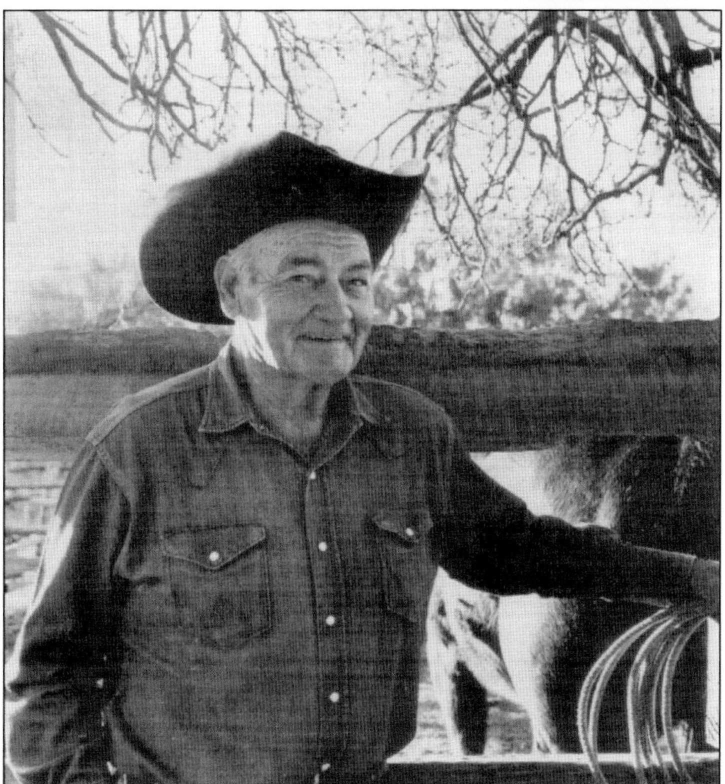

Hube Yates was a Renaissance man in a cowboy hat. He was a rancher, minister, raconteur, fireman, and the winner of the Carnegie Hero Medal for rescuing a man stranded on a sandbar during the 1931 flooding of the Salt River. His greatest attribute was his kindness, and for that, he was most beloved.

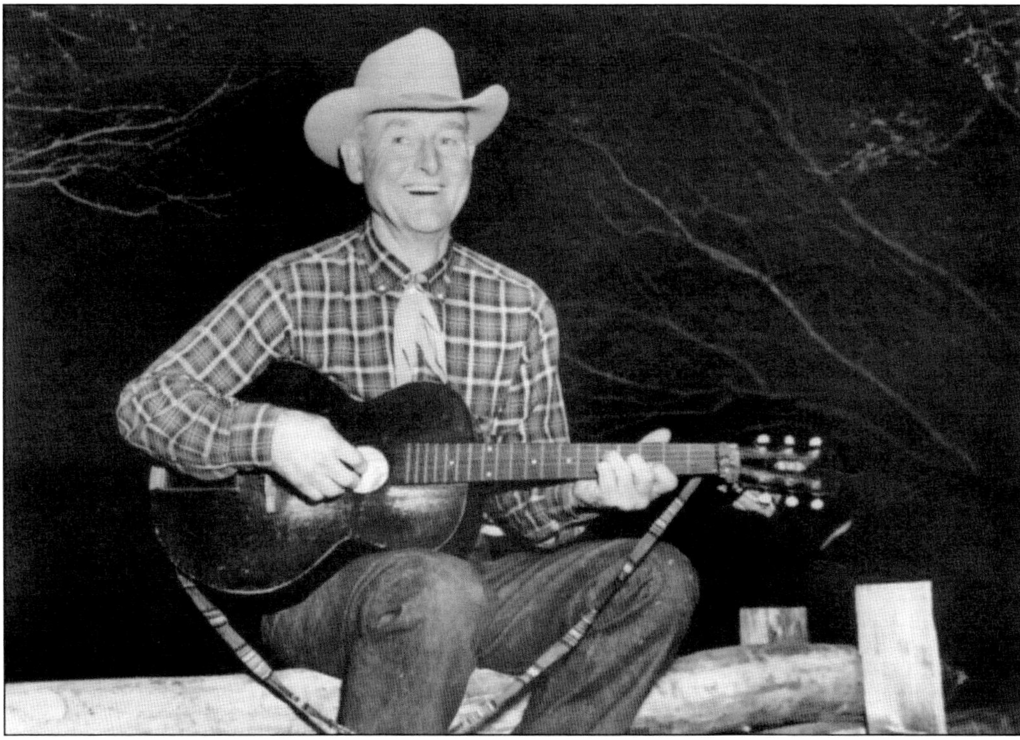

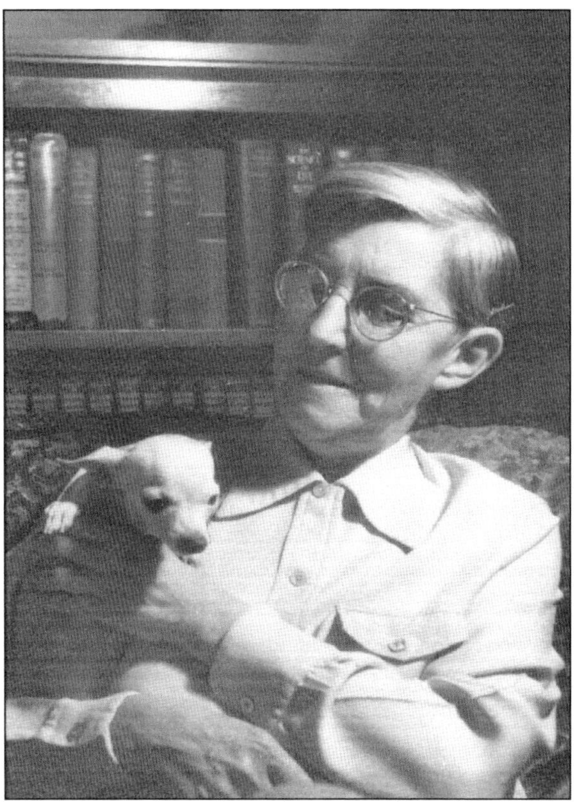

Romaine "Romy" Lowdermilk (above) was known as the "father of dude ranches." In the 1940s, he began entertaining "dudes" intent on experiencing the Wild West on the 750-acre Rancho Mañana dude ranch. A real working cowboy, Lowdermilk was a dynamic entertainer, singing lively cowboy songs, performing rope tricks, and organizing outings. A published songwriter, he performed on local and national radio programs as the Singing Rancher.

Pat Bradley came to Cave Creek in 1934 seeking relief from poor health. She was an experienced surgical nurse who became the community nurse for all emergencies. In addition, she served as town postmaster from 1941 to 1954. According to stories, the remote small-town setting allowed postal employees leeway in their duties, and they often tucked a piece of pie or other non-stamped item into a postal patron's box.

The pipe-smoking, effervescent ErnaMarie Smith defined organization. The self-employed businesswoman ran several enterprises, including designing and creating stylish Western wear. While she wore many hats in the community, Smith's favorite was as the organizer for both the Fiesta Days and Fourth of July parades. Local celebrities Dick Van Dyke and Hugh Downs rode the routes. Tragically, ErnaMarie Smith was murdered by a thief who broke into her home.

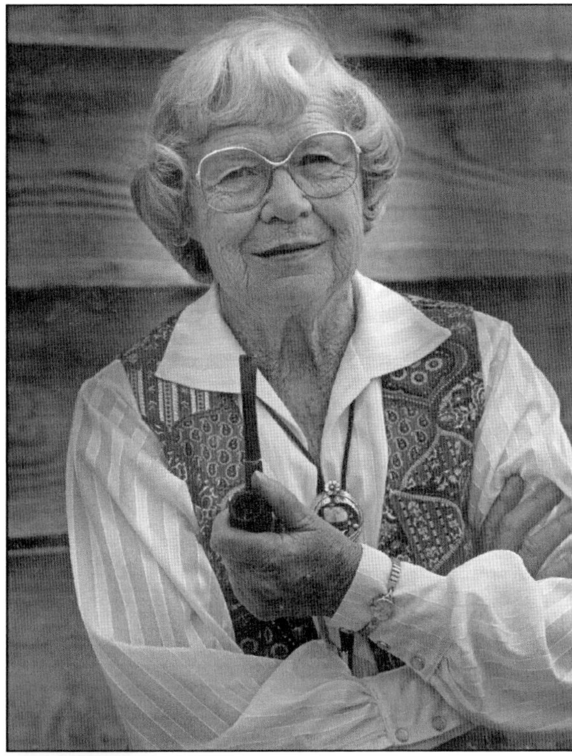

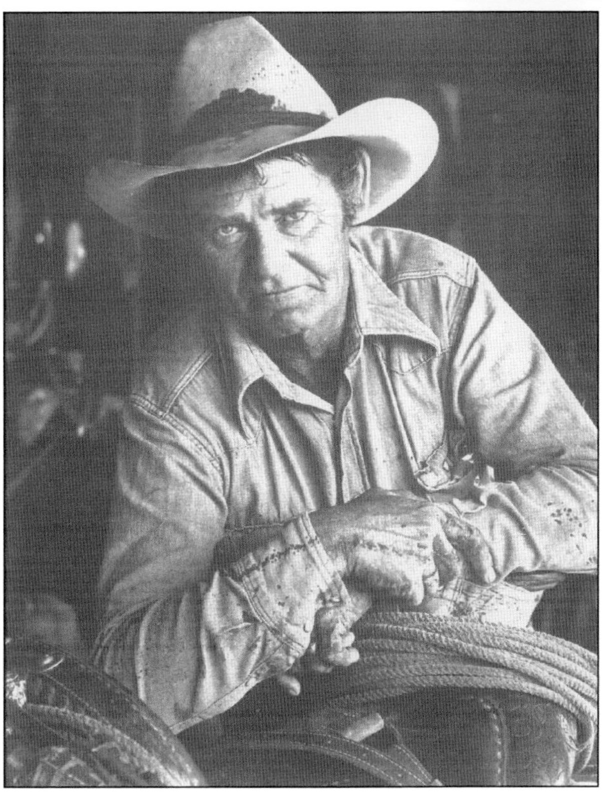

George Mileham, who was called "the last cowboy," described himself as "stoved up" because he had been gored by cattle, was shot three times in World War II, and spent 14 to 16 hours a day in a saddle. On some of those days, he was tossed from his horse, and horses even landed on him several times. Mileham was known for punching cows and, on occasion, fellow cowboys during rowdy nights at Harold's Corral.

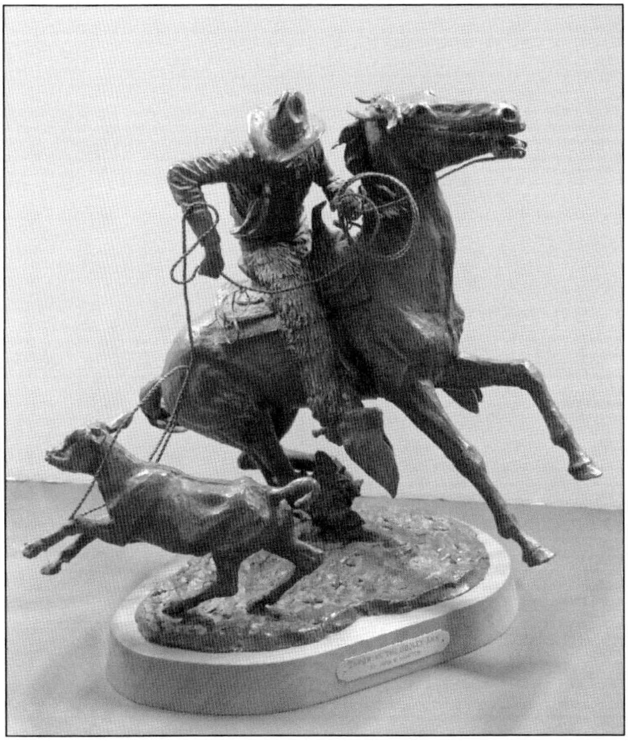

John Wade Hampton wanted greater respect for Western artists. In 1965, while walking near his Cave Creek home, he envisioned the Cowboy Artists of America. He shared his idea with artist friends Joe Beeler, George Phippen, and Charlie Dye. Today, the exclusive, invitation-only artist's organization perpetuates the memory and culture of the Old West. Seen here is Hampton's bronze *Throwing the Hooley-Ann*, from the Cave Creek Museum's collection.

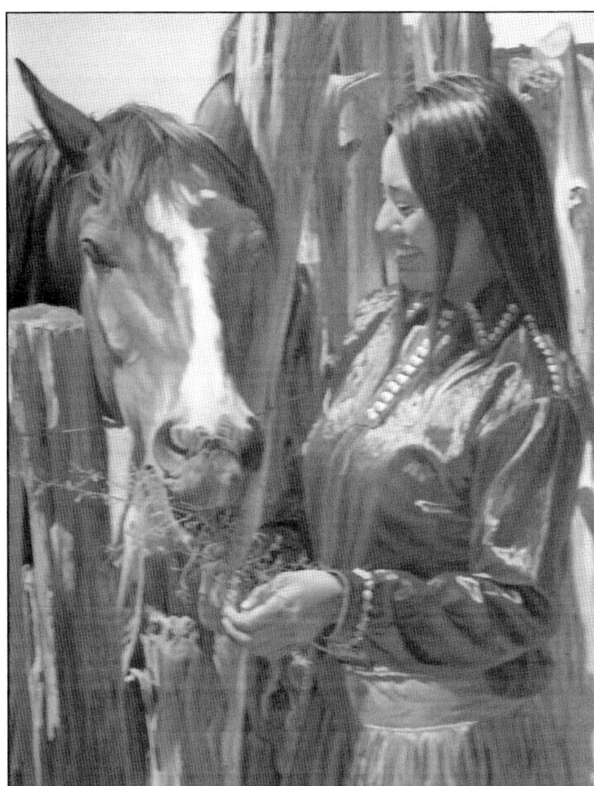

Carefree resident Ray Swanson, a two-time president of the Cowboy Artists of America, was a prolific painter whose favorite subjects were the Navajo. One of his many pieces, *Fresh Greens*, is seen here.

Lon Megargee was born in Philadelphia, the son of a wealthy philanderer who was killed by a jealous husband. On his own at age 13, Megargee headed west, becoming a cowboy in the 1920s. During his rough and lonely life in the saddle, he sketched, trading pictures for food. Droughts turned him from cowboying to painting full time. His art ranged from commercial posters to classical murals for the Arizona capitol.

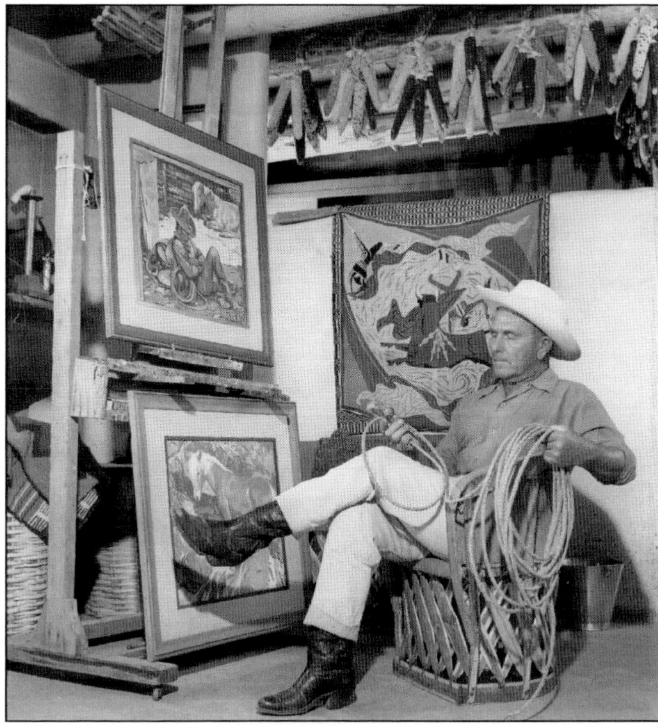

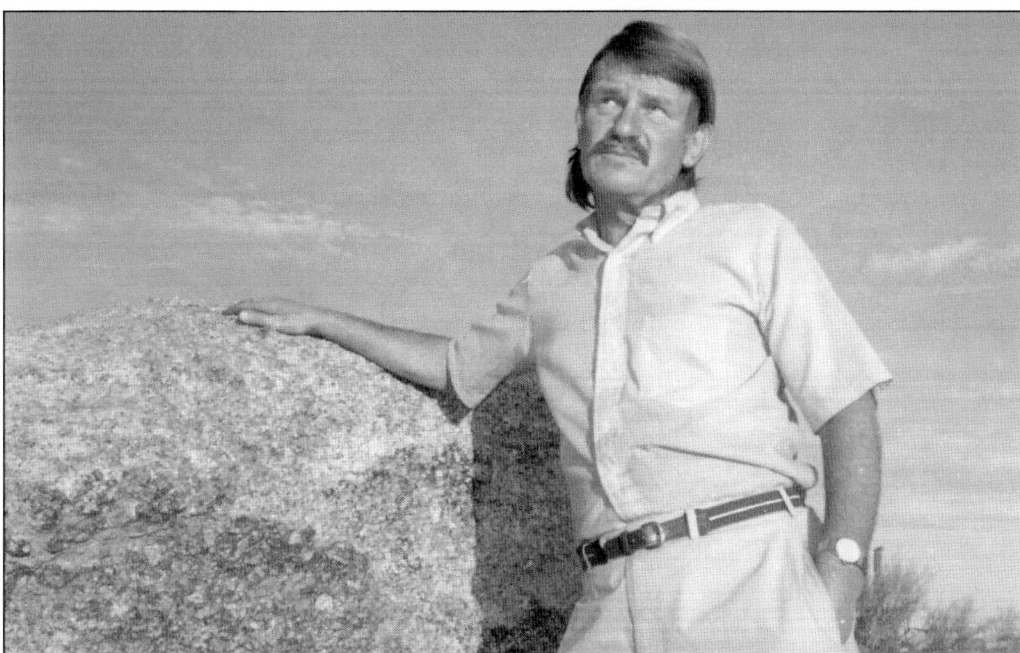

Geoffrey Platts, the poet laureate of Scottsdale, was a lively raconteur and a passionate writer. Transplanted from England, Platts embraced the desert and bemoaned the development that created what he termed a "Disney desert." A 20th-century Thoreau, he lived in a rustic cabin in the desert without plumbing or electricity. A man of adventure, he died tragically in 2000, drowning while trying to save a friend in the raging Verde River. (Courtesy of Jack Grenard.)

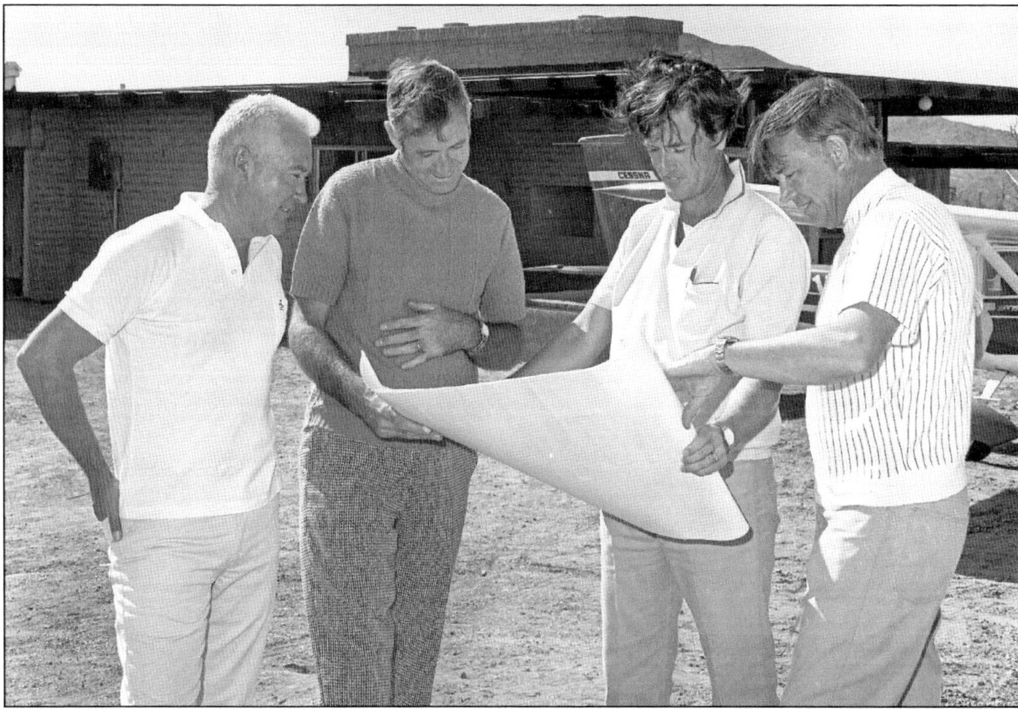

Gerry Jones, a respected architect, built the first home in Carefree. He went on to build many more, including homes for Carefree founders Tom Darlington and K.T. Palmer and celebrities Hugh Downs and Paul Harvey. Here, Charles Turek (left) and an unidentified Cessna pilot watch as Hugh Downs (right) consults with Gerry Jones (holding plans) about the creation of the first "fly-in" home in America, built at the Carefree airport. (Courtesy of Gerry Jones.)

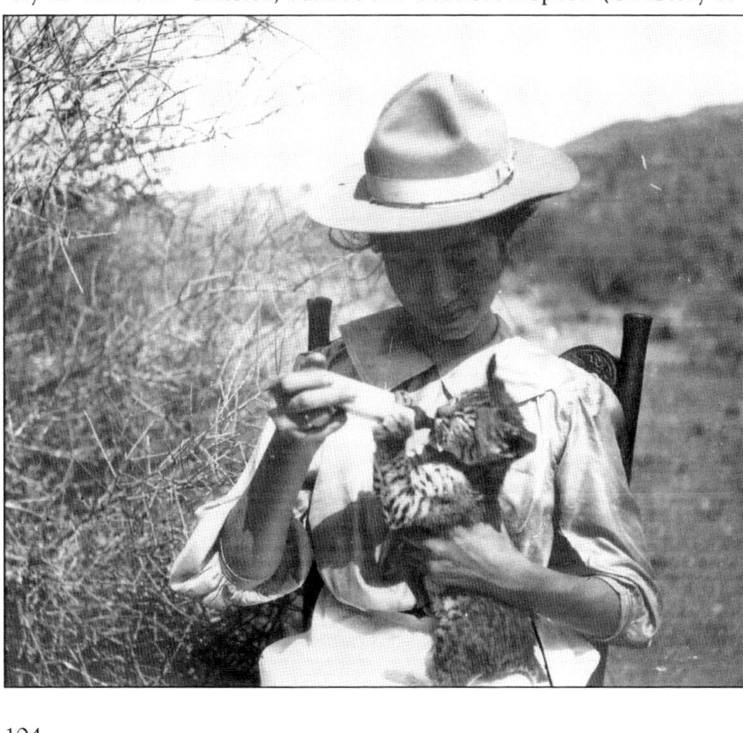

Dulcy Houck was the daughter of James Houck, who, among his other enterprises, ran a sheep ranch in early Cave Creek. As the business grew, workers arrived for shearing. A stagecoach run evolved, and what had been a lonely outpost became quite lively. Thanks to her interest in photography, Dulcy Houck documented many aspects of early-20th-century Cave Creek life. She is seen here with an orphaned bobcat kitten.

Dorothy Smith, a retired librarian from New York, was the first director of what is now the Desert Foothills Library. Despite having grown up in East Coast refinement and in the company of Rockefellers, she loved Cave Creek. With her friend Corolyn Cox, Smith started the library in 1954. She trekked into Phoenix to get books from the Maricopa County Library. Initial circulation was often done from her car trunk, as no permanent building existed yet.

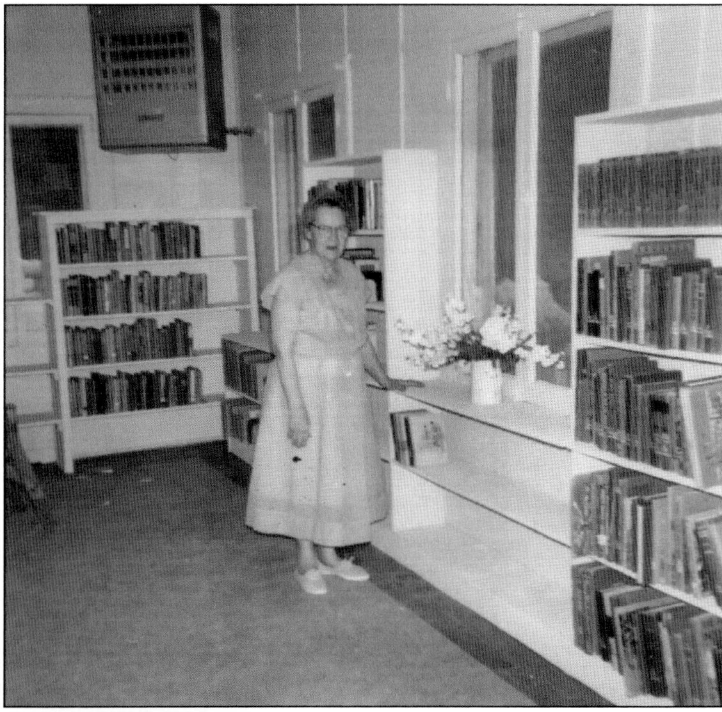

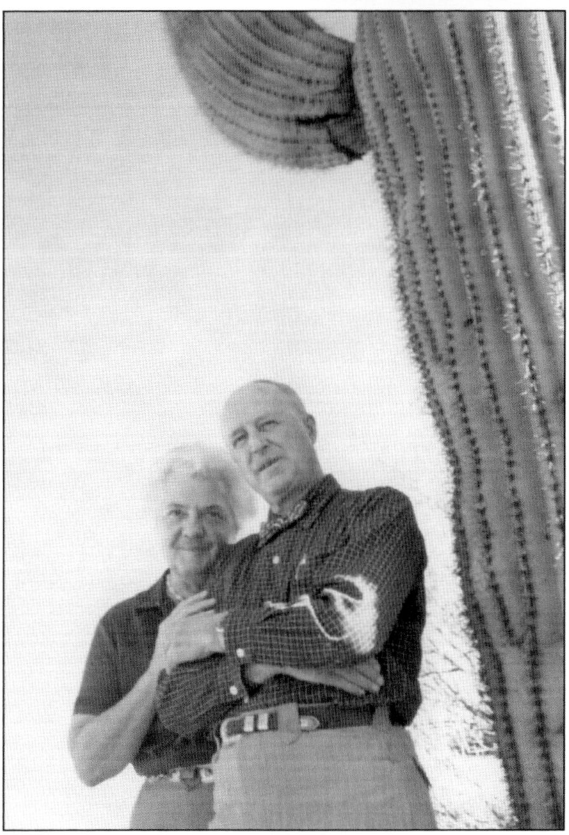

Jack and Corolyn Cox came to Cave Creek in 1948 to soothe Jack's lungs after he was gassed in World War I. The gregarious couple soon integrated into the community, boldly accepting a blanket invitation to a town-wide barbecue at Doc Hudson's. There, they met townsfolk, including the host. Corolyn wrote prolifically about people and "doings" in her "Cave Creek Calling" newspaper column, and, with Dorothy Smith, was instrumental in founding the library. (Courtesy of Eileen Santlal.)

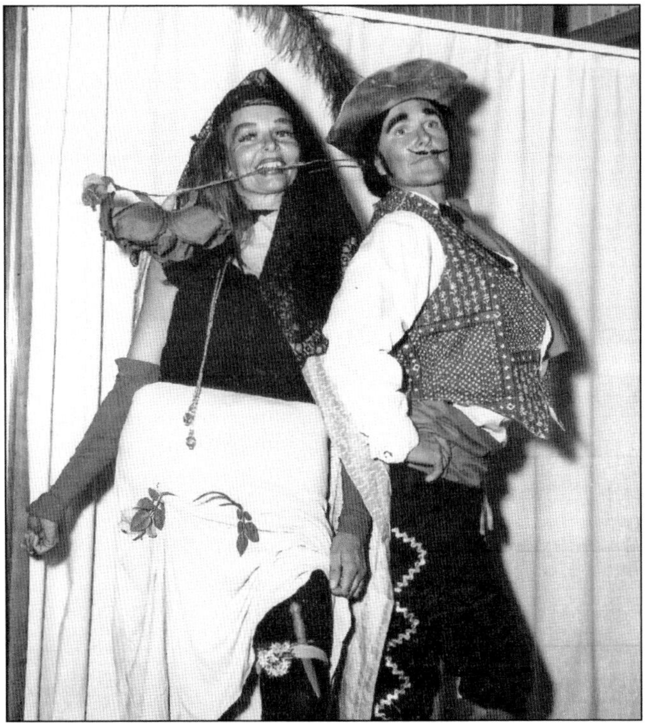

Mothers' Club members Marianne Davis (left) and Corky Cockburn ham it up at a 1965 fundraiser to create a kindergarten for area children. In addition to Mothers' Club, Cockburn was a leader in the formation of the Cave Creek Improvement Association and the library. Her famous parties featured fare harvested from the desert. Late risers, Cockburn and her husband, Curt, left the key to their lumberyard for construction workers to get in early and pay later. (Courtesy of Beverly Metcalfe Brooks.)

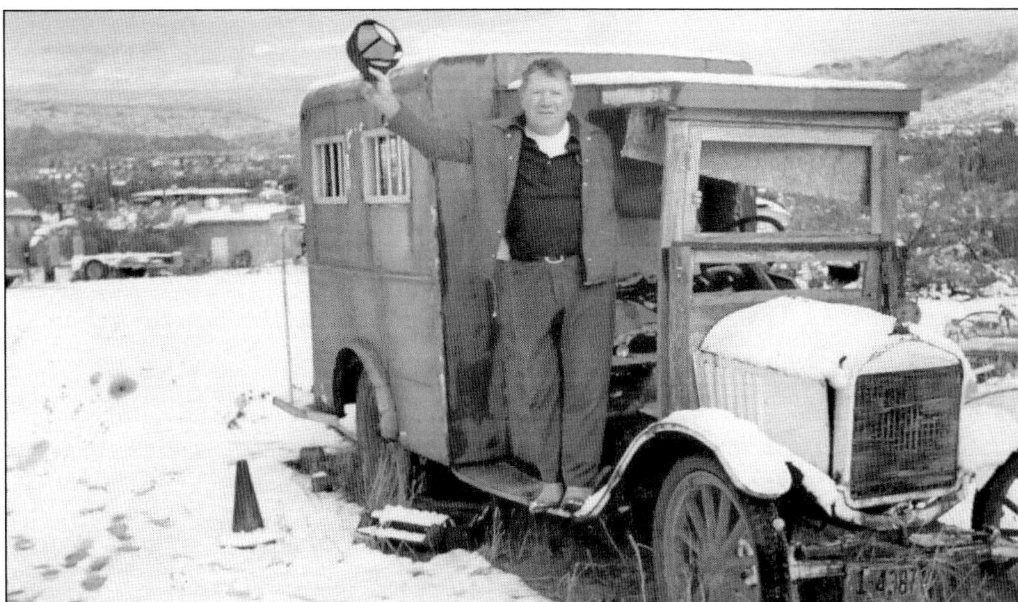

In 1950, Harold and Ruth Gavagan bought the Cave Creek Corral, Cave Creek's oldest continually operating business. In addition to cowboys, construction workers, celebrities, townsfolk, and tourists, the colorful landmark hosted lions and tigers in a large outdoor circus cage. The renamed Harold's Corral grew with add-ons and relocated buildings. Built in the same piecemeal fashion, Harold Gavagan was also proud of this half-1924 Ford Model T, half-trailer creation, seen in a rare Cave Creek snow. (Courtesy of the Gavagan family.)

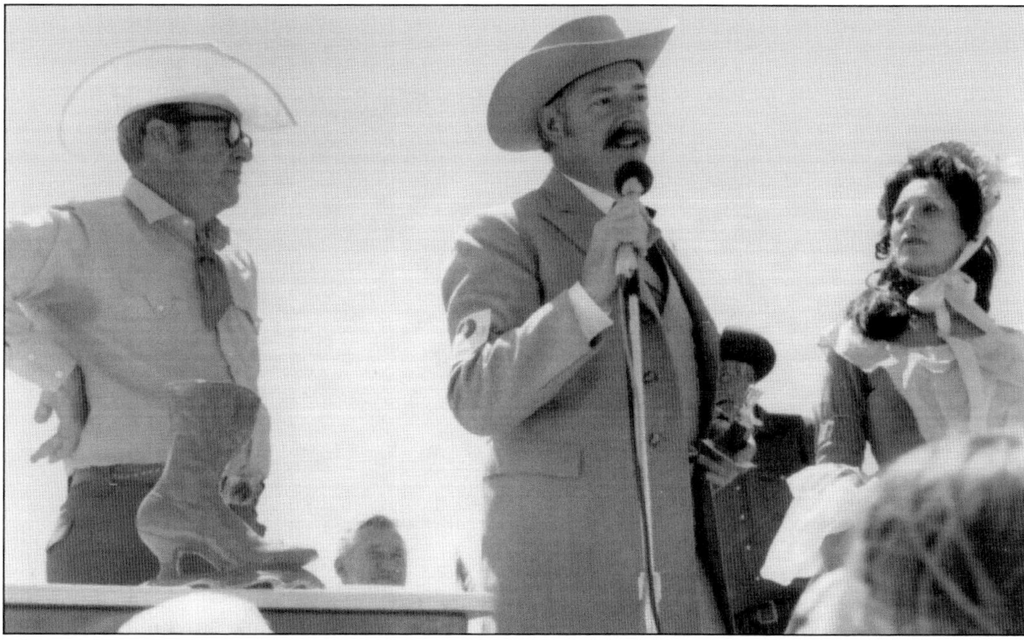

Mustachioed Hugh Downs, the six-time Emmy Award–winning broadcaster, television anchor, producer, author, and game show host, was one of the initial investors and early residents in Carefree. He financed the first speculation home at the Carefree Airport. He is seen here speaking at the Cave Creek centennial parade in 1970.

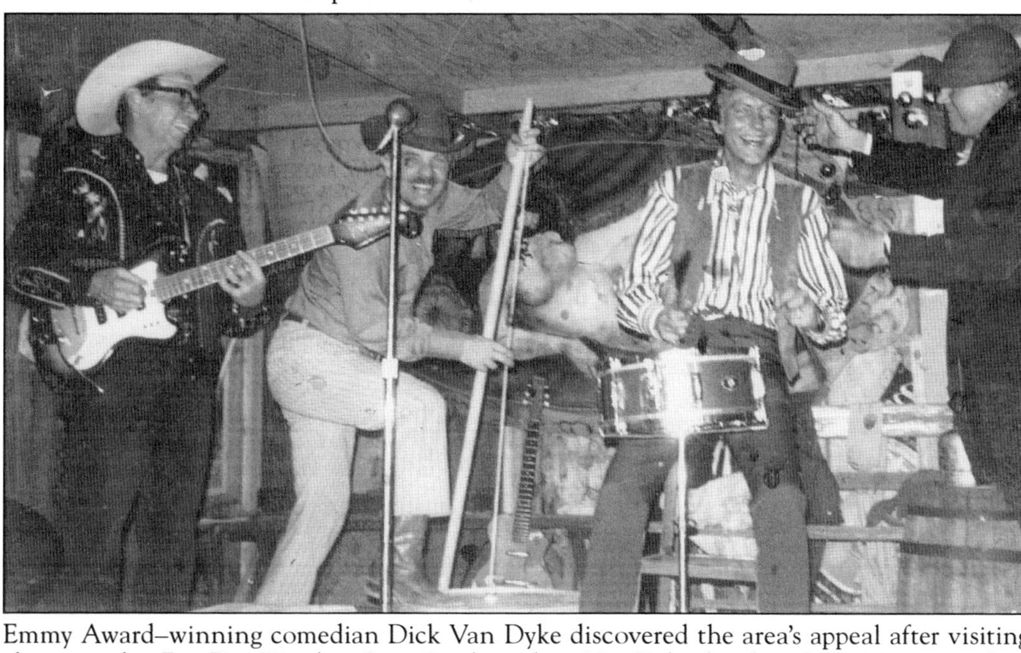

Emmy Award–winning comedian Dick Van Dyke discovered the area's appeal after visiting choreographer Dee Dee Woods, a Cave Creek resident. Van Dyke then bought a 180-acre ranch in the area. He quickly adopted the town, participating in parades and frequenting Harold's Corral, where this photograph was taken of Van Dyke playing the drums. While Hollywood beckoned, Van Dyke decided to film *The New Dick Van Dyke Show*, which ran from 1971 to 1974, at the Graham Studios, which were built here for that purpose.

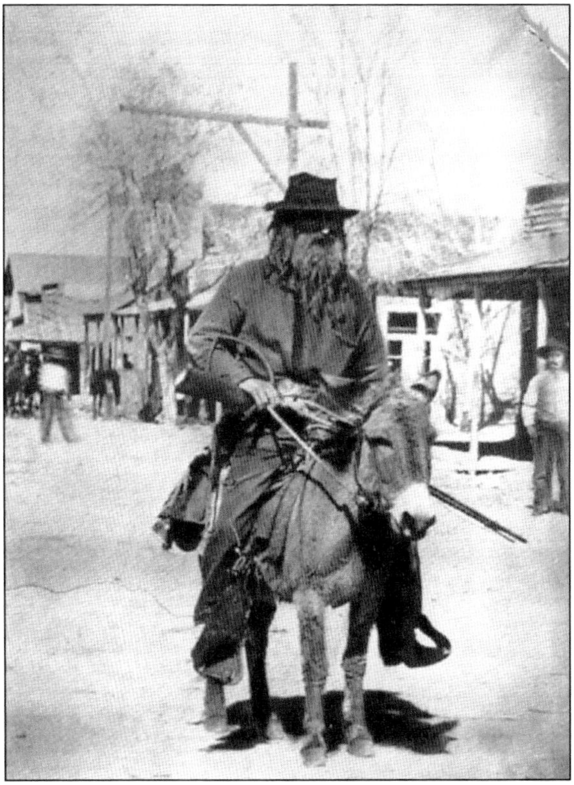

Known as Old Rackensack, Edward Cave considered cities to be prisons, so he spent much of his life prospecting. A former Confederate soldier, he had Southern wit and shared tales with appreciative friends when he came to town. In his wanderings, he discovered signs of early mining, sites worked perhaps by 17th-century Spanish or Mexican people. Some speculate that Cave Creek was named for him, but the town was already named when he arrived.

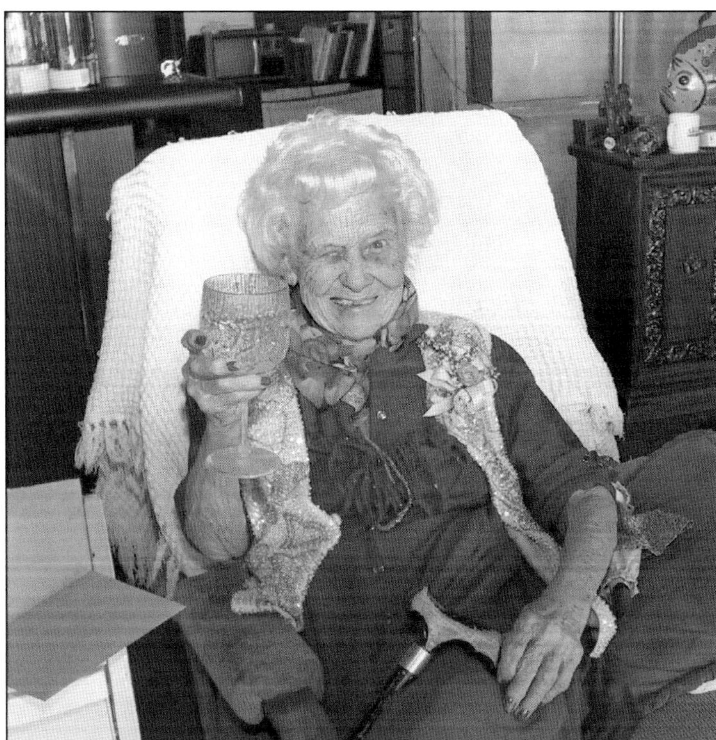

Grace Voss Frederick was a colorful, lively actress whose career included work in vaudeville and television. She and her husband, Claude, moved to Cave Creek in 1971 for his health. She applied her considerable energy to environmental causes, and then began collecting an eclectic array of memorabilia. In her 90s, she created the Grace Museum for the Preservation of Americana, which housed her vast collections in an 180,000-square-foot building. She died at the age of 103. (Courtesy of the *Sonoran News*.)

Nine

Carefree

K.T. Palmer and Tom Darlington first shared their vision for creating a town in 1946 at a Kiwanis luncheon at the Adams Hotel in Phoenix. It may have been the first time the two men met. In the early 1950s, they found themselves as partners in a Scottsdale real estate firm and deeply entrenched in civic affairs. Palmer, the president of the Scottsdale Chamber of Commerce, and Darlington, the president of the Paradise Valley Improvement Association, were unsuccessful in convincing the town leaders of Scottsdale that they needed a master plan to guide future development.

The time had come to move out of Scottsdale and build their own master-planned community. The two men considered the Pinnacle Peak area, where both had sizeable real estate holdings, but water in commercial quantities was not to be found. Farther north, where deep, plentiful aquifers existed, they made their first purchase in 1954, buying 400 acres owned by Helen Allen of Phoenix. In 1955, this was supplemented by the purchase of a portion of the Old Goat Ranch, owned by Ruth Clark. Together, this initial land became the Carefree town center. Eventually, Palmer and Darlington controlled, through purchase or lease, 2,200 acres.

The Carefree Development Corporation was formed in 1955. Although other names for the town were considered, including the one-letter name of O, the name Carefree persisted. Professional engineers and town planners were hired, and by 1957, their recommendations were made to the board. In 1959, the original plat of Carefree was recorded. Roads were graded, waterlines were placed, and residential lots were offered for sale from the Darlington-Palmer Building, the first structure completed in the town center. By 1963, a world-class golf course, an airport, an inn, and a restaurant were open and ready to welcome the prominent, wealthy people Palmer and Darlington wanted to attract.

Carefree's street names deserve a special place in its history. Easy Street, Ho and Hum Roads, Peaceful Place, Breathless Drive, and other charming monikers were "shook out of a gin bottle," it is said, at one of Darlington's tented cocktail parties. Carefree and its street names caught the attention of travel editors, tourists, and prospective buyers from around the world.

In 1984, Carefree incorporated. Created in the beauty of lush, native desert, the town is forever protected from commercial sprawl and annexation because it is governed by deed restrictions and strict zoning, just as Palmer and Darlington envisioned.

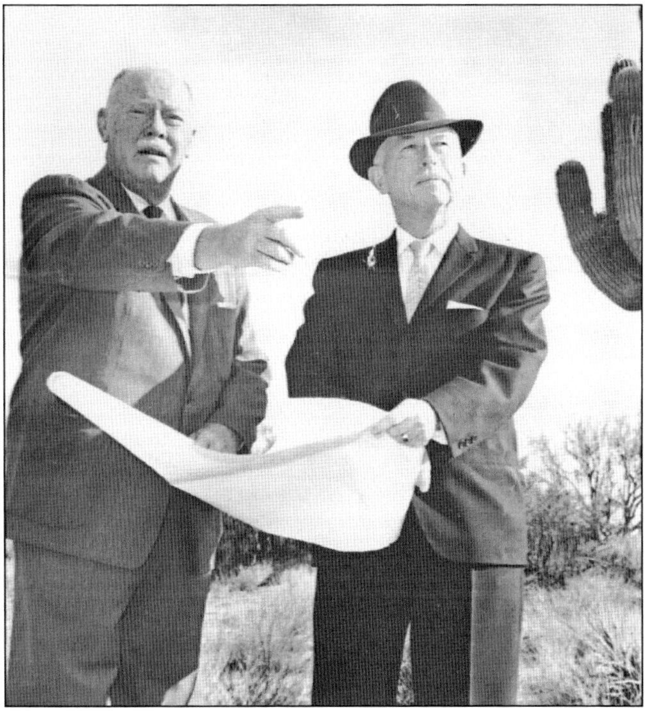

Carefree's founders and developers, Tom Darlington (left) and K.T. Palmer, oversee plans in 1959, when the first 1,400-acre subdivision was complete. One-, two-, and five-acre residential lots went on sale, in addition to commercial development sites in the town center. Beautiful 2.5-acre residential sites on Black Mountain with underground utilities sold for $2,700.

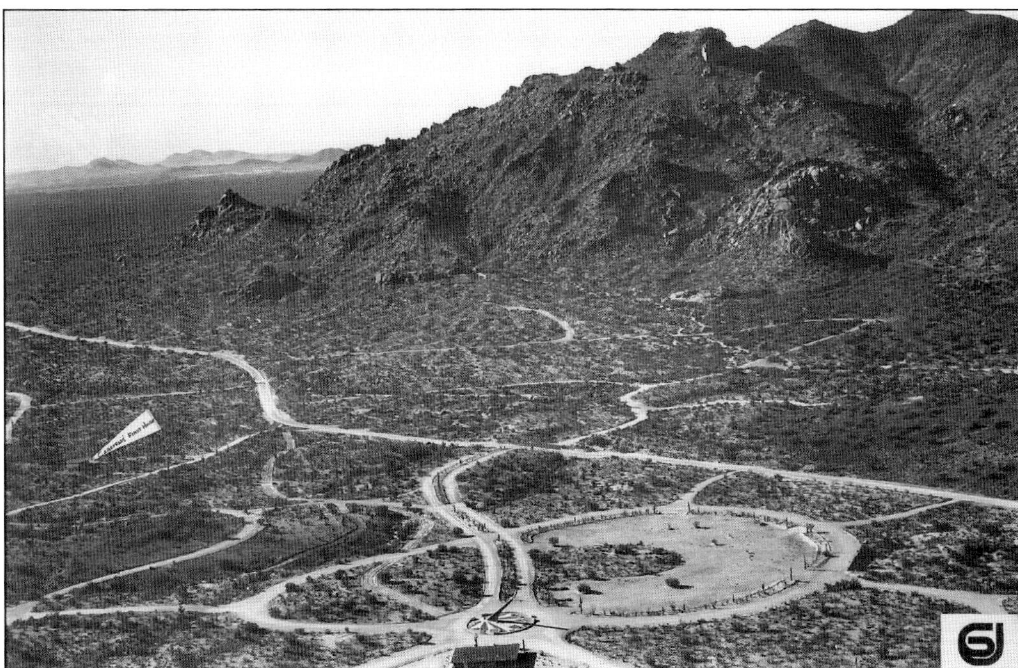

This 1959 aerial photograph shows gravel roads that were laid out and excavated between 1957 and 1959. The Darlington-Palmer Building, designed by Joe Wong, is in the lower center, directly underneath the sundial. The white arrow on the left identifies the first residence, designed and built by Gerry Jones, when it was under construction. It was sold to Bill and Newie DeMille, who became Carefree's first residents. (Courtesy of Gerry Jones.)

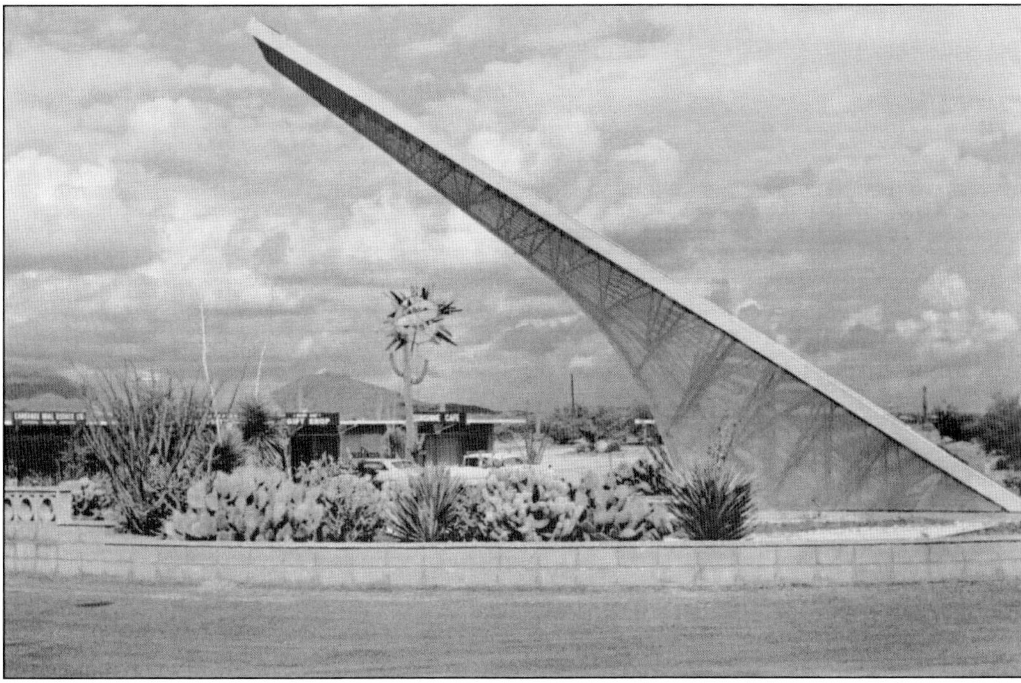

Solar engineer John Yellot and architect Joe Wong designed the sundial for K.T. Palmer in 1959. It was the attention-getter Palmer knew would draw people to Carefree. The landmark structure combined time telling with a solar water heater. Heated water was pumped across the street to the Darlington-Palmer Building, which also housed the Sunshine Café, the Quien Sabe Gift Shop, and the Tonto National Forest ranger's office.

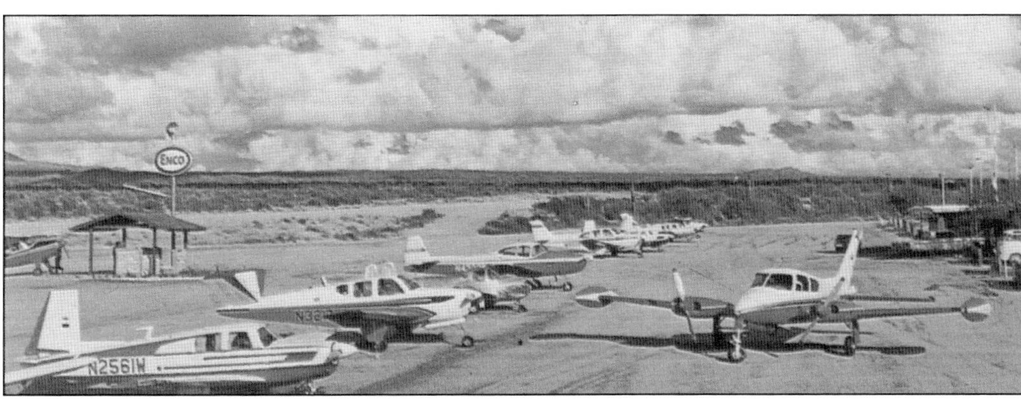

With no direct roads, paved or otherwise, travel to Carefree was initially a challenge. The airport was an early addition to the town's plan, allowing well-heeled residents and potential residents to arrive in style and live an exclusive lifestyle. In 1965, Sam Mosher, the chairman of Signal Oil & Gas, needed a paved runway to land his corporate jet, so his wife, Maggie, led the effort to pave the 4,000-foot runway.

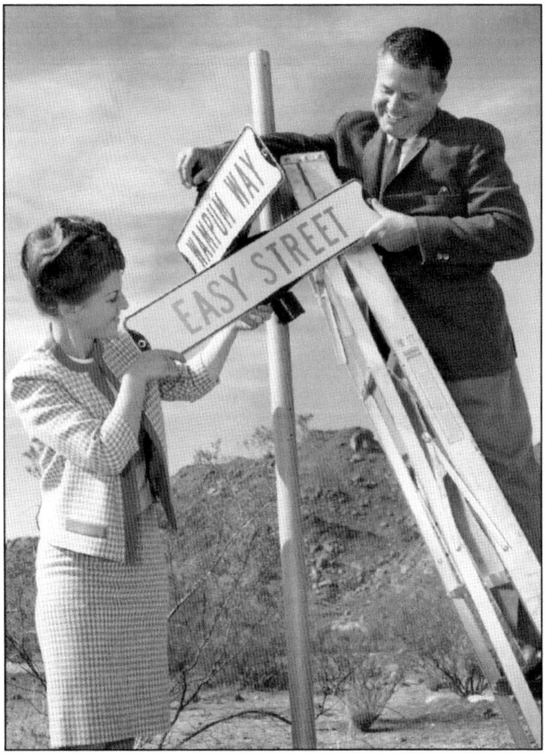

Jim Patrick, a Carefree resident and the president of the Valley National Bank (now Chase Bank), obtained approval to build a branch on the corner of Easy Street and Wampum Way. It became known as the Easy Wampum Bank. Here, during the ground-breaking ceremony for Carefree's first bank, teller Kathy Blair adjusts street signs with manager Carl Gleason. Carefree's whimsical street names are a hallmark of the town.

Below, horseback riders Pete Moot (left) and Hube Yates are greeted by, from left to right, bank manager Carl Gleason, Betty Bianchi, and Elba Smith in front of the bank. In 1968, bandits made off with $52,000 from the bank after herding employees into the vault. The perpetrators headed down Cave Creek Road and were intercepted around Union Hills Road by numerous sheriffs' deputies returning from weapons practice at Ben Avery Gun Range. The roadblock stopped them, and a shoot-out ensued.

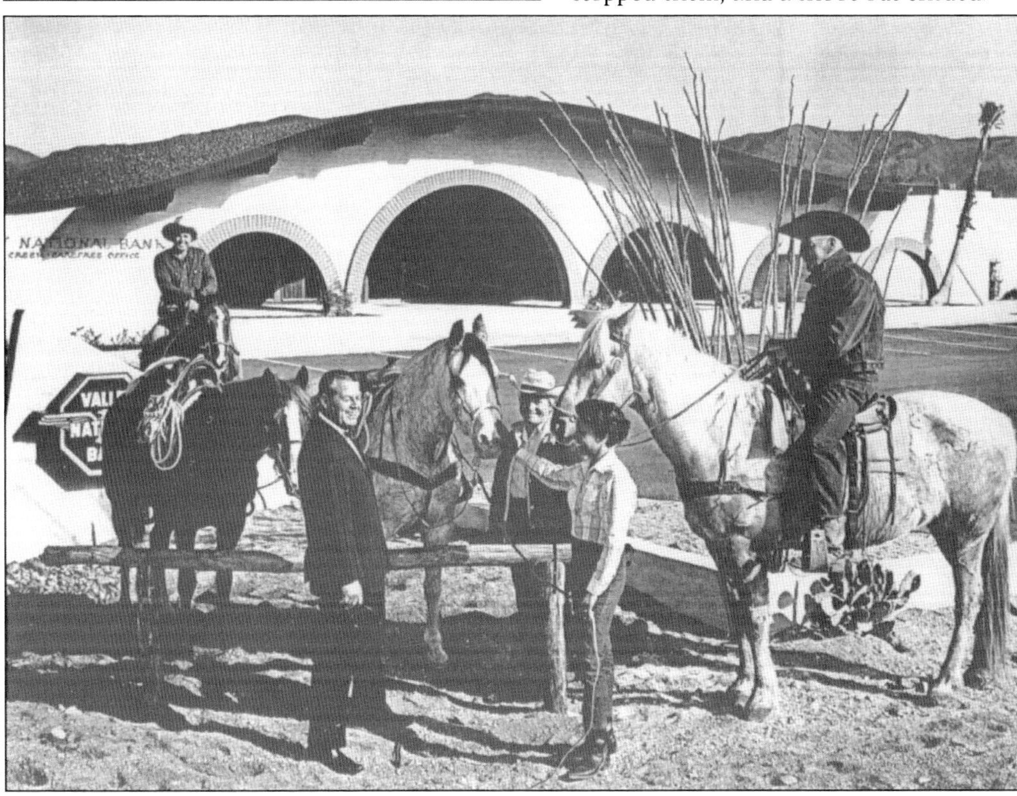

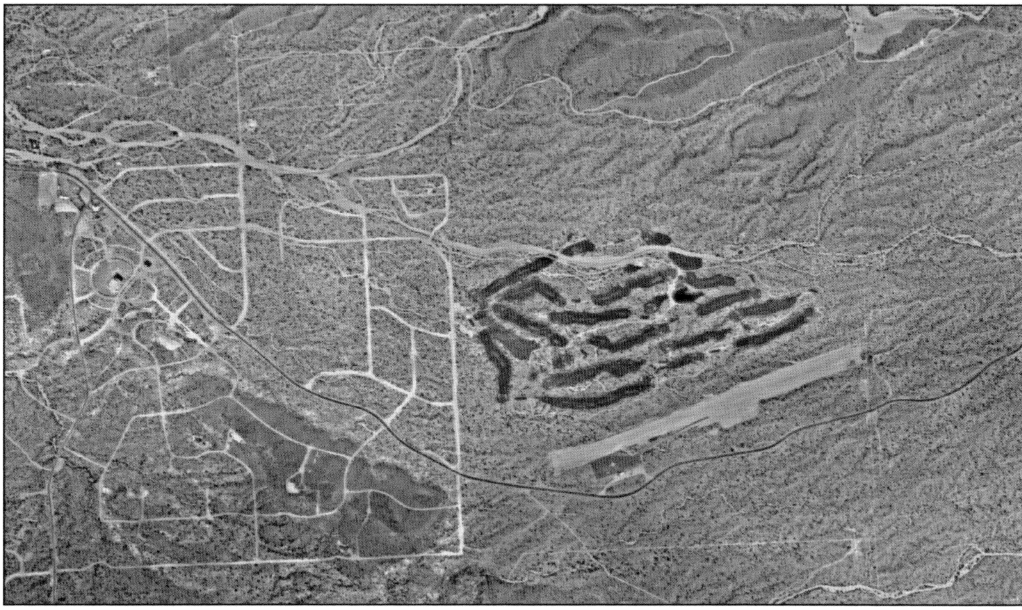

This aerial photograph shows the outline of early Carefree roads (left). The dark mottling in the center marks the Desert Forest Golf Club. Below it, the long strip is the original dirt runway of the Carefree Airport, known as the Sky Ranch, which was built in the early 1960s. In 1965, the runway was paved. In the 1980s, the Carefree Flying Museum, featuring restored vintage aircraft, offered rides to the public on Saturday afternoons. (Courtesy of Arizona State University.)

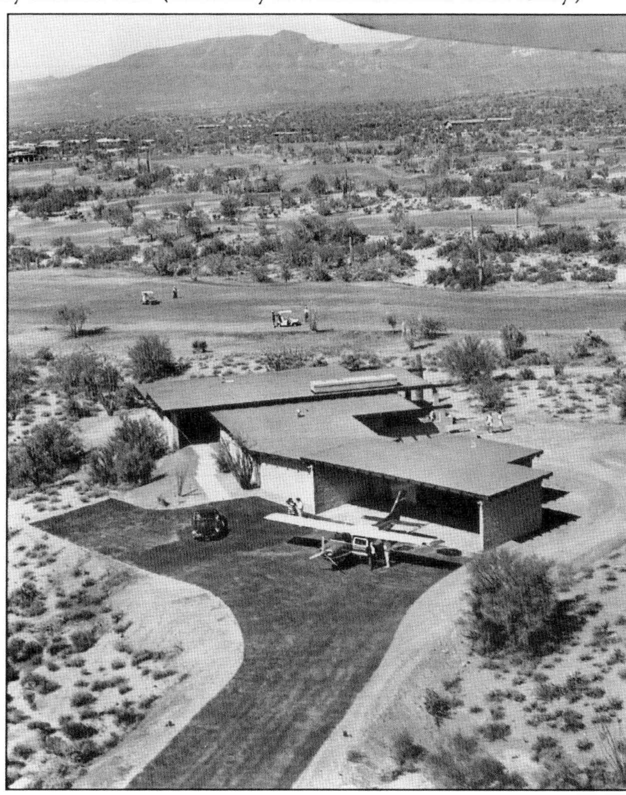

In 1968, architect Gerry Jones and Hugh Downs decided to design and build the first "fly-in" home in America. A twin-engine aircraft could taxi from the runway directly to the home and its attached hangar. The concept was a sensation that drew national attention. A few months later, the home sold to Earl Bartholomew, who did not fly, own an airplane, or golf. He loved the hangar, however, and converted it into a workshop. (Courtesy of Gerry Jones.)

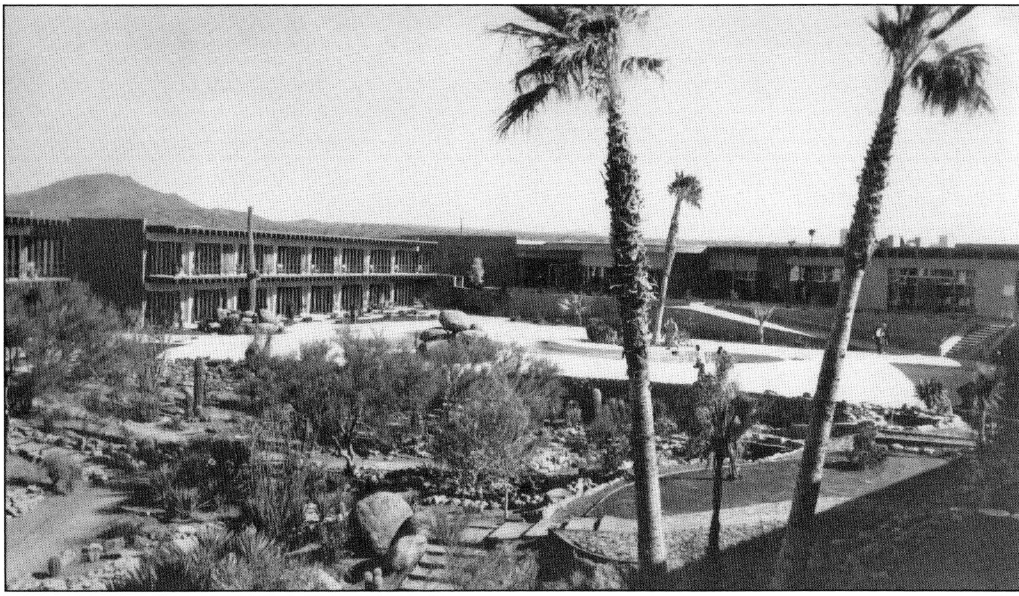

The Carefree Inn (now the Carefree Resort and Conference Center) was built opposite the Desert Forest Golf Club. A luxury resort with 105 rooms, it soon became the social center of Carefree. Investors' wives would call every name in the 20-page phone book and invite them to parties.

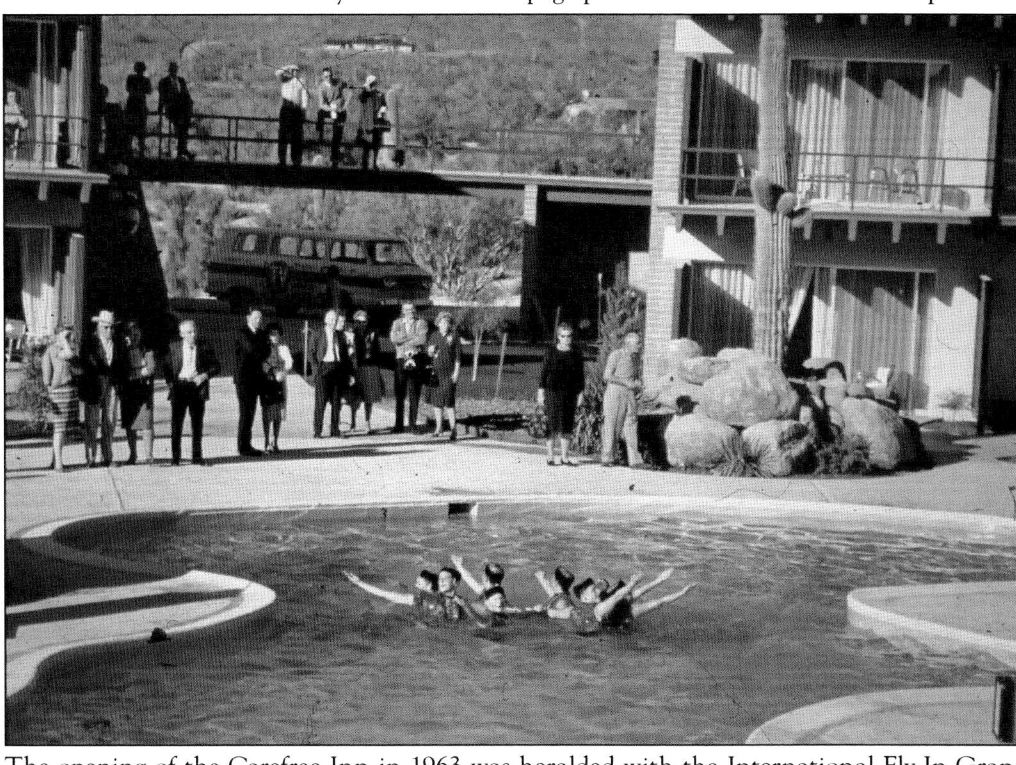

The opening of the Carefree Inn in 1963 was heralded with the International Fly-In Grand Event. The Carefree Inn Aqua Maids synchronized swimming team, seen here, was part of the show. Carefree and the Carefree Inn became a fly-in playground for celebrities. (Courtesy of Gerry Jones.)

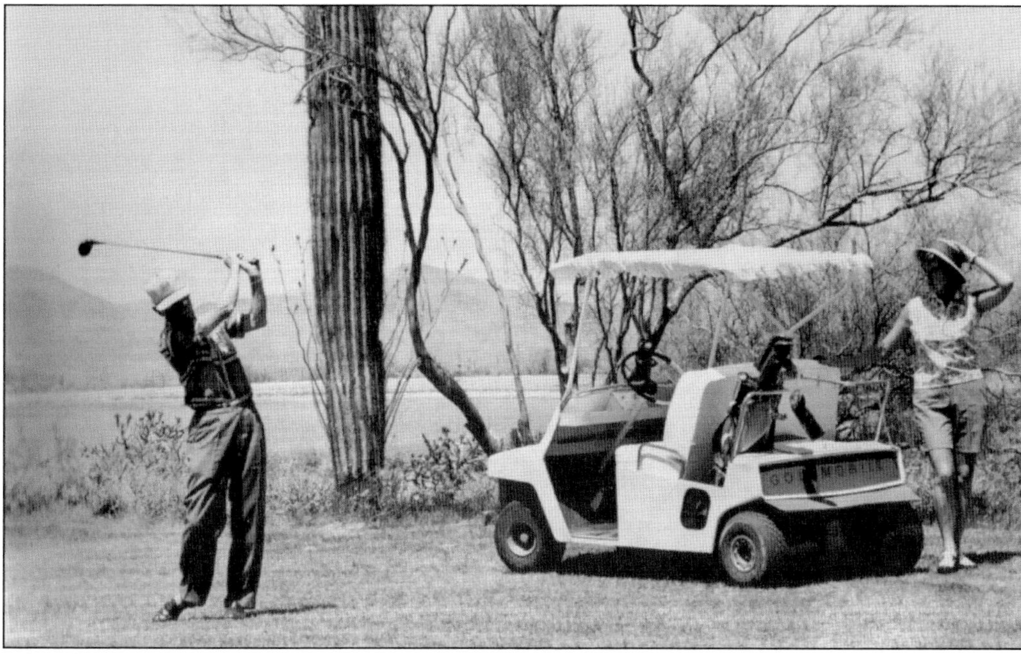

After the Desert Forest Golf Club opened in 1962, there were more golf carts than cars in Carefree. Open range cattle often had to be chased off the fairways before golfers arrived. Seen here in mid-swing is K.T Palmer, the first club president. The club has always been private and owned by its members. In 1962, there were 100 members and a membership cost $1,500. Property owners received a $250 discount.

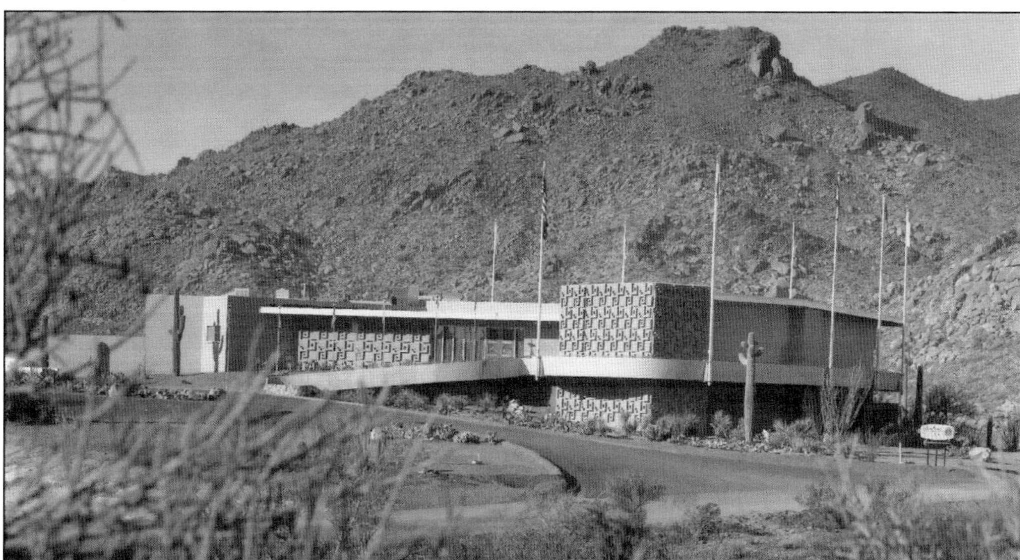

The International Restaurant cost $500,000 to construct. Billed as one of the world's finest places to dine, its seven dining rooms were decorated in African, Mediterranean, Nordic, North and South American, German, and Asian styles, respectively. The 1963 grand opening was so widely marketed that huge crowds traveled to Carefree. Unprepared, the staff could not properly serve all the guests, and many never returned. It closed in 1965 and is now a retreat center.

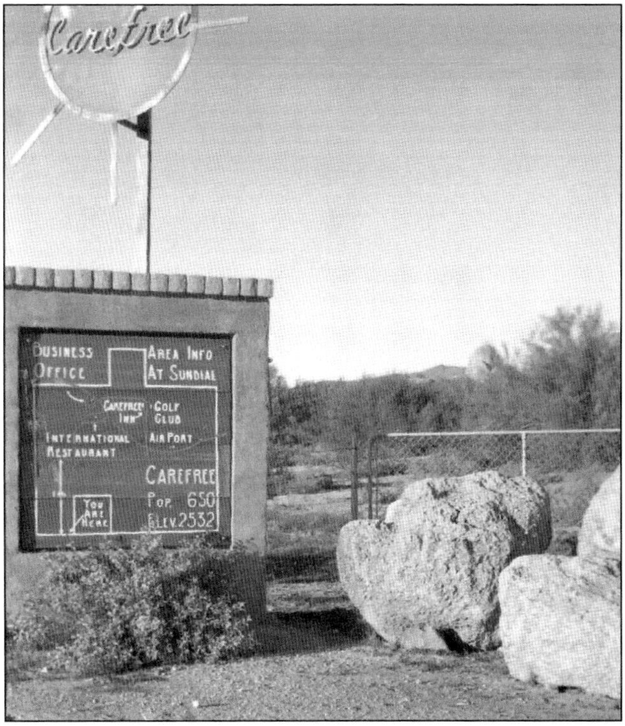

Resident architect Gerry Jones recalls that this wooden sign was located on the northeast corner of Scottsdale Road and Carefree Highway. The "You Are Here" box designated the acreage K.T. Palmer donated for the Presbyterian church. The Carefree sun sign was designed and welded by Palmer in his shop, which Jones had built. The sign welcomed all to world-class desert golf, a unique place to dine, and lodging.

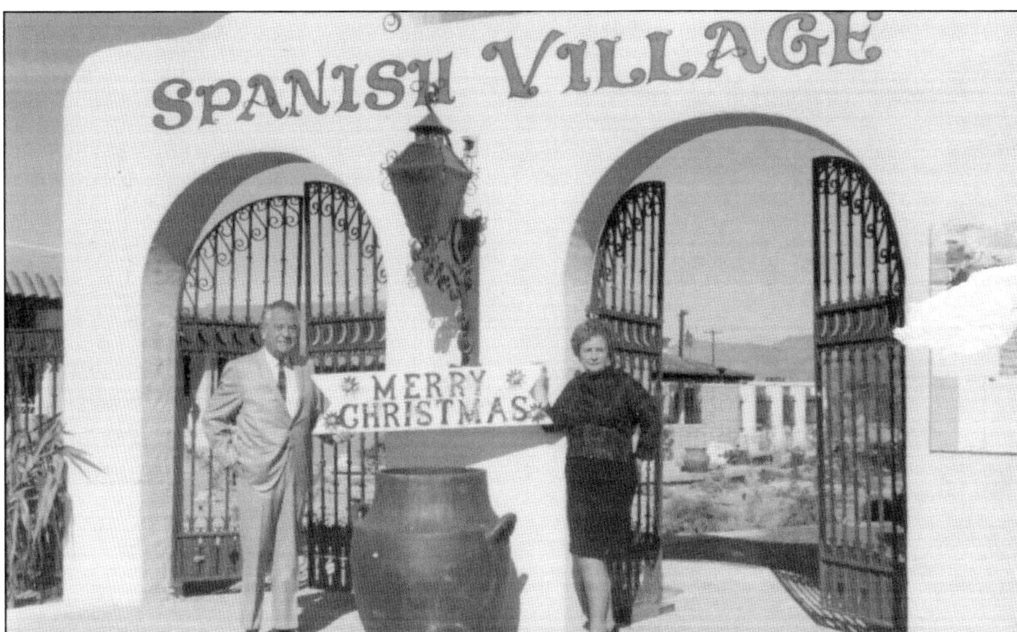

K.T. Palmer's personal influence on Carefree ended with the completion of Spanish Village. Recognizing the need for interesting business buildings but not getting support from the development company, he partnered with Rex Howard and the owners of Foster International Gifts to bring a bit of old Spain to the heart of Carefree. In 1968, the first 10 shops, El Toro Restaurant, and Bull Ring Bar opened.

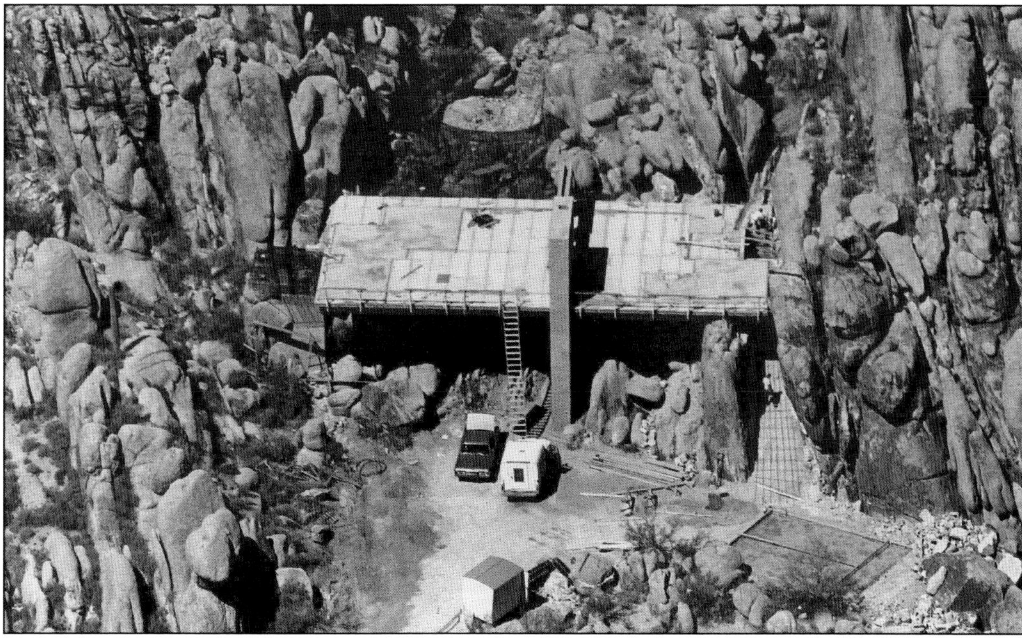

Carefree became known for its severe terrain architecture. Gerry Jones wrote the original architectural guidelines for Carefree and led the way with new and inventive architectural solutions to build beautiful and practical homes on rocky and steep terrain that many had considered unbuildable. This Stage Coach Pass residence, shown under construction in 1970, was designed and constructed by Jones and demonstrates some of the site's difficulties. (Courtesy of Gerry Jones.)

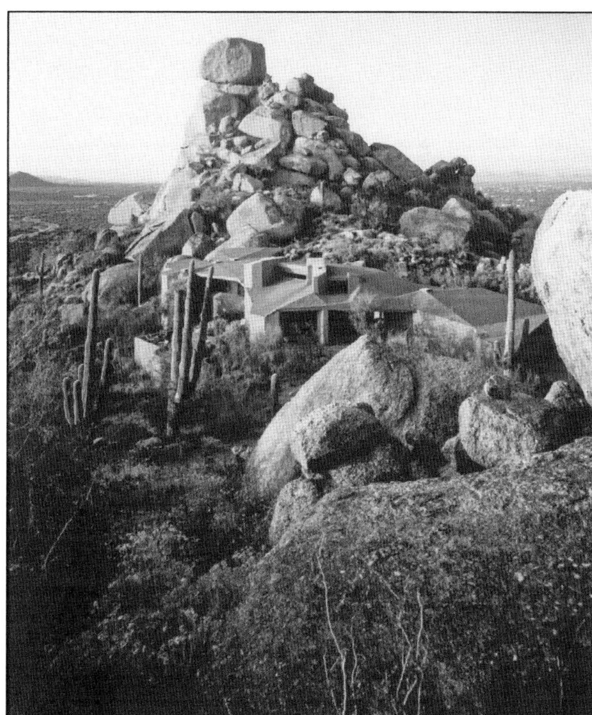

The Lipman residence, designed and built by Gerry Jones, was completed on Black Mountain in Carefree in 1969. The owners had important connections to the art world and wanted to house major art pieces within while conforming to the massive boulders without. Jones solved the complex architectural puzzle by creating a totally new asymmetrical architectural design. The residence was the first in Carefree to receive international recognition. (Courtesy of Peter Bloomer and Gerry Jones.)

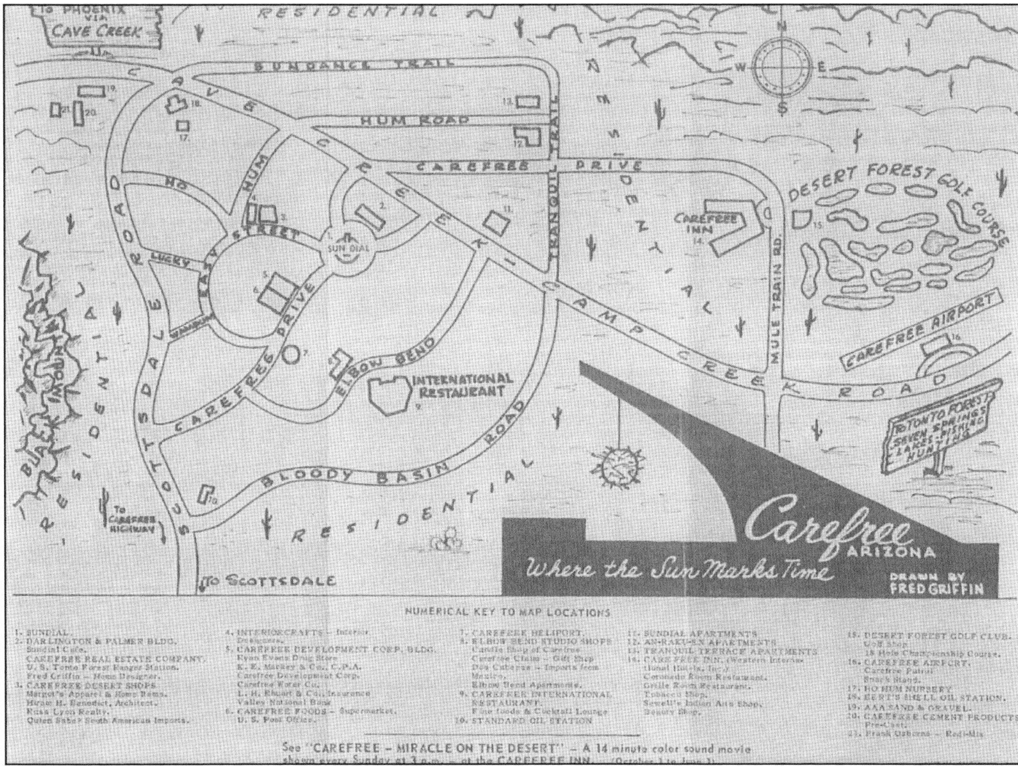

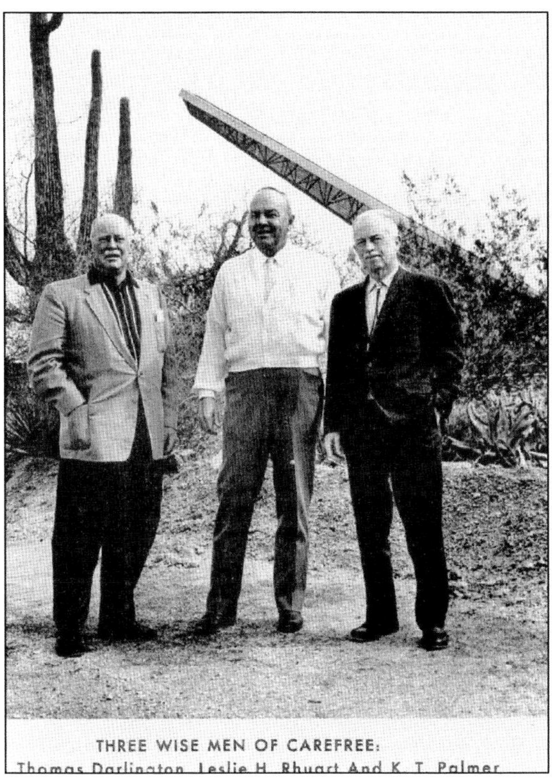

The map above, taken from the Carefree sales brochure and drawn by Fred Griffin, noted the 14-minute color and sound movie *Carefree: Miracle on the Desert*, which was shown at the Carefree Inn every Sunday at 3:00 p.m. between October 1 and June 1. A heliport, a Standard Oil station, a Shell station, Carefree Foods, and a variety of specialty shops marked the early beginnings of Carefree.

Tom Darlington (left) and K.T. Palmer (right) received the most public recognition for developing Carefree. Others also made major contributions; none more so than Leslie "Les" Rhuart (center). President of the Carefree Inn and Development Corporation and the Desert Forest Golf, he filed the petition to name Carefree Highway, saw the Carefree Inn and Desert Foothills Scenic Drive to completion, and led the organizational meeting that chartered the Carefree Kiwanis Club. (Courtesy of Carolyn Rhuart Saxer.)

Ten

Cave Creek Museum

Cave Creek Museum sits like a hidden treasure on a quiet street near the center of town. The museum, largely run by volunteers, represents more than 40 years of work by devoted Cave Creek and Carefree residents.

Begun as a historical society in 1968 by a small group of volunteers, the museum was born when land was donated by Frank and Hazel Wright and Cave Creek's original church was relocated to that site. Donations and gifts of local historical significance poured in.

In April 1970, the museum opened the doors of the former church to visitors. This small building served as the museum for more than 10 years before a new building was constructed. Now grown into a collection of structures, the museum is surrounded by the beauty of the Sonoran Desert, full of the history and prehistory of people who once lived here, and offers educational programs and community activities.

At its front on Basin Road, the low Pueblo-inspired building competes for the eye with the three-story Golden Reef Stamp Mill, relocated from the site of a defunct gold mine. A stone *arrastre* nearby shows an earlier phase of mining. A meandering path traverses a desert garden.

Inside, the central auditorium contains Trails through Time, exhibits with themes of local history dating back to the 1870s. There is also an annual art exhibit featuring a different well-known local artist each year, close-up exhibits of desert life, and the busy little museum store.

The Pioneer Wing features exhibits of mining, ranching, and pioneer life, plus a case of beautiful Arizona minerals. There is also a recreation of the entrance to the Mormon Girl Mine on Black Mountain.

The Archaeology Wing presents exhibits of magnificent prehistoric Native American pottery and other prehistoric artifacts. Artifacts from recent local archaeological projects are prominently displayed. The west wall is dedicated to a living native culture. On the north wall, a room from the Sears-Kay ruin in the Tonto National Forest is also re-created. In a mini-wing near the rear entrance, visitors can see photographs reflecting the histories of Cave Creek and Carefree.

The museum's collection continues outside in the rear. Another collection of mining and ranching equipment patiently waits in the sun. The small tubercular cabin, listed in the National Register of Historic Places, is the last of thousands of cabins and tents that were once used by people hoping to recover from lung ailments. Beside it sits the restored church where the museum started.

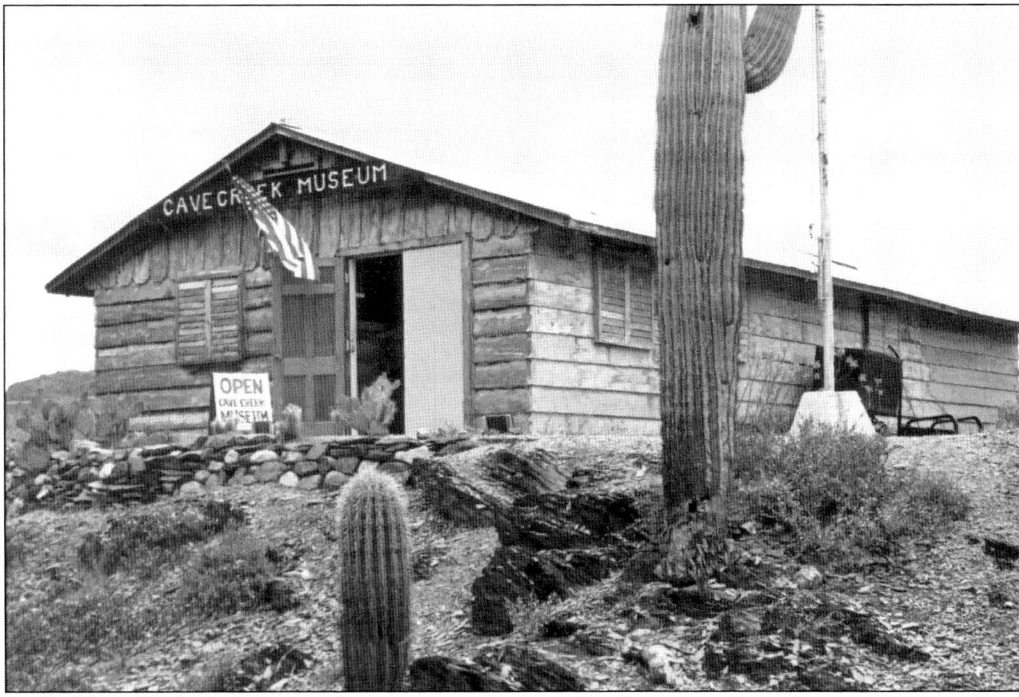

The former Community Church opened its doors as the Cave Creek Museum in April 1970 on land donated by Frank and Hazel Wright. The community donated money to move the building, and volunteers used log rollers to relocate the structure from Cave Creek Road to the museum site. Townsfolk donated historical items to begin the museum's collections.

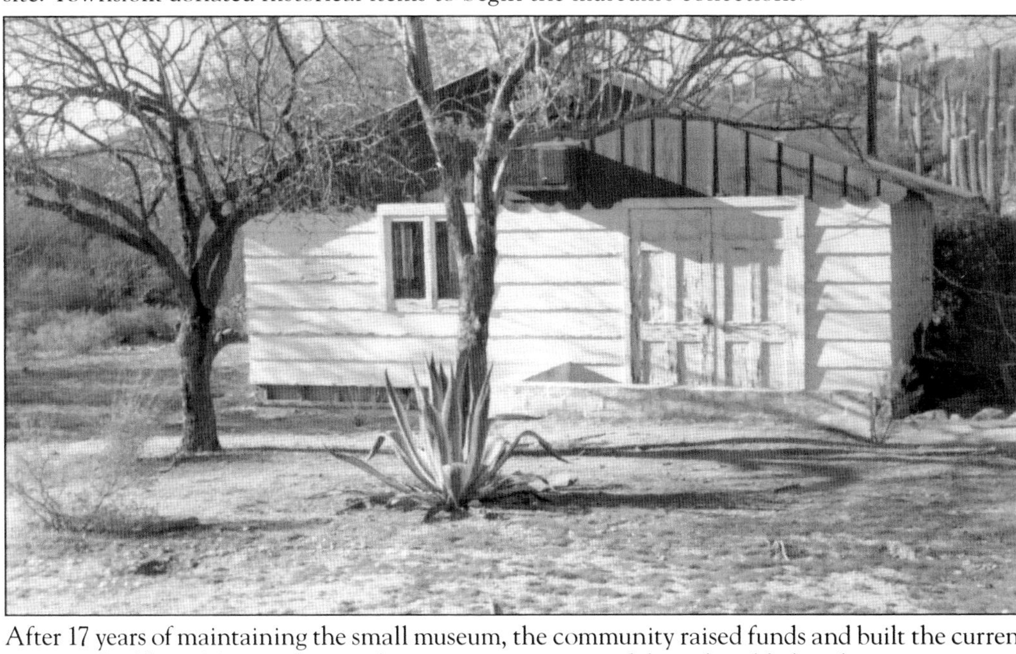

After 17 years of maintaining the small museum, the community raised funds and built the current museum building. Many volunteer hours were spent remodeling the old church into a museum, and remodeling it once again back into a church. Restored to its original appearance, the church is now used for weddings, funerals, and museum programs.

One of Cave Creek Museum's founders and one of its most ardent proponents, Iveanne Scruggs, a former beauty queen, poses with her cigarette holder for her portrait as museum board president. She served as president from 1984 to 1987.

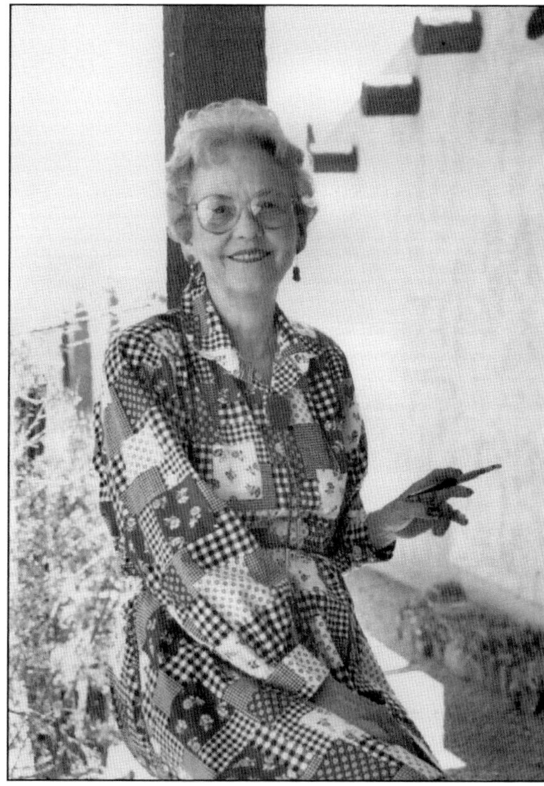

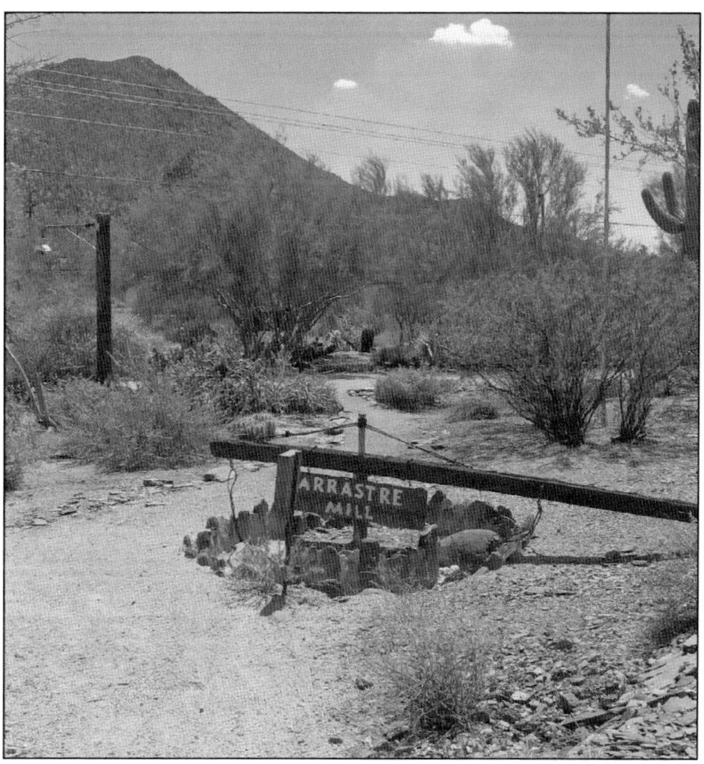

This historic *arrastre* was moved to its current location in 1978 from the Linville ranch. The *arrastre* was a primitive ore crusher that used donkey or mule power to drag a heavy stone over the ore to pulverize it before further processing.

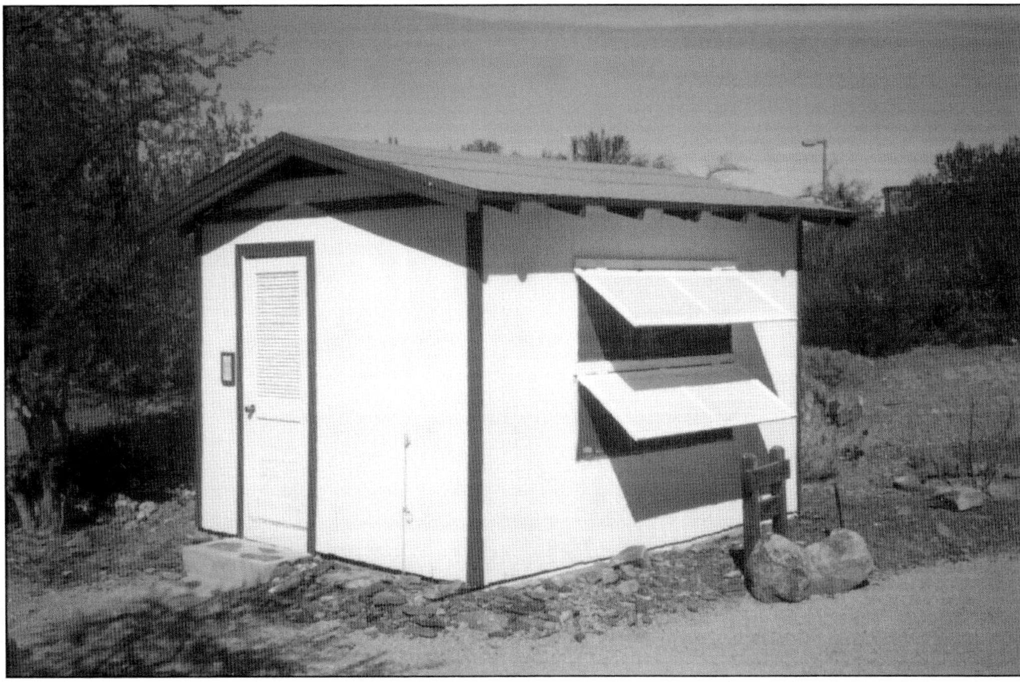

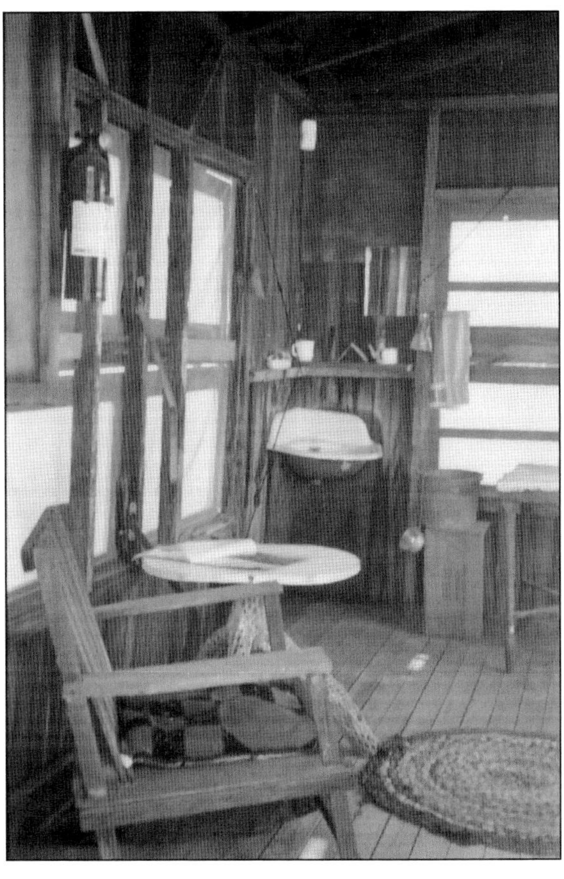

The tubercular cabin (above), listed in the National Register of Historic Places, is the last known original tuberculosis cabin in Arizona. Clusters of buildings such as this one were built in camps, where those with lung diseases would stay in hopes of improving their health. Cave Creek was a well-known destination for "lungers."

This photograph shows part of the interior of the tubercular cabin with some of its original furnishings and fittings. Not shown is the rustic bed.

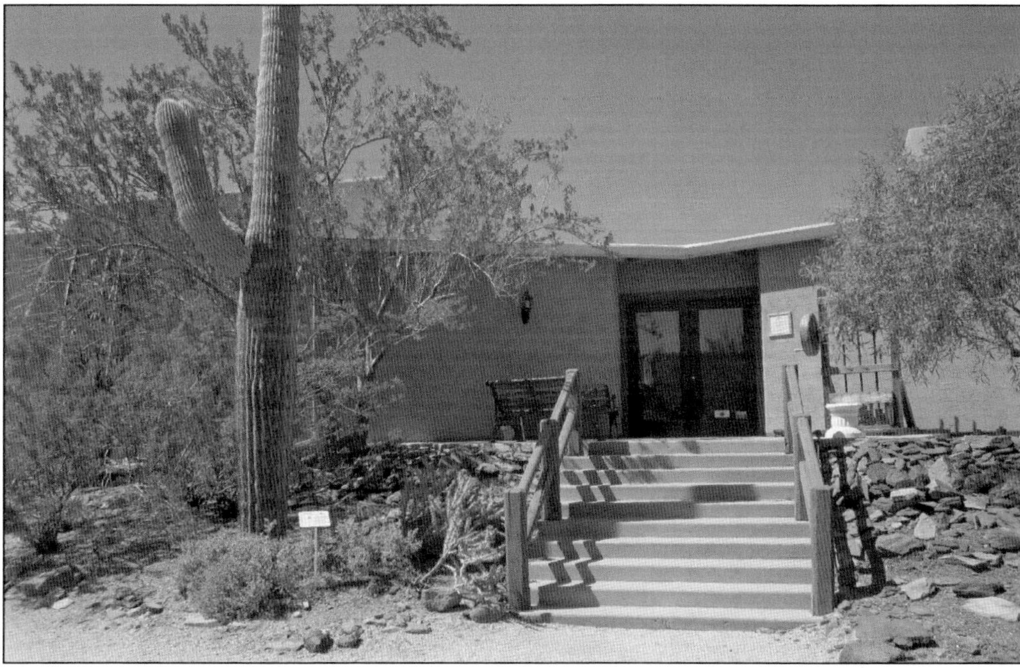

The Cave Creek Museum is now housed in a Pueblo-inspired building designed by the late Rali Albright. The building opened in 1986 with a central core. Two wings were added a few years later. The museum complex also includes additional buildings and outdoor exhibits that are part of its collections.

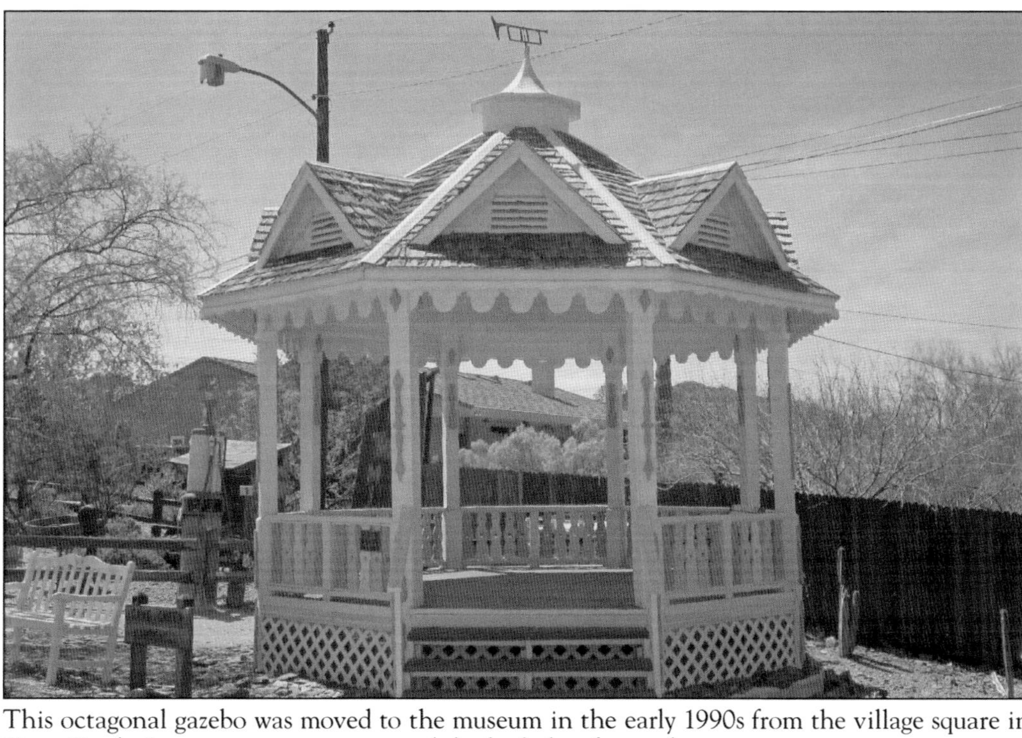

This octagonal gazebo was moved to the museum in the early 1990s from the village square in Cave Creek. It now serves as a stage and shade shelter for outdoor events.

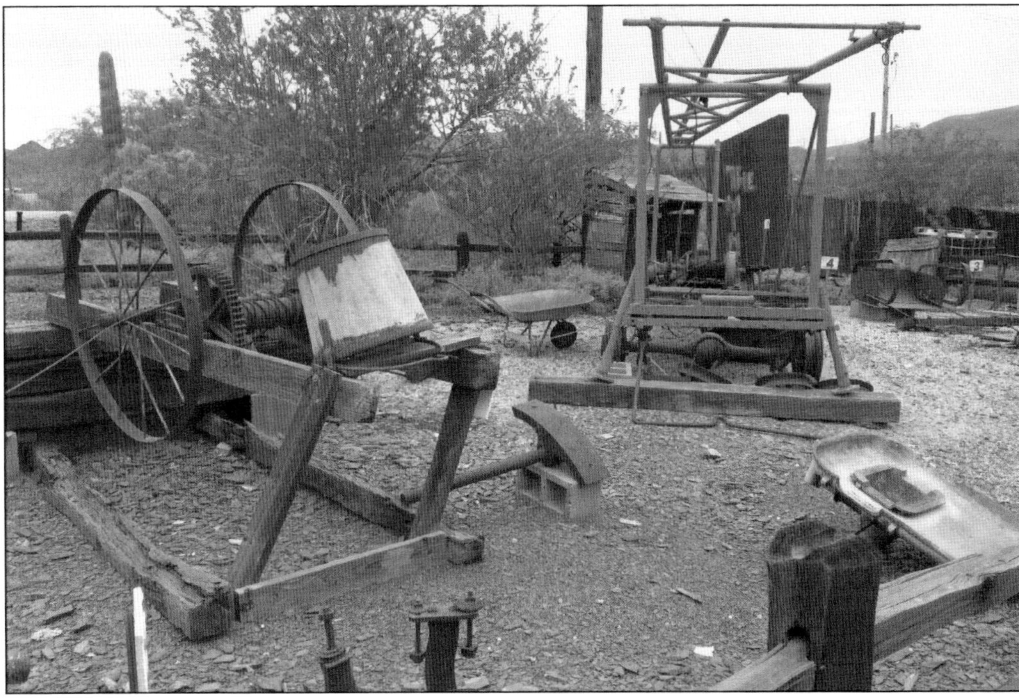

Outdoor exhibits include rarely seen items such as the mine head windlass and ore bucket (left) and the well repair rig used from the 1930s to the 1950s (right). The rig is mounted on a 1933 Chevrolet chassis.

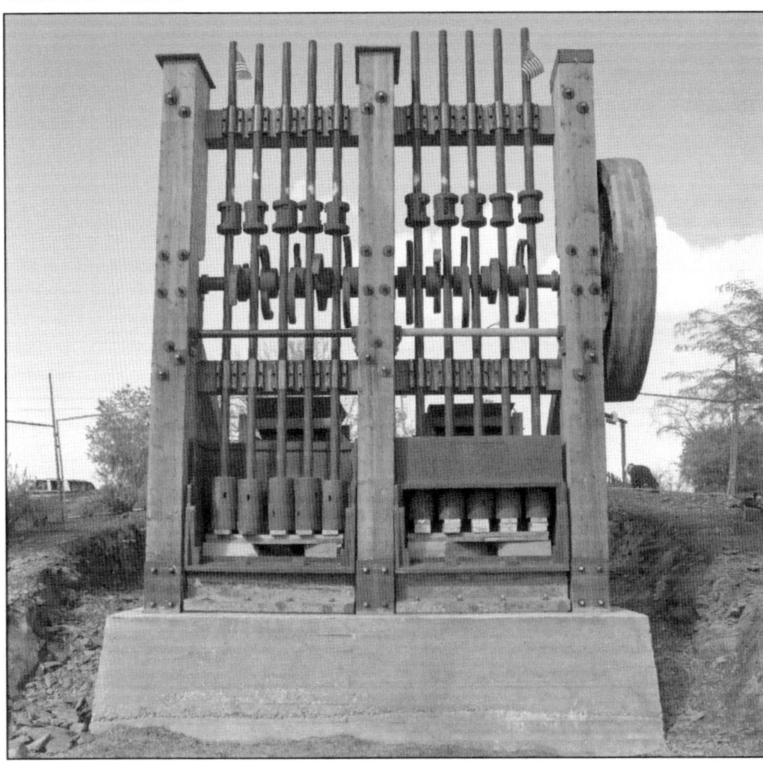

The stamp mill from the former Golden Reef Mine, dating from the 1880s, was donated by Dr. Martin and Joni Chattman. The huge structure crushed ore. The massive components of the mill were transported to the museum in 2009 using cranes from Arizona Public Service and museum volunteers. The restoration of the mill to full operation has been a labor of love and ingenuity by a cadre of dedicated volunteers.

About the Author

Author and historian Patrick Grady writes and speaks on topics related to Arizona territorial history. His professional career was in city community and economic development, with an emphasis on downtown revitalization, and he served in Tampa; College Park, Maryland; Columbus, Ohio; and Phoenix. Upon retirement, he returned to his passion for history. Grady has a bachelor of arts in history from DePauw University as well as a master's degree in history and PhD work in urban history from Kent State University.

His first book, *Homesteading Along the Creek*, portrayed pioneer life in early Cave Creek. *Out of the Ruins*, a history of frontier Phoenix from 1867 to 1881, was released in 2012. Later that same year, he served as a historical consultant to the wonderful Arizona Centennial Legacy production of *In the Devil's Frying Pan*, written by Lori Vander Maten and presented by the Desert Foothills Theater. Grady has also contributed articles for the Cave Creek Museum newsletter, *Nuggets*, and serves on the museum board.

INDEX